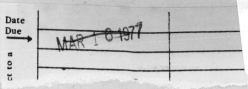

DT
21
U53
1969

Universities of East Africa Social Science Conference, 5th, Nairobi, 1969.

War and society in Africa; ten studies, edited by Bethwell A. Ogot.   London, F. Cass [1972]

268 p.   maps.   22 cm.   B***

Selected papers from the 5th Annual Social Science Conference of the University of East Africa held at the University College, Nairobi, from 8-12 December 1969.

Includes bibliographical references.

1. Africa—History, Military—Congresses.   I. Ogot, Bethwell A., ed.   II. Title.

DT21.U53   1969   960   72-92974
ISBN 0-7146-2921-9   MARC

Library of Congress   73

WAR AND SOCIETY IN AFRICA

WAR AND SOCIETY
IN AFRICA

Ten Studies

Edited by
Bethwell A. Ogot
University of Nairobi, Kenya

FRANK CASS : LONDON

First published 1972 in Great Britain by
FRANK CASS AND COMPANY LIMITED
67 Great Russell Street, London WC1B 3BT, England

and in United States of America by
FRANK CASS AND COMPANY LIMITED
c/o International Scholarly Book Services, Inc.
P.O. Box 4347, Portland, Oregon 97208

ISBN 0 7146 2921 9

MADE AND PRINTED IN GREAT BRITAIN BY
THE GARDEN CITY PRESS LIMITED
LETCHWORTH, HERTFORDSHIRE
SG6 1JS

Contents

Maps

Introduction

Bethwell A. Ogot

At the 5th Annual Social Science Conference of the University of East Africa held at the then University College, Nairobi between the 8th to 12th December, 1969, I was put in charge of the historical section whose theme was *War and Society in Africa*. Twenty-nine papers were submitted under this theme, the majority of them written by historians. I have selected ten of these papers for the present volume and I hope their publication will intensify the debate on this little-studied aspect of African history.

During the last few years, many books and articles have been written on "The Nature and Role of the Military in Africa", largely as a result of the many coups that have taken place on the continent since 1960. Most of the authors of these works are primarily interested in the role of the military in African politics. They have all concluded that the most colonial institution which the "successor states" in Africa have inherited from their former masters is the African army. Ruth First, for example, has argued in her book, *Power in Africa* (1970) that to a large extent "Africa's armies were an extension of the West". They were created by the European powers, who still provide the military training as well as modern weapons to the new states, whose heads are the new Commanders-in-Chief.

But we are not likely to understand the nature and role of the military in post-independence Africa unless we also study the nature and role of the military in pre-colonial as well as in colonial Africa. Indeed, historians and other Africanists must go further and attempt to understand the dynamics of warfare in the pre-colonial and colonial periods before they can hope to understand why even the modern civilian regimes in Africa have to rely on the military for survival.

An important start has been made in this direction by two books which have dealt with some aspects of the indigenous military organisation in West Africa. The first of these is *Yoruba Warfare in the Nineteenth Century* (1964) written jointly by Professor J. F. A. Ajayi and Dr. Robert S. Smith. It is a study of the Ijaye war of 1860–65 and the art of war in Yoruba country from 1817–93 which throws much light on the interaction of war and

politics in pre-colonial Africa. The second book was published in
1971. Written by Dr. Jack Goody, *Technology, Tradition and the
State in Africa* is ostensibly a discussion of the now fashionable
concept of "intermediate technology" in relation to the African
traditional background by a social anthropologist. Goody, however,
devotes a section of the book to a discussion of military technology
and military organisation in pre-colonial Africa, drawing most of
his illustrations from West Africa. In a most illuminating manner,
he attempts to relate the nature of the polity to the means of destruction available to it, by examining differences in the political systems
in West Africa with the aim of linking such differences with their
technological base. He writes: "In West Africa we are basically
concerned with four military technologies: (i) bow and arrow;
(ii) spear and sword; (iii) horse; (iv) gun." He concludes that for
social organisation, "the most significant aspect of distinction between acephalous societies, forest kingdoms and savannah states
lay in their military technologies rather than their productive techniques . . . it is because the crucial control of force was the first
element of the systems to disappear under the colonial regime that
this factor has so often been underplayed in retrospective analyses
and post-colonial reconstructions".

The veracity of such a statement which seems to contradict
Marxist and other theories about state-formation should be established through a systematic study of the military history of the
region. The theory reminds one, for example, of the military revolution that took place in Europe in the fifteenth century when heavy
cavalry gave place to firearms. And as has been said by the military
historians of Europe, firearms battered down the feudal castle,
resulting in far-reaching social and constitutional changes.

There are also other questions relating to the theme of "War and
Society in Africa" which historians should investigate. For example,
what were African attitudes towards warfare in general? Many
successes in history, including African history, are often attributed
to successful warfare. Most national heroes such as George
Washington, Nelson, Churchill, Napoleon, de Gaulle, Bismarck,
Cavour, Mazzini, Mao tse-Tung and de Valera are often war-
leaders. English schoolboys know the names of Poictiers, Crecy,
and Agincourt, and in the same way the French schoolboys know
the names of the French victories. The attitudes of the various
nations towards warfare has affected the writing of history, in that
the historian becomes conscious of the need to demonstrate the
military success of his nation. Taken to its absurd end, such an
exercise leads to political propaganda and historical myths.

But in Africa this is an important question in that most non-African historians have portrayed pre-colonial Africa as a continent of warring natives. The impression has therefore been created that the Chaka wars were senseless and inhumane while the Thirty Years' War was fought for a noble cause. Hence Chaka is portrayed as a blood-thirsty savage. A proper study of the dynamics of warfare in Africa may enable us to appreciate more the problems that faced Chaka in his attempt to build the Zulu nation. He may even emerge as the Napoleon of Africa.

Secondly, the historian should be interested in assessing the role of violence in pre-colonial African societies. This could perhaps be achieved by examining the relationship between social ideas, the organisation of society and the love for violence in Africa.

Moreover, a study of the kind of wars which were fought in Africa should pay dividends to any assiduous researcher. We tend to write about warfare in pre-colonial Africa as if they were simply an aspect of the phenomenon of "territorial expansion". One would therefore like to know what kinds of wars were fought in Africa and by whom. We know religion—especially Muslim religion—was an important factor, particularly in West and North Africa where it led to a series of *jihads*. But to what extent were traditional religions an important factor in the dynamics of warfare? In the same way, were there any wars which were inspired by economic motives? I would suggest that in order to answer such questions, a typology of pre-colonial wars in Africa is needed.

Another aspect of this theme which should be explored is the genesis of the different types of armies. For example, what historical circumstances led to the rise of the mercenary armies in pre-colonial Africa? What led to the rise of standing armies? To what extent was the large standing army a force for political stability?

In this book we have explored some of these themes by considering ten different wars selected from Ethiopia, Kenya, Uganda, Tanzania, Rhodesia and South Africa. The wars fall into three distinct categories: (i) the civil wars in Nkore, Usuku and Ethiopia; (ii) the anti-colonial wars: Mbiru, Mumboism, Giriama, Maji Maji, Kyanyangire and the land wars in Rhodesia; (iii) a war between two European powers: the Boer War. Each of these types of war can be further divided according to their descriptions.

Looking at the first category, we see that three types of civil war are represented in this volume. The civil wars in Nkore, Uganda, were caused by succession disputes. Max Gluckman had examined this kind of war among the Bemba of Central Africa, in Chapter Two of his book entitled *Order and Rebellion in Tribal Africa* (1963). Under the title "Succession and Civil War Among the

Bemba" Gluckman tried to apply an anthropological theory that had been developed by Evans-Pritchard, Fortes and himself amongst the Nuer, Anuak, Tallensi and Zulu—all patrilineal societies, to the Bemba who are matrilineal. According to this theory, "societies which have a stagnant techno-economy have conflicts which can be resolved by changing the individuals occupying office or in relationship with one another, without changing the pattern of the offices or relationships". Karugire, on the other hand, does not set out to prove any historical theory. Indeed, the whole chapter is a warning against the use of such theories to explain succession wars in Africa.

In Usuku, also in Uganda, the civil war was related to settlement patterns. Different origins, migrations and other historical experiences of the northern and southern sections of Usuku were potential sources of hostility. These differences led to war because of the devastation of the great famine and its aftermath. The two sections were also at different stages of agricultural development—a fact which tended to emphasise the differences.

In the case of Tewodros, the civil war was caused by the use of violence which was unique in that it was directed against his own people. Increased terrorism led to increased resistance. Tewodros's personality led to the policy, and the policy to the failure.

Six different wars fall into the second category. In the case of the Mbiru, traditional methods of resistance were combined with modern techniques (hiring a lawyer and presenting a petition) learned from the colonial period. People resented tax and blamed it on their chiefs for allowing themselves to be corrupted by the colonial government. They were opposed to the submission of their chiefs to European corruption, rather than to their position as traditional leaders.

In the case of the Rhodesian revolt of 1896, we learn that land grievances were not a major factor; other more pressing issues were the hut tax, forced labour and harsh working conditions. Nevertheless the uprisings convinced administrators of the urgent need to assign land for African use (the best land had already been given away to European settlers). The Imperial Government had two main objectives: to ensure that adequate native reserves were established throughout the country, and to protect as far as possible those Africans living on land owned by Europeans. "While Africans in Rhodesia lost the war, they at least achieved some tangible gains from the peace."

In a similar manner the Giriama wars were largely caused by attempts made by the British to force the Giriama into the labour market by instituting tax. The Giriama were economically independent; hence they were able to pay tax and resist forced labour. Like the Rhodesians, while they did not win the war, they won important concessions.

In the case of the Maji Maji war, we have a situation where there was no central authority, as the clans were politically equal. There was thus a need for a new ideology to bring about unity against the common enemy. Already a common religious belief and cultural similarities existed among the clans. Hence, as far as organisation was concerned, the unity of the movement was more a matter of faith rather than practical military administration. Theory and practice did not harmonise, as they were united by ideology and not by central administration. Hence, warfare was mostly guerrilla rather than pitched battles.

Turning to the Kyanyangire in Bunyoro where a central authority existed, we find that the revolt was mainly against British overrule rather than Buganda subimperialism. But Bunyoro concentrated the onslaught on the Baganda rather than the government officials, thus creating the false impression that the movement was a purely anti-Ganda affair. Their chiefs were in the middle between the people and the colonial administration.

Mumboism resembles the Kyanyangire in certain respects in that both were secondary resistance movements, the primary stage having resulted in total defeat for both groups. What was needed among the Gusii of Western Kenya was an ideology which could unite them against the British overrule, and this need was met by borrowing a traditional religion of their neighbours, the Luo, and using it to bring about unity.

The last category is represented by one war only—the Boer war. "In many respects the war between Boer and Britain marked a truce in the undeclared war between black and white, and the end of the white war was the end of that truce." Neither side wanted the Africans to fight, but the Africans tended to side with the British. The Afrikaners did not want African participation because it was more important to them to keep Africans subjugated than to fight against the British. The approach adopted by Denoon in his chapter could, for example, be used to study African participation in the First World War in East Africa, for like the Boer war, the former was a war fought on both sides by Africans.

From these ten studies, three important themes have emerged: (i) the role of the prophets was important in several wars: Maji Maji, Mumboism, Giriama war and Usuku. There is a need to study these personalities who seem to have wielded considerable influence, especially in the nineteenth and early twentieth centuries in Africa. (ii) The anti-colonial uprisings were usually precipitated by taxes and/or forced labour. (iii) We have three examples of people losing the war but winning important concessions: Rhodesia, Giriama and Kyanyangire.

1

SUCCESSION WARS IN THE PRE-COLONIAL KINGDOM OF NKORE[1]

S. Karugire

The Kingdom of Nkore,[2] in Western Uganda, came into being around the beginning of the sixteenth century[3] as a result of the political transmutations caused by the arrival of the Luo immigrants in the present Bunyoro district of Uganda, where they established a dynasty—the Babito dynasty. It appears that the attempts of the new arrivals to extend their hegemony further south was met by a consolidation of small communities into viable polities to resist the extension of Babito rule. One of the families which founded a chain of local dynasties in this area was that of the Bahinda clan, whose leader, Ruhinda, founded the Kingdom of Nkore and several other kingdoms in the north-west of Tanzania. Whereas, it appears, the establishment of these dynasties was accomplished by the founder with relative ease, the consolidation of their power was an entirely different question. This chapter outlines the succession wars in Nkore against the background of the political conventions which gave form to these conflicts and also shows, contrary to what many diffusionist analysts have said, that whatever else may have been common among the interlacustrine kingdoms, the rules governing succession to the throne were not the same.

Ruhinda, the founder of the Kingdom of Nkore, seems to have been a distant overlord rather than a ruler of Nkore, and the local traditions of Nkore and of the Buhaya states indicate that he was much more a ruler of Karagwe than or Nkore.[4] When his death was known in Nkore, the restless clan heads, who do not appear to have been subjected to any higher authority before the advent of Ruhinda, promptly rebelled against Nkuba, his son and successor in Nkore. These rebellions were easily put down and for the next six reigns there was internal calm which was disturbed by a serious invasion of Nkore by Bunyoro during the reign of Nyabugaro (see Table, p. 34). It appears that this invasion strengthened the shaky dynasty by uniting the tiny Kingdom behind its rulers against the invaders. On the whole, however, the Bahinda dynasty exhibits a singular lack of administrative imagination and military ruthlessness. The fairness of this general statement is borne out by the fact that, up to the coming of the Europeans, Nkore had not developed an efficient system of administration like that of Buganda and had not reached the military sophistication of Rwanda.[5] Nevertheless, the loose system of government which the Bahinda evolved in Nkore was sufficient to hold the Kingdom together. The reign of Ntare IV, around the beginning of the eighteenth century, gave the Kingdom a definite shape. The enterprising character of that monarch established the dynasty as the unquestionable rulers of Nkore and gave the Kingdom a definite identity as a nation. But even then the essential strength of the dynasty largely rested on a double myth which appears to have been carefully nursed over the first two centuries of the Kingdom's existence. The first of these was the belief that the Bahinda were direct descendants of the Bacwezi—a dynasty believed to have ruled the area prior to the arrival of the Luo invaders and which the Banyankore had worshipped since their departure. The second was the belief held about the royal drum of Nkore, the Bagyendanwa, which was also believed to have been made by the Bacwezi. The possession of that drum by a prince was the greatest single qualification for ruling Nkore as far as the Banyankore were concerned. So long as the dynasty was unsure of its moral authority over an essentially hostile and unruly but small population, the rulers could hardly afford family squabbles among themselves and, for this reason, the first few reigns of the dynasty were free of succession disputes. No sooner had the measures taken by Ntare IV been seen to be effective, than the Kingdom stumbled into what can only be described as an epidemic of succession wars.

The causes and results of succession conflicts are best discussed against the background of what constituted "legitimate" succession in Nkore. A careful examination of written sources tends to show that the question of "legitimacy" in the interlacustrine region has been simplified into uniformity by a diffusionist approach to its analysis. A clue to this approach is to be found in what Frazer termed "Divine Kingship" and which he defined as a system in which the king has power over nature, which power he might exert voluntarily or involuntarily. He is considered to be the centre of the universe so that the wellbeing of the universe depends upon his actions and course of life—both of which have, therefore, to be carefully regulated.[6] Seligman accepts this definition for, among other kings, the Bagabe of Nkore and adds, "The customs applying to the Mugabe ... presents a close and interesting parallel to those applying to the Shilluk King, particularly do they agree with the belief of the Shilluk that at one time anyone of the royal house

... might kill the King and succeed to his throne".[7] Ford and Hall agree with this general reasoning in respect of Karagwe and Nkore and they conclude, "Just as the custom of suicide ensured that the throne should not be held by a King lacking the full possession of his powers, so the civil wars which broke out at his death ensured that he should be succeeded by the strongest among his sons."[8] At this stage it is necessary to separate two issues that are not automatically related and which, in the case of Nkore, appear not to have been related at all. These are the supernatural powers that a king might be believed to possess and the criteria upon which a successor was chosen. In so far as the Mugabe, for example, was regarded as a symbol of the well-being of his subjects and in so far as he was believed capable of "performing miracles", he could be termed a "divine king". But this statement is subject to crippling qualifications. In the first place, the royal drum of Nkore was the essential embodiment of the Society's welfare and not the person of the Mugabe as such. The Mugabe was merely the embodiment of the political life of the country. Secondly, the Mugabe himself took no active part in ritual ceremonies and for many of these ceremonies, his physical absence was traditionally decreed. Thus in no sense can he be said to have been a spiritual leader of his country. The general conclusion here seems to be that the only reason why the Mugabe was credited with supernatural powers, denied to his subjects, was the belief, unfounded or otherwise, that he was descended from the "wonderful" Bacwezi.

So far as Nkore is concerned, the question of "royal suicide" appears to be a myth, despite the fact that it has been accepted by many writers in the past. The present writer was unable to get a single example, in oral traditions, of a single Mugabe who ended his life by that means. Traditional accounts abound with examples to the contrary. For example, of the twenty-three Bagabe, whose reigns are covered by this study, at least twelve are said to have died of old age or common ailments, and this includes Nkuba, who died a blind and senile man, Ntare II, who was ill throughout his reign, and Kahaya I, who lived and ruled so long that he saw his great-grandchildren mature into manhood.[9] The single reference to royal suicide by Katate and Kamugungunu, in connection with the Mugabe Rwebishengye (c. 1640–70), was not confirmed by any of my informants, who included Kamugungunu himself. Thus if one accepts the existence of royal suicide in Nkore, one would also be bound to say that the rule allowed liberal exceptions, and this would divest the whole concept of whatever divine aspects that may have been enshrined in the "rule", since the practice is then reduced to nothing more than an alternative expedient available to the individual rulers beset by different problems.

In Karagwe, too, we are told that Ruhinda VI and his grandson Rumanyika committed suicide—Ruhinda because he felt it was time he made room for his son to succeed him, and Rumanyika because of an affliction of the eyes and because of the grief for his son's death. "We may be reasonably sure that both suicides were committed to prevent the failing powers of the King from being reflected in disasters to the country."[10] In the case of Rumanyika at least it is possible to argue that his suicide could be attributed to the mundane causes as the traditions of Karagwe say, rather than to the mystical disasters that would befall the country if he died from natural causes. We have no evidence to suggest that these kings were preoccupied with the welfare of their kingdoms after their own deaths. The suicide of Ruhinda VI, however, seems to offer the real reason for the few cases of royal suicide in this region. When a king grew very old and had grown-up sons who were impatient to succeed him, there was a real danger that the sons could dispose of him. Rather than face this indignity in old age, the old ruler might well have opted to forestall the move by taking his own life. It is also to be appreciated that an ageing ruler in this region had no real alternative to taking his own life when faced with such a challenge. He had no military force to count on, since there were no standing armies which could be called upon to back the civil authority of a legitimate ruler in such a crisis. Even on these grounds, royal suicide does not seem to have been a common political instrument in this region. If we take the example of Buganda, particularly in the eighteenth century, we find that the insecurity of the tenure of the throne drove kings to extreme cruelty. But this took the form of putting to death all possible rivals whether or not these had any ambitions for the throne. Thus, for instance, from the reign of Kagulu to that of Semakookiro, kings were either assassinated or died in battle and the single exception to these violent deaths was Namugala, who abdicated in order to forestall a contest with his brother, Kyabaggu.[11] One can therefore reasonably conclude that the suicides, where they occurred in this region, were individual responses to specific problems by those kings who committed suicide, and were not an expression of obedience to mystical rules, which appear not to have existed. Secondly, whatever mystical aspects might have been associated with the king's person or office, they did not have much influence on the king's decision to take his life and had even much less in determining a successor to the throne.

The concept of "legitimacy" is even more involved, because it is affected by the sociological and the political conventions of the society, for which the past writers do not seem to have made adequate allowances. Thus Oberg tells us that two considerations governed the choice of a Mugabe: he had to be in the royal line, which criterion was ensured by patrilineal succession, and he had to be the strongest of the late king's sons, a criterion that was ensured by a succession war.[12] To accept this as the role of succession wars is the equivalent of elevating them to the status of a permanent institution, which they were not. It is also to presuppose a condition that did not apply to the dynasty of Nkore—the condition that a succession war followed the death of every king. Stenning recognises this point although he, too, qualifies it by saying, "It is fair to say in a general way that the succession war was an institution of the dynasty of the Bahinda and of course it is always associated with an upstart King."[13] In Nkore fourteen out of the twenty-three Bagabe, covered by this study, came to the throne without resort to violence and the causes and course of the remaining nine contests are too varied to be subjected to a single generalisation. Moreover the throne did not always go to the strongest of the late king's sons. Thus we find that Karara and Karaiga (See Table, p. 34) and then Kayungu gained the throne over the heads of their stronger rivals, while Macwa had stronger brothers and yet gained the throne without fighting for it.

So far the explanations given to distinguish between "legitimate" and "illegitimate" successions have only served to emphasise the unreality of this distinction. Stenning, for example, suggests that once a Mugabe had been installed, and had organised his "warbands" and the internal administrative structure suited to them, he became legitimate.[14] There are two objections, at least, to this observation. In the first place, it would be difficult to establish that Nkore had any administrative/military organisation of the precision implied by Stenning, before the reign of Mutambuka. Secondly, of the nine "pretenders" listed by the same author, at least eight were installed, established capitals of their own and, since they then fought to retain their thrones, they must have established some form of military organisation however rudimentary this might have been. The logical conclusion seems to be that these were not pretenders. Nor can we look for help from Katete and Kamugungunu on this issue, since the criteria they set down are contradicted by what they write. For example, they tell us that in order for a ruler to be considered legitimate, he had to die on the throne and from natural causes and he had also to be buried in the royal burial ground at Ishanje. And yet one of their listed "pretenders" was buried in Ishanje while three "legitimate" Bagabe were not. A much more serious objection to these explanations is that, in terms of succession, legitimacy can only be meaningful as a part of a continuous political system if it is acquired by the prince concerned at the onset of his reign or never at all. For Gorju, "A patriarchal benediction is very highly esteemed by the Bahima and the benediction of a dying father is literally sacred, so much so that in this case (of Ntare V who fought for the throne around 1875) as to prevail against the innate pastoral exclusivism."[16] His argument is that Ntare V should have been excluded from the throne on the grounds that his mother was a foreigner, which she was, but that he was nevertheless accepted because he had been willed the throne by his father. In fact Ntare V came to the throne after fighting the longest and the bitterest succession war remembered in Nkore traditions and, contrary to what all the written sources suggest, Ntare was not a son but a grandson of Mutambuka to whose throne he succeeded. Thus the "benediction", if it was given at all, was of no consequence in this case.

A comparison with the neighbouring states whose political systems resembled that of Nkore tends to show that there were variations in what constituted "legitimate" successions. In Karagwe it is said by Cezard that the king chose his favourite son to succeed him[17] and by Speke that the system of primogeniture applied, but only to those sons born *after* the accession of the father.[18] The two statements are of course contradictory, since it does not follow that the favourite son was necessarily the firstborn. The point is that neither criterion appears to have been the basis of determining successions in Nkore, since we have examples not only of sons who succeeded their fathers though they were born *before* their father's accession, but also of princes coming to the throne before their elder brothers. In Buganda, we are told, it was normal for succession to pass through two or three brothers before passing on to the next generation,[19] and this stands in contrast to Nkore, where it was more common for sons to succeed their fathers. Nyakatura gives criteria for determining which kings of Bunyoro were legitimate, such as whether they died a natural death, whether they buried the bodies of their predecessors and, most dubious of all, whether they occupied the throne for at least nine years. Apart from the objections raised above, which apply in this case also, none of the three criteria can be said to be consistent with what Nyakatura writes of the individual successions in Bunyoro.[20] Low makes the valid observation that the chief cause of succession wars in the interlacustrine region was the shared disability that most male relatives of the ruler and almost all his sons were equally legitimate successors to his throne.[21]

In Nkore all the sons of the ruling Mugabe, whether born before or after their father's accession, were equally legitimate claimants to his throne when he died. But they had to be grown-up sons, so that they could rule on their own, since the idea of regency was unknown in Nkore. Furthermore, the brothers of the deceased Mugabe were not legitimate contenders for his throne unless the Mugabe had failed to leave a son old enough to succeed him. If a Mugabe died without leaving a son or a brother to succeed him, then and only then could his uncle be in line for succession. This practice was as true for the succession to the throne as it was for the inheritance of property among the common people. It would appear that what gave rise to the classification of certain Bagabe of Nkore as "pretenders" or "upstarts" was the inadequate translation of the term *Ekyebumbe* into English, rather than any misconception of the institutional system of succession. The term is derived from the verb *okubumba, to build up* in the same way as ants built up anthills. It is used thus because when a king died, the sons intending to contend for the throne marshalled the different clan elements around them for support, i.e. they *built* support around themselves. Because it was the princes who solicited for the support, they were called *Ebyebumbe*, the plural form of *ekyebumbe* which literally means "those who have built support around themselves". Again, not all these princes could be called "unsuccessful claimants" because some of them actually came to the throne, ruled for some period and were then deposed by their rivals. Thus in this context, the term can neither be adequately rendered "pretender" nor be given a single expression in English. During the time the fighting was in progress, each candidate was regarded as legitimate even by those fighting on the opposite side and it was only *after* the victor had emerged that the term *ekyebumbe* was used to describe the loser. It is precisely at this point, in the progress of the succession disputes, that we come to a myth which was accepted, or rather believed, by the whole tribe as a constitutional norm governing successions. This was the belief that a prince born to come to the throne was born with a miniature "drum and bow", collectively called "the things of the kingdom", i.e. the signs of kingship, right from his mother's womb. Naturally, my informants insist, this was a strictly guarded secret, known to the father, mother and to the nurses present during delivery, to prevent possible harm to the prince by any ill-wishers. There was little likelihood of the nurses leaking the information since the royal wives, like all other women, were normally delivered by their own blood relatives. It is conceivable that if the reigning Mugabe communicated this "knowledge" to the public, there would have been little, or no grounds at all for fighting for the throne since the people themselves believed in the "authenticity" of these signs of kingship. But this would have been tantamount to making a will while in health—a practice that was abhorrent to all the Banyankore in the past and to a great many of them even today. By custom a person, be he king or commoner, did not will his property while he lived as this was, and to some extent is, regarded as inviting death or some other type of misfortune.[22] It was for this reason that the tribe had fixed conventions governing the distribution of property after the death of the head of the household, and these conventions are still recognised by the western-type law courts.

This, then, means that up to the time when the deceased Mugabe was buried, his former subjects were not sure who their next ruler would be. It was only after the succession war, in the case of contested successions, had decided this issue, that we see myth and political reality blended into a constitutional practice. It was believed that a prince born with the right signs could not possibly lose a succession war. "How could a prince born with the right signs of the kingdom lose the war for the drum?" informant after informant asked me in amazement. If there was a peaceful succession, then obviously God Rugaba had saved the people from "useless spears" to determine the issue, but the prince with the right signs had succeeded to the throne all the same. In other words, wars of succession were meant to prove a point which was already decided and proven, but which had been kept secret from the public. What this belief did for Nkore was not to give the basis for legitimacy but rather to place the nomination of a successor to the throne outside the control of any one individual or group. Against this background it is reasonable to conclude that there were no "pretenders" in the history of the dynasty of Nkore, because those who lost their thrones to their rivals were as legitimate as those who supplanted them.

The political reality to be considered in this context is the fact that the outcome of any given succession was determined by the number of men who could be put on the field against an opponent, more particularly by the size of the maternal clans. Various factors influenced the clan groupings around the princes fighting for the throne. A person might fight for a particular prince, even if the majority of his clansmen were fighting on the opposite side, because the prince was his personal friend; or some men joined a particular side to fight alongside their friends who were already committed to fighting on that side, etc. Maternal clans aside, the part that could be played by the uncommitted clans, fighting as clan groups, was subject to severe limitations. Firstly, the probability of severe reprisals against such a clan by the successful candidate for the throne weighed heavily against hasty commitment for or against royal candidates. Secondly, members of such clans, and indeed of all clans, were usually so scattered all over the country that they could hardly plan to act in concert when the war broke out. But the maternal clans, owing to their exalted position at court while their daughter was the wife of the ruling Mugabe, were in a position to keep links between the court and the countryside very much alive, so that their kinsmen were usually aware of the events at court. This then meant that a prince who embarked on a war with the biggest maternal clan behind him was at least sure of the first round of the contest, and the number of spears the prince could call upon were the ultimate arbiter of the contest, rather than the possession of the "right signs".

When we turn to the royal family itself, we find that the princes who had the same maternal clans, and this includes all the uterine brothers, did not fight against each other, but that they fought on the same side. Within the circle of princes who had the same maternal clan, the eldest of the group was supported by the rest. Thus the principle of primogeniture could be said to have been recognised on the maternal side. The succession struggle in Nkore, as in most African states, was quite simply a consequence of polygamy. Each maternal clan backed its own "eldest" prince. But then polygamy was further complicated by the social conventions of Nkore society. A man started having children when he was barely out of adolescence and went on having them until his hair turned grey and even beyond. He himself might have ceased being virile, but his younger blood relatives slept with his wives and the children born of such intimacies were, for all practical purposes, considered as his own. Their right to inherit his throne or his property was equal to those of his other physical sons. Their legitimacy was beyond question because the practice itself was legitimate for the rulers as well as for the ruled. The practical result of this convention was that the age range between the brothers varied enormously. This then was the basic mechanism by which succession was worked out in traditional Nkore.

We can now examine the succession wars. The death of Ntare IV was not followed by a succession war and this appears to have been due to two factors. By all accounts Macwa, who succeeded Ntare IV, was greatly loved by all his younger brothers on account of his gentle nature. Secondly, and more decisively, all the sons of Ntare IV, including Macwa, had the same maternal clan, the Bashambo, because both wives of Ntare were uterine sisters. This,

we have seen, tended to make brothers or half-brothers stand together rather than fight each other. Thus this peaceful accession
was not due, as Stenning suggests, to the fact that "Of the four
sons of Ntare IV, only Macwa survived the Buhweju wars".[23] All
his sons, Macwa, Bujuga, Murari and Nyakakoko survived Ntare
IV, and Bujuga did conduct a raid against Bwera on behalf of
his brother the Omugabe Macwa.[24] Nor indeed can we attribute this
peaceful succession to the rather bizarre episode recorded by Katate
and Kamugungunu. These authors tell us that a friend of Macwa
since childhood named Jejere came to the palace soon after the
death of Ntare IV and a great number of people gathered there. He
went into the house and asked Macwa which of the late king's sons
had been willed the throne, and threatened to commit suicide if he
was not given an immediate answer. Macwa assured him that he,
Macwa, had been willed the throne. Thereupon Jejere went before
the multitude outside and declared Macwa to be the rightful king
and "everyone agreed. Jejere then rose and sat him on the royal
stool". For one thing Jejere was a Mukimbiri by clan and therefore
he could not possibly have sat Macwa on the royal stool, since this
was always done by the Bayangwe clan. Secondly it is improbable
that Ntare IV had made his will known for reasons already indicated, and it is even less likely that this could have affected the
intentions of any princes who might have wanted to fight for the
throne.

All traditional accounts are agreed that Macwa, of all the remembered Bagabe of Ankole, had the greatest number of children
—those mostly remembered were sixteen, of whom three were
girls.[25] Despite this factor no war followed his death. His son
Rwabirere succeeded him peacefully. Then misfortune struck because Rwabirere died from a fall shortly after coming to the throne,
apparently because, it is said, he was very fat. His younger brother
Karara succeeded him and, all traditionalists say, ruled for "six
Kinyankore years".

He was then murdered by another brother Karaiga. Since
Kinyankore reckoning is by dry and wet seasons, six Kinyankore
years would be about three calendar years. It might be noted in
passing that Karaiga is the only example in the dynasty of a prince
who sought to gain the throne by underhand methods, and that
he also seems to have been born with more than a moderate measure of gratuitous malice because, soon after the murder of Karara,
who seems to have loved him, he unsuccessfully poisoned Kahaya,
his younger brother who had not shown himself in any way to be
unfriendly. The greatest single factor which made the succession
war between Karaiga and Kahaya inevitable was not so much

that there were still several of Macwa's sons living, but that neither Rwabirere nor Karara had left a son old enough to succeed to the throne. Had either of them done so, the rest of Macwa's sons would have been automatically disqualified, and his grandsons either by Rwabirere or by Karara would have been in line for succession. It is thus difficult to "view the succession wars down to Mutambuka as the working out of Macwa's virility..."[26] for if this were the case, one would not find a reasonable explanation for two peaceful successions out of three involving the very sons of Macwa.

It is after the defeat of Karaiga by Kahaya that considerable confusion creeps into the course of subsequent disputes. Kahaya's son, Rwebishengye, had done most of the fighting for his father, and had succeeded in driving Karaiga out of the kingdom to Busoga, where he is presumed to have died. It is at this point that Katate and Kamugungunu, and after them Stenning, make two mistakes that are hard to explain. Firstly, Katate and Kamugungunu imply,[27] and Stenning actually states,[28] that Rwebishengye challenged his father for the throne on the grounds that he had defeated Karaiga. Secondly, the three authorities describe the subsequent succession war between Rwebishengye and Nyakashaija as if it was a continuation of the war between Karaiga and Kahaya. To take the second point first, one only needs to point out that Kahaya and Karaiga were sons of Macwa, whereas the other two were Macwa's grandsons, so that they are separated by at least one generation (see Table, p. 34). Rwebishengye, according to my informants, did not and could not challenge his father for the throne. What he did was to refuse to bring the royal drum to his father immediately after securing it from Karaiga, but he did not attempt to strike it and thus to declare himself the king, which he could have done. One may note here that one of the chief differences between the Buganda and Nkore dynasties was that while in Buganda the sons could and did challenge their fathers for the throne, in Nkore this could not and did not happen. In the latter case it is reasonable to attribute this fact to two causes. In the first instance a son, whether of a king or of a commoner, could succeed to his father's property only after the death of the latter. By this convention, too, such death could not be at the hands of the son, whose obedience to the father had to be absolutely impeccable if he was to inherit the property at all. Secondly, a prince challenging his father could hardly raise an army, for nobody would conceivably support a son against his own father. Any slight disobedience to one's father—Runyankore expressed it as "beating one's father"—was, and is, held in such universal odium that no one could hope to advance his ambitions through it. What these authors missed was the obvious point that Rwebishengye, despite his personal prowess on the battlefield, was an erratic character, and erratic he remained even after securing the throne. For this assessment of his character Katate and Kamugungunu supply ample evidence. For example, it is hard to understand why, after he had succeeded in driving his younger brother Nyakashaija into exile, he did not take the throne. He merely went back to herd his cattle.[29] This is but one of his several incomprehensible actions.

Kahaya I came to the throne when he was a very old man and held it, by all traditional accounts, for a very long time. He lived to see his great grandchildren mature into manhood. When he died, he left several sons, of whom Rwebishengye was the eldest, but they were not of the same mother. What is more, Rwebish-engye, who was already a famous warrior, seems not to have been in Nkore when his father died. He seems to have been absent herding his cattle in Buganda, although Buganda sources do not mention him. This is not a surprising omission, if he was merely there to graze his cattle like all other pastoralists. There are good grounds for assuming that had Rwebishengye been in Nkore, and had he been less irresponsible at the time of his father's death, he would have taken his father's throne without war. Firstly, of all his brothers, and all seven were younger than he, he was the only one who had become a famous warrior and who had an Omutwe[30] of his own. Besides, he had already procured success-ful treatment for his father when the latter was suffering from poison, and had defeated Karaiga, thus enabling his father to get the throne. None of his brothers had achieved anything com-parable to this, and for that reason it would have been unlikely for the brothers to take on such a rival. We now come to con-sider what appears to be the second mistake made by Katate and Kamugungunu and accepted by Stenning. According to these authors Nyakashaija, Rwebishengye's younger brother, came to the throne in succession to his father Kahaya I. After some period Rwebishengye challenged Nyakashaija, but he was defeated and he fled to Buganda. He obtained aid from Kabaka Kamanya of Buganda with which he overran Nkore and then, for some in-comprehensible reason, returned to Buganda. We are not told of what had happened to the Omutwe that Rwebishengye had per-sonally led several times in his father's lifetime. The reasonable conclusion seems to be that Rwebishengye was in Bwera when his father died, and that he merely carried out a raid against Nyakashaija. It was the other brother Bwarenga who challenged and then defeated Nyakashaija. All my informants, including Mr. Kamugungunu, insist that Bwarenga fought for the throne on his own behalf and not as a deputy of Rwebishengye as it is recorded in "Abagabe b'Ankola".[31] It is also said by Katate and Kamugungunu[32] and by Stenning[33] that when Rwebishengye returned from Buganda, he requested the leaders of the Emitwe to unseat Bwarenga in his favour and that these leaders refused. Stenning goes even further to say that one of the reasons the request was turned down was that Rwebishengye was already old and that he had married a Muganda woman by whom he had had a son, Kayungu, who was to be involved in the next succession war. This story, too, is rejected by all my informants and seems to be substantially inaccurate. The chief objection to the story is that a study of the military organisation of Nkore shows that the Emitwe were creations of a ruling Mugabe, and that their effective corporate existence ceased with the death of their creator, so that they could not have influenced the choice of a prince for the throne. Neither in the earlier nor in the subsequent reigns can we find examples of Emitwe of the previous reigns siding with a candidate for the throne. On the death of the Omugabe, his Emitwe dissolved and the constituent members dispersed. Moreover all traditional accounts are agreed that Rwebishengye never married a Muganda and that the mother of Kayungu was not a Muganda. Finally, Rwebishengye secured the throne after the death—from natural causes—of Bwarenga, not because the Emitwe leaders had changed their mind, but because Bwarenga did not leave a son old enough to succeed him.

Like his father, Rwebishengye lived long on the throne and had several children both before and after his accession. But his death was followed by the single uncharacteristic war of the dynasty. It was uncharacteristic because the initiative was not taken by the princes, but by the clans which promoted the candidates, in particular by the maternal clan of Kayungu, one of the candidates. The two "eldest" sons of Rwebishengye were Gasyonga and Kayungu. After the death of their father, the maternal clan of Kayungu incited him to take the throne. With this backing he was able to hold on to the throne for some time, but he was eventually defeated by the forces of his elder brother, Gasyonga. The latter had an already grown-up son, Mutambuka, who was to be the greatest martial king of the dynasty. It was this son, already a famous general, who fought and won the throne for his father, assisted by his father's half-brother.

But this victory did not give the throne to Gasyonga immediately because his uncle, Rwanga, contrived to steal the drum before the new king was properly installed. This, too, was due to events outside the control of the royal family. The version of this episode given by Katate and Kamugungunu and by Stenning is that Rwanga himself challenged Gasyonga and secured the drum with the support of the drum keepers and of most clans, because he was a maternal son of the Baitira clan "from whom the Bagahe had come in the past", whereas Gasyonga's maternal clan had never produced a Mugabe before.[34] This account seems to be substantially incorrect. If Rwanga had been supported by "most" clans, why did he lose so quickly in light of the fact that the Bagabe clan, the maternal clan of his opponent, was still very small in Nkore? (This clan was of Mpororo origin.) Furthermore, we know from traditions that since the reign of Ntare IV several Bagabe were born of women from Mpororo clans—not of the Batwa or Baitira clans as in the preceding reigns. Thus neither Macwa, Karara, Kahaya I, nor Rwebishengye had Batwa or Baitira as their maternal clans. This being so, how could it have become a material consideration, as late as this in the dynasty, whether or not a particular clan had produced a Mugabe before? The answer to these questions seems to be supplied in a different version of the same episode given by some of my informants to explain Rwanga's behaviour.

According to this source, Rwebishengye had a brave courtier named Kitunda, who was also the leader of the Omutwe of *Abashandura*. When Mutambuka grew up, he virtually controlled all the Emitwe under his father's nominal command. For this reason he fell out with Kitunda, who tried to force Mutambuka into a subordinate role. Mutambuka, however, was overbearing, as his later actions at Mugabe amply show. He managed, by influencing his father, to relegate Kitunda to a position of second in command of the Mutwe which Kitunda had formerly led; and Mutambuka himself assumed its leadership. Kitunda naturally took this as a personal affront and, in pique, incited the maternal clan of Rwanga to steal the drum so that Gasyonga should not become king, for he knew if this happened, his opponent, Mutambuka, would be in an unassailable position in the whole kingdom. Kitunda himself stole the drum, but he was overtaken and killed. In despair, Rwanga committed suicide and thus Gasyonga secured the throne. The point to note is that Rwanga was not a "pretender" in the sense Katate and Kamugungunu define the rest of the "Bagabe pretenders" because he did not conduct purification ceremonies and he did not strike the drum. In fact, if the traditional accounts are correct, Rwanga is the only pretender in the real sense of the word because, by the conventions governing successions as we have just seen, he did not have a valid claim to the throne since the previous Mugabe had left grown-up sons. Only the sons of Rwebishengye could claim the throne, but not their uncle. It was for this reason that Rwanga's flight with the drum was short-lived, because he could not have recruited sufficient support for a claim which most of the population regarded as invalid.

One further point remains to be made, about the parentage of Gasyonga, which illustrates the conception of legitimacy peculiar to the Banyankore as a whole. Bukundu, who was Gasyonga's mother, was not Rwebishengye's wife. She was married in Mpororo but her younger sister was married to Rwebishengye. Then Bukundu came to Nkore to visit her sister and, during her stay, she slept with Rwebishengye, which was a perfectly normal thing by the social conventions of Nkore, and she conceived Gasyonga. Back in Mpororo she gave birth to that son, but her husband insisted on sending back the child to his physical father because, it is said, he had "no wish to be the father of the Omugabe's child". Thus Gasyonga was sent back to Nkore and when he grew up, his half-brother Rwakarimirwa, that is to say the son of his mother by her substantive marriage in Mpororo, came to live in Nkore, and it was this brother whom we saw fighting for Gasyonga. The point to note is that no one questioned the right of Gasyonga to succeed his father on the grounds that his mother was not married to his father, because he was unquestionably the son of his father and that was all that counted.

Gasyonga's death was not followed by a succession war, and this was due to the fact that Mutambuka, his son who succeeded him, did not have any brothers who could match the fame which he had already achieved as a prince. He had personally led several Emitwe in fighting for his father to gain the throne and in repelling several raids which the Baganda had made during his father's lifetime. None of his brothers had achieved so much, so that it would have been difficult for any of them to raise an army to challenge him, since such a contest would have appeared to most Banyankore as the "suffering of the spears for nothing". But Mutambuka's court was full of intrigues which disturbed the kingdom. These are too involved to go into here. Suffice to mention that Mutambuka was given false information which led him to execute or expel a number of his uncles from the kingdom and also to execute one of his own brothers. This created some discontent, but was nothing compared to what was to follow.

Mutambuka's official sister was Kibangura, and she was married in one of the most powerful clans of those days—the clan of

Bene Itanzi. By that marriage she had a son called Nyinabujwahire. But she conceived a great hatred for Mutambuka's eldest son, Bacwa, for reasons that are far from clear. Bacwa was not merely Mutambuka's eldest son, he was also the greatest general of Nkore at the time. He had successfully led the campaigns against Isansa of Kooki and Rwegira of Karagwe and had had several Emitwe under his personal command during his father's lifetime. Moreover, by virtue of leading the Emitwe, he had also made many influential personal friends and followers in the country. Thus he was regarded as the obvious successor to his father by most people. This uncomfortable feud in the royal family was further complicated by the fact that Nyinabujwahire, Kibangura's son, married Mutambuka's daughter, Bakarangwire—then as now a permissible marriage in Nkore. This then meant that Mutambuka was both Nyinabujwahire's maternal uncle as well as his father-in-law. While the silent feud between Bacwa and his aunt Kibangura was going on, there was a drinking party at the palace to which both Bacwa and Nyinabujwahire went. Bacwa got drunk and Nyinbujwahire tried to persuade him to go home in order that he should not be seen to be drunk in front of his father (this was regarded as showing disrespect to one's father). Bacwa, in a fit of drunken temper, speared Nyinabujwahire to death and the chain of misfortunes was set in motion. At the instance of Kibangura, Bacwa was banished from the kingdom by his father, and he went to live in Mpororo and then in Rwanda, where he was murdered, it is said by Kibangura's agents. But, before Bacwa's death was known in Nkore, Kibangura had threatened to "defile" the royal drum[35] unless one of Bacwa's sons was put to death in atonement for the death of her own son. Mutambuka yielded and Rukamisa, the eldest son of Bacwa, was put to death. When Mutambuka learnt of his son's murder in Rwanda, he was furious. He banished the whole clan of Bene Itanzi from the kingdom—this being the clan into which Kibangura was married—and, consequently, those members of the clan who did not flee the Kingdom had to disguise themselves by joining other clans. This is why this clan is one of the most insignificant in Nkore today.

Bacwa had already had several children by the time he was banished from the Kingdom and he had left these behind in Nkore. His children were: Rukamisa, Igumira, Ntare, Bikwatsi, Rwakarombe and a daughter, Magwende. After the death of Rukamisa, Mutambuka divided the rest of Bacwa's children among his own sons for upbringing. Igumira was given to Makumbi, Ntare to Rukongyi, Rwakarombe to Nkuranga, Bikwatsi to

Gandiga and Mutambuka himself brought up the daughter Magwende. This in Kinyankore parlance, meant that the sons of
Bacwa were "adopted" by their uncles and the daughter by her
grandfather. Because Mukwenda, Muhikira and their sister,
Bakarangwire, the wife of Nyinabujwahire, were of the same
mother, they were regarded as enemies of Bacwa's family and
for that reason they were not given any of Bacwa's children for
upbringing.

Against this unhappy background it is possible to understand
the bitterest succession war of the dynasty, which followed the
death of Mutambuka. All my informants are united in saying
that, if Bacwa had not predeceased his father, he would have
taken the throne without fighting for it. This seems to be a very
reasonable assumption, because Bacwa was in the same position
as his father had occupied a generation before, so that there was
little likelihood of his candidacy being challenged by any of his
brothers, for none of them had his public stature. But Bacwa
had died before his father and in very unhappy circumstances.
The death of Mutambuka left Nkore with several grown-up princes
who were not only divided along the traditional maternal align-
ments, but who were also embittered by the death of Bacwa and
Rukamisa. On one side was Rukongyi, the eldest son of Mutambuka on that side, with Makumbi and Nkuranga lined up behind
him. On the other side was ranged Mukwenda and Muhikira, the
former being the elder of the two uterine brothers on that side.
Most of the other princes were behind Rukongyi, probably for the
reason that most people, and not just the princes alone, associated
Bacwa's misfortunes with Mukwenda's side.

During the purification ceremonies following upon the death of
Mutambuka, against all rules of conduct in succession wars and
known precedents, Rukongyi was murdered by one of Mukwenda's supporters.[36] Because of this element of surprise, Mukwenda's party managed to scatter the supporters of Rukongyi who
fled towards the border of Buganda under the leadership of
Makumbi, the other younger brother of Rukongyi. Once in
Kabula, Makumbi's party sent emmissaries to Buganda for assistance, but, unknown to them, Mukwenda had beaten them to that
source. The Muganda chief who came to Kabula, ostensibly to
make blood brotherhood with Makumbi (to ensure that there
would not be any treachery in the transactions from either side)
had secret instructions from Kabaka Mutesa of Buganda to kill
as many as he could of Makumbi's supporters. Makumbi went to
Kabula with the senior princes and the leading warriors of his
party to meet Mukasa, the chief of Buddu, who had made

elaborate plans for their reception. He had had a large house built, the inside walls of which were lined with barkcloths. Between the barkcloths and the actual walls of the house, there were huge spaces where armed men were hidden before the arrival of Makumbi and his party. When the latter arrived, they were asked to leave their spears outside the house, because, the Baganda said, since they were coming to make blood brotherhood, they need not carry offensive weapons into the house where they were to be received. The request was complied with without hesitation because it seemed reasonable. When they settled down inside the house, the chief from Buganda signalled to the hidden men and they fell on to the unsuspecting party and massacred them to a man.[37] "Only the Baganda could have thought of such a thing", some elderly Banyankore remark bitterly. The effect of this massacre on the political system of Nkore was disastrous. It is, however, necessary to point out that the massacre itself was not planned to have the long term effect on Nkore—political instability arising out of the fact that the death of so many princes in line for the throne, left Nkore without an obvious successor after the death of Ntare V. In the first place, neither the Baganda nor their allies in Nkore could have foreseen such a consequence or the fact that Ntare would win and then die without an heir. In the second place, the success of the trap itself was an accident. The slightest suspicion on the part of the victims could have broken the whole conspiracy wide open prematurely and the massacre, then, would not have been so complete. The immediate result of the massacre was counter-productive, since it seems to be the sole incident which made Ntare resolve to carry on the struggle unto death if necessary. The military significance of this and the subsequent dispatch of Baganda troops to aid Mukwenda was negative—it prolonged the war, but did not decide its outcome because Mukwenda did not even win it. One can in fact argue that this massacre sealed Mukwenda's fate because it embittered many people who decided to fight and die rather than live in an Nkore ruled over by Mukwenda.

Up to this point Ntare had not been considered as a candidate for the throne, not because of his age—he was younger than most of Mutambuka's sons—but because he was not Mutambuka's son. It was for that reason that he had not gone to Kabula to negotiate the terms and plans of Buganda's assistance. This fact alone saved him from being killed along with the other princes, as it did two other sons of Mutambuka, Nkuranga and Gandiga, who stayed behind in their camp because they were younger than all the other princes who went to Kabula. It was not, as Stenning suggests, on account of being forewarned of the treacherous intentions of the Baganda that Ntare had stayed behind.[38] If he had been fore-warned, there is no reason to suppose that he would have let his kinsmen walk unsuspectingly into a lethal trap. Nor indeed did Ntare owe his life to being distrusted by the other princes of his party on account of being a son of a "captive" mother as Morris suggests.[39] If they had not trusted him, they would not have fled with him and lived in the same camp with him in the first place; and in the second place, Kiboga, his mother, was not a captive. It was after the massacre of Kabula that Ntare came into the lime-light.

When the news got to the camp of the massacred party, its remaining members decided that any more fighting was pointless and they agreed to disperse and go into exile. This mood of des-pair is understandable when one considers that this party had so far lost two actual candidates and several potential ones in mas-sacre, before they even had the chance to fight their opponents in a straight battle; and yet the ranks of their opponents were still intact. Few people at this stage, could have had any doubts as to which side the gods were on, because every Munyankore believed that bad luck was always caused by divine intervention. Worse still, nearly all the senior princes and the leaders of the Emitwe who had first backed Rukongyi and then Makumbi, had been massacred at Kabula, and this deprived their side of the seasoned warriors around whom other warriors were gradually collecting. Both Nkuranga and Gandiga, the only surviving sons of Mutam-buka in this party, were in full agreement with the decision not to fight any more. Not Ntare, however. He is said to have told his colleagues that any or all of them could go to Bwera into exile, but that he would never go to Buganda again, since the Baganda had treacherously murdered his kinsmen, and that he was deter-mined to return to Nkore to die at the hands of Mukwenda as several of his uncles had done before him. In those circumstances, this spirited rejection of the prevailing counsels of despair was an act of courage, which impressed his demoralised party. It was then that the men present, including Ntare's two uncles, decided that they would fight behind him and, if necessary, die in the at-tempt to put him on the throne. Most people would have been unwilling to back any of the sons of Mutambuka in this party be-cause it was felt that "the sons of Mutambuka were cursed by the gods," as informant after informant put it to me. And yet the members of his party, and particularly the princes, could never have lived in Nkore if the other sons of Mutambuka— Mukwenda and Muhikira—had become the rulers, because these had shed the blood of their own kinsmen away from the battle-field—they had killed their half brothers in cold blood. This consideration was largely responsible for many people coming to Ntare's side and for his eventual triumph. Nor could the question of Ntare's legitimacy arise. Since he was a son of Bacwa who, in the opinion of most people, would have been certain to succeed to his father's throne, and since he had been adopted by his uncle Rukongyi, and hence he could legitimately inherit his property, he was amply qualified to succeed both of them. He now succeeded to their claim to a throne neither of them had occupied. We have already discussed the general concept of legitimacy in Nkore and one might add here that, by losing the will to fight in the middle of the conflict, Nkuranga and Gandiga had surrendered their claims as the legitimate successors of Mutambuka to the next generation, but this is only to consider the finer points of the system. The decisive factor was that Ntare was willing to challenge his rivals when his uncles were not, with the supplementary consideration that his uncles were considered to be too unlucky to be fought for by most people. Ntare also had a personal stake in this contest beside the throne because, by fighting Mukwenda and his party, he was also avenging the death of his own father Bacwa. From the time it was decided to fight behind Ntare, this battered band returned to Nkore, and Ntare had several narrow escapes with his life, largely due to the relentless energy of his mother and to the courage of a band of a few devoted followers. The story of Ntare's defeat in the next two battles, his being unsuccessfully poisoned by Mukwenda's agents and his final victory at Mugoye, in the modern county of Ibanda, is told by Katate and Kamugungunu and by Morris.[40]

When Ntare eventually got the throne, he ruled over a very embittered population. The few survivors of the royal family were split right through the middle, and so were his subjects, by the bitter memories of the blood relations who had perished in the war. It was to his great credit that he was able to weld together such a divided society to the extent that he did. He was able to raid his neighbours and to expand the boundaries of his Kingdom despite this great setback. Nevertheless, the Kingdom, or rather the political system, rested on a foundation that was basically fragile, because the cream of the ruling class—and this included nearly all the sons of Mutambuka—had perished in the carnage of the civil war. A class society without a ruling class is always a dangerous anomaly, but this danger to the whole structure was not immediately apparent. It was only after Ntare's sudden death without leaving a son that the inherent weakness of a

kingdom without princes in direct line for the throne nearly broke
the Kingdom into pieces.

One more question remains to be asked about Nkore in this
period and that is: What prevented Nkore from being broken up
into smaller units, each under a different prince, or just from being swallowed up by any of her more powerful neighbours? Any
of these courses might appear to be a logical possibility in the light
of the civil wars and the external raids which Nkore weathered in
this period. A partial answer to the second part of the question
is that the most likely countries which could have annexed Nkore
—Bunyoro and Buganda—were too engrossed in their own problems to exert sufficient pressure to break up Nkore. To this lucky
circumstance may also be added the fighting qualities of the
Banyankore themselves. Though never organised as tightly disci-
plined groups of warriors, the Banyankore individually were great
fighters on the field. This quality was enhanced by their rather
quixotic code of conduct during the actual fighting. It was regarded
as a standing disgrace to run away or to sustain an injury in the
back (in Kinyankore parlance this was also running away) in
battle, and the stigma of doing so was passed on to the descendants of such a man. This meant that they could fight against
heavy odds. Even after the advent of the gun, most of the tribe's
warriors remained attached to their traditional weapons, because
the gun was universally despised as the "weapon of those who
could kill from a distance before the adversary had a chance to
fight." Thus it is not certain that Buganda or Bunyoro could have
succeeded in annexing Nkore in this period if such a course had
been attempted.

We have also to consider the point that Nkore was too small
for any portion of it to be a substantial attraction to any prince intending to carve out a kingdom for himself. A comparison with
nineteenth century Bunyoro tends to show that Toro could break
away from the parent state under a rebel prince, largely because
Bunyoro was an extensive territory, ineffectively administered by
a variety of chiefs, who enjoyed different degrees of neglect, from
the control of the king. On the other hand, the expansion of
Buganda was matched by the almost simultaneous development of
administrative control by the setting up of *Ebitongole* in the
newly acquired areas and then the appointment of Baganda chiefs
to man them. Thus it can be said that the chief difference between
Buganda and Bunyoro was that the former had what may be
termed political cohesion, which the latter did not attain because
the institutions were designed to suit neither an agricultural
society nor a pastoral one. In this lies the chief weakness of pre-

colonial Bunyoro, rather than the celebrated princely rivalry and weak kings[41] from which weakness no single kingdom, in this region, was specifically exempt, nor to which was it patently prone. Thus whereas the administrative structure of Nkore was loose, it suited a pastoralist-dominated society whose territory was not large enough to permit partial disintegration under warring princes.

The course of the succession wars and the concept of kingship supply the answer to the first part of our question. Succession wars on their own do not guarantee any form of polity or the non-existence of one. They did not, in the case of Nkore, ensure the accession of strong kings as some writers have suggested, just as much as they did not ensure the accession of weak ones. In fact the strongest kings of the dynasty, Ntare IV and Mutambuka, did not emerge from succession wars. Even if Nkore had had an automatic system of succession, this could only have removed the grounds for civil wars for the throne, but would not necessarily have ensured a particular brand of rulers or policy. This means that the amount of damage or benefits to the political system which could be caused by the succession wars is best understood against the background of the entire system of ideas on which the political system itself rests.

Stenning states that the belief in the royal drum was strong enough to prevent the break-up of Nkore into smaller states under different princes.[42] In so far as the drum symbolised Nkore as a state, separate from and independent of other states, this is a valid interpretation, but it amounts to a partial explanation on its own. Since no prince could become king in Nkore without the royal drum and since the drum was one and indivisible, only one prince at a time could become Mugabe. In this sense the drum was regarded as a symbol of authority belonging to the whole country and not simply to the kings, so that without it, a prince could hardly find subjects to rule over. This is the sense in which the drum served to preserve the unity of Nkore as a state.

Finally one has to consider the mechanisms within the social fabric which militated against disintegration. We have already noted that the outcome of any succession war was not determined, as Stenning and Oberg suggest, by the Emitwe or by the drum keepers since these did not participate in succession wars as organised groups. The maternal clans of the rival candidates, around which the other clans rallied in war, were the decisive factor. But the maternal clans of any rival group of candidates were always heavily outnumbered by the rest of the uncommitted clans and these uncommitted clans had to exercise great restraint on their members to refrain from hasty intervention in princely quarrels as compact groups, owing to the almost certain reprisals that would be visited on the clans if the candidate they supported did not win. Generally speaking there was always reluctance, even in the quarrels of the common people, to intervene in the family quarrels of other people and this is expressed in the Kinyankore saying that "When you find brothers fighting, you are well advised to stand aside" (i.e. do not try to separate them as they might then turn on you). This also explains why, for instance, the murder of a popular Mugabe, Karara, was not immediately followed by a civil war—the crime had been committed by another prince. Karaiga. It was thus the inertia of the uncommitted clans that acted as a deterrent, in civil war conditions, to prevent general chaos in the country. It is perhaps necessary to observe that not *all* princes took part in *all* succession wars because the princes who did not have ambitions for the throne and who were not attracted to the support of either of the contestants, were usually left in peace by the victorious candidates. Thus despite the frequency of the succession wars in this period, Nkore remained intact as a country owing to the in-built mechanisms of her political and social institutions which militated against the breakdown of social order during periods of internal disquiet. The trying out in practice and the confirmation of these mechanisms may well be the greatest achievement of this period of Nkore history.

But it seems fairly certain that these mechanisms could not have held the kingdom together after the death of Ntare V in 1895. Then the circumstances were such that no established system could have coped effectively. The last decade of Ntare's reign was a very unhappy one both for himself and for his people. In rapid succession the country suffered from disabling epidemics—tetanus, the jigger epidemic (up to then unknown in Nkore so that no one had any idea of how to fight it), and an outbreak of rinderpest. These struck a people just recovering from an epidemic of smallpox which had taken a heavy toll, including Ntare's only son Kabumbire. Moreover, the epidemics struck just at the point where the economic axis of the society was most vulnerable. By almost wiping out the cattle, the rinderpest had made the pastoralists—the ruling class and the soldiers—economically destitute and physically weak because they were not used to eating vegetable food. Worse still, the jigger epidemic had crippled the agricultural population so that food production was also decreased and, in some places, halted altogether. This then meant that the once proud and excitable people were now the sick and hungry population over whom Ntare ruled in the twilight of his reign. As if that was not enough, the Banyankore had also to cope with Buganda raids which, towards the end of the reign, were of a high nuisance value rather than of material harm. Towards the end of 1894 the Banyarwanda invaded Nkore in large numbers and they advanced far into Nkore territory before they met any real opposition. The final blow was the sudden death of Ntare V, in 1895, without leaving a male heir. The civil war of the generation before and the peculiar succession rules of Nkore[43] plunged the country into chaos and gloom.

NOTES

1. This chapter is a part of a wider thesis on the history of Nkore which was submitted for the degree of Ph.D. University of London in November 1969. The author spent a year in Nkore collecting traditions which form the backbone of the thesis and wishes to express his gratitude to the Rockefeller Foundation whose generous grant enabled him to carry out the research in Uganda and in London between 1966 and 1969.
2. Nkore is the traditional name of the present Ankole district of Uganda. Its inhabitants are Banyankore (Sing., Munyankore) and their language is Runyankore.
3. See for example: Roland Oliver, in *History of East Africa*, Vol. 1 (Oxford, 1963), p. 180. B. A. Ogot, *History of the Southern Luo*, Vol. 1 (Nairobi, 1967), p. 46. M. Posnansky, "Kingship, Archaeology and Historical Myth", *Uganda Journal*, 30 January 1966, p. 5.
4. See for example: Katate and Kamugungunu, *Abagabe b'Ankole* (Kampala, 1955) F. X. Lwamugira "The History of Karagwe, Ihangiro, Kyamutwala etc.", (a MS. in Luhaya).
5. See for example: M. S. M. Kiwanuka, Ph.D. Thesis (1965); A. Kagame, *Le code des institutions politiques du Rwanda precolonial* (Bruxelles, 1952).
6. Sir James G. Frazer, *The Golden Bough*, Part III (London, 1957) pp. 9–10.
7. C. G. Seligman, *Egypt and Negro Africa* (London, 1934), pp. 2–5; 33.
8. Ford and Hall, "The History of Karagwe", *T.N. and R.*, No. 24 (December 1947).
9. See for example: Katate and Kamugungunu, *op. cit.*, pp. 52, 94.
10. Ford and Hall, *op. cit.*, p. 9.
11. M. S. M. Kiwanuka, *op. cit.*
12. K. Oberg, "The Kingdom of Ankole in Uganda", in *African Political Systems*, edited by Fortes and Evans-Pritchard (London, 1966), pp. 157–8.
13. D. J. Stenning, "Succession wars in pre-protectorate Ankole" (African History Seminar Paper, University of Sussex), p. 7.
14. *Ibid.*, p. 9.
15. Katate and Kamugungunu, *op. cit.*, pp. 47, 97.
16. Gorju, *Entre le Victoria, l'Albert et l'Edouard* (Rennes, 1920), p. 35.
17. Cezard, "Le Muhaya", *Anthropos* (1937), p. 30.
18. Speke, *Journal of the Discovery of the Source of the Nile* (Edinburgh and London, 1863), p. 207.
19. M. S. M. Kiwanuka, *op. cit.*

20. J. W. Nyakatura, *Abakama ba Bunyoro-Kitara* (Canada, 1947), p. 80.
21. D. A. Low, "The Northern Interior 1840–1884", in *History of East Africa*, Vol. 1, p. 329.
22. A man was free to disown his child or wife while he lived but he could not distribute his property to his likely successors.
23. D. J. Stenning, *op. cit.*, p. 8.
24. Katate and Kamugungunu, *op. cit.*, p. 83.
25. *Ibid.*, p. 84.
26. D. J. Stenning, *op. cit.*, p. 8.
27. Katate and Kamugungunu, *op. cit.*, pp. 93–8.
28. D. J. Stenning, *op. cit.*, p. 8.
29. Katate and Kamugungunu, *op. cit.*, pp. 93–8.
30. Omutwe (Pl. Emitwe) was the basic military unit in Nkore.
31. Katate and Kamugungunu, *op. cit.*, p. 96.
32. *Ibid.*, pp. 96–7.
33. D. J. Stenning, *op. cit.*, p. 9.
34. Stenning, *op. cit.*, p. 9: Katate and Kamugungunu, *op. cit.*, pp. 102–3.
35. To "defile" the drum by striking it with a woman's sash or, among the common people to "strike a home" was believed to cause great misfortunes to the families involved.
36. Purification ceremonies were undertaken by every family in Nkore, not just by the royal family alone, after the death of the head of the family. The object was to "cleanse" the property, relatives and friends of the departed so that his successor should not live under the shadow of death. It was the last act of mourning and, after the conclusion of that ceremony, mourning, in any form, was forbidden. During the ceremony itself no hostile gestures or acts, including quarrelling, were allowed as this was disrespectful to the dead, hence the enormity of this murder.
37. Katate and Kamugungunu record 20 princes and 58 other people killed.
38. D. J. Stenning. *op. cit.*, p. 10.
39. H. F. Morris, *A History of Ankole* (Kampala, 1962), p. 13.
40. Katate and Kamugungunu, *op. cit.*, pp. 119–25; H. F. Morris, *op cit.*, p. 13.
41. See for example: R. A. Dunbar, *A History of Bunyoro-Kitara* (Nairobi, 1965).
42. D. J. Stenning, *op. cit.*, p. 11.
43. In these circumstances there were only two princes who would have furnished the country with a choice. One was prince Igumira, a son of Bacwa and then the most popular and famous living general of Nkore. The other was Kahitsi, a son of Makumbi who had died in the massacre of Kabula. But Igumira had a defective eye and Kahitsi was left-handed and custom decreed that no one with a physical deformity could strike the Bagyendanwa. Both of them were thus effectively disqualified.

TABLE: COMPARATIVE CHRONOLOGIES OF BUGANDA AND NKORE

Buganda	A	B	C	D
Kimera	20	19	1420–1447; ±60	
Tembo	19	17	1447–1474; ±58	
Kigala	18	16	1474–1501; ±56	
Kyimba	17	15	1501–1528: ±54	
Kayima	16	14	1528–1555: ±52	
Nakibinge	15	13	1555–1582: +50	
Mulondo, Jemba, Suna I	14	11, 12	1582–1609; ±48	
Sekamanya, Kimbygwe	13	10	1609–1636; ±46	
Katerega	12	9	1636–1663; ±44	
Mutebi, Juko, Kayemba	11	8	1663–1690; ±42	
Tebandeke, Ndaula	10	7	1690–1717; ±40	
Kagulu, Kikulwe, Mawanda	9	6	1717–1744; ±38	
Mwanga I, Namugala, Kyabagu	8	5	1744–1771; ±36	
Junju, Semakokiro	7	4	1771–1798; ±34	
Kamanya	6	3	1798–1825; ±32	
Suna II	5	2	1825–1852; ±30	
Mutesa I (died 1884)	4	1	1852–1879; ±28	
Ruhinda	—	—	—	—
Nkuba	—	16	—	1447–1475; ±40
Nyaika	—	15	—	1475–1503; ±39
Nyabugaro (Ntarel)	16	14	1528–1555; ±52	1503–1531; ±37
Rushango	15	13	1555–1582; ±50	1531–1559; ±36
Ntare II	14	12	1582–1609; ±48	1559–1587; ±35
Ntare III	13	11	1609–1636: ±46	1587–1615; ±33
Kasasira	12	10	1636–1663; ±44	1615–1643; ±32
Kitera, Rumongye	11	9	1663–1690; ±42	1643–1671; ±30
Mirindi	10	8	1690–1717; ±40	1671–1699; ±28
Ntare IV	9	7	1717–1744; ±38	1699–1727; ±26
Macwa	8	6	1744–1771; ±36	1727–1755; ±24
Rwabirere, Karara, Karaiga, Kahaya	1– 7–	5	1771–1798; ±34	1755–1783; ±22
Nyakashaija, Bwarenga, Rwebishengye	6	4	1798–1825; ±32	1783–1811; ±20
Kayungu, Gasyonga I	5	3	1825–1852; ±30	1811–1839; ±17
Mutambuka	4	2	1852–1879; ±28	1839–1867; ±14
Ntare V (died 1895)	3	1	1879–1906; ±26	1867–1895; ±10

KEY TO TABLE

A. Generations for Buganda: R. A. Oliver, "The Royal Tombs of Buganda", *Ug. Jnl.*, 23 February 1959, pp. 124–33.

Generations for Nkore: R. A. Oliver, "Ancient Capital Sites of Ankole", *Ug. Jnl.*, 23 March 1959, p. 52.

B. Generations for Buganda: M. S. M. Kiwanuka, Ph.D. Thesis (1955). Reigns for Nkore according to the present writer.

C. Calculations by Oliver and accepted by Kiwanuka for Buganda. Calculations by Oliver for Nkore.

D. Calculations by the present writer for Nkore.

2

THE CIVIL WAR IN USUKU

J. B. Webster

The Iteso of modern Uganda belong to a family of peoples which may be called the Ateker and include the Jie, Karimojong, Turkana, Dodos and Toposa. The Ateker refer to those peoples who speak an understandable dialect of the same language. The Ateker in turn belong to the larger Paranilotic linguistic grouping.[1] About 1600, one section of the Ateker, called the Iseera, inhabited most of north-central Karamoja. They were agriculturalists who kept goats and possessed few cattle. The Iseera were probably segmentary in political organisation, with age sets and military confederacies resembling nineteenth-century Iteso organisation. The word "Iseera" refers to a cultural group in which many subgroups knew themselves by distinctive names, two of which may have been Atekok and Ikarebwok—groups which figure very largely as clan names in Teso and Lango. From about 1600 the Iseera slowly spread out, settling the modern area of Teso, especially southern Usuku and probably Ngora and Kumi. The major gateway into Teso was through Magoro. Periodically the migration was accelerated by prolonged famines which afflicted the area. Major famines have been identified around the 1620s and 1720s, as well as the Laparanat famine of c. 1785–92.

Lwo-speaking peoples moved into northern Karamoja and by 1600 had moved south to the area of Mt. Otuke and Labwor. About the same time these Lwo were joined at Otuke by others who had come from the Nile area in the west, passed through modern Lango and moved east to Otuke.[2] Possibly as a result of the Nyandere famine of about the 1720s, pastoralist elements began an expansion from their concentration at Koten.[3] The same famine set in motion a southward movement of people whom the Acholi call Lango Tiro from the area of Agoro and Lotuho. The Lango Tiro were an Ateker people but they spoke a slightly different dialect from the Iseera living in Karamoja. Nevertheless the Lango

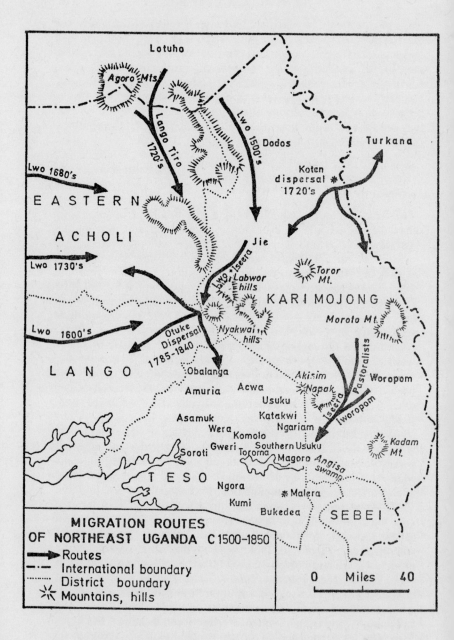

MIGRATION ROUTES
OF NORTHEAST UGANDA C 1500–1850

Routes
International boundary
District boundary
Mountains, hills

0   Miles   40

Tiro may probably be classified as Iseera. From the 1720s onward
the Iseera, Lwo, Koten pastoralists and Lango Tiro began to fuse
and mix in different proportions, and out of this fusion emerged a
number of modern ethnic groups of north-eastern Uganda:
Karimojong, Jie, Dodos, Nyakwai, Labwor, Langi, Iteso and
Eastern Acholi. The following equations representing the fusion
process carry generalisations almost to the point of absurdity. But
they are offered in the hope that they will help clarify the complex
pattern of ethnic fusion.

Koten + Iseera + small Lwo = Karimojong	Ateker-speaking
Koten + Iseera + larger Lwo = Jie	today
Iseera + Koten + small Lwo = Iteso	

Iseera + Lwo + Lango Tiro + small Koten = Langi	Lwo-
Lwo + Iseera + Lango Tiro + small Koten = Eastern Acholi	speaking today

From the time of the expansion of the Koten pastoralists, they
began a process of absorption of the Iseera and Lwo inhabitants.
Iseera and Lwo, Iseera-ised Lwo and Lwo-ised Iseera who were
not absorbed moved away to the west and south. Some went to
east Acholi, others to Labwor and yet others to Teso. This migration was greatly accelerated by the Laparanat famine of c. 1785–92.
This was when the Lwo-ised Iseera—later Langi—moved west and
south out of Otuke and began the settlement of their present homeland, and the non-Lwo-ised Iseera also moved south into Teso.
The Laparanat famine caused such a mass migration that it has
been wrongly believed that the first settlement of Teso began during this period.

Probably over half of the Iteso people belong to the Atekok and
Ikarebwok clans. The Koten pastoralists conquered and defeated
the Atekok and Ikarawok and absorbed some of them as two clans
into Karimojong society. However, by far the largest number of
these two Iseera peoples migrated away from the advance of the
Koten pastoralists. The majority remained Iseera and became
Iteso, but a substantial proportion became Lwo-ised and moved
through Labwor to become Langi. Just prior to the Laparanat
famine (c. 1785–92), the Atekok people appear to have been in the
Lakwar area of Nyakwai. The next largest group among the Iteso
are the Irarak. They would appear to have been an age set among
the Karimojong who drove the cattle away to the west and joined
the migrating Langi or Iteso, never to return to their elders. The
Irarak clan probably represents the Koten element among the Iteso,
and it was their tradition of origin which has been accepted as
the tradition for all the Iteso—namely, that the Iteso broke away

from the Karimojong. Small Lwo elements (the Ikomolo clan) and possibly even Lango Tiro (Igoria from Agoro?) are also present in modern Teso. But the Lwo and Lango Tiro are far more important elements in Langi than in Iteso society.

The Laparanat famine also seems to have driven the Karimojong to expand from their southern frontier in the Moroto area and drive southwards, engaging in a series of wars against the Iworopom people. By c. 1830 the Iworopom were destroyed as a coherent ethnic entity. Some were absorbed into the Karimojong, while others fled to northern Usuku where today their descendants form the majority of the population. The Laparanat famine and the Iworopom wars produced the last and greatest of the population movements into Magoro and from thence west to Soroti and south into Kumi and Bukedea.[4]

THE SETTLEMENT OF USUKU[5]

Almost every Iteso elder can recount a family migration story; out of fifty-six informants in Toroma only two could not; in Nyero, Kumi only three out of thirty; and in Katakwi, only three out of thirty-eight. The average elder can give precise names of his fore-fathers and when they lived to either his grandfather's or great-grandfather's generation. Thus they normally go back three to four generations, and many then go on to say that the family tradition is that they originated in such and such place. Out of fifty-six informants in Toroma, nineteen gave precise details to the grand-father; twenty to the great-grandfather; with seven going even further back. In Nyero, out of thirty, six went to the grandfathers; fourteen to the great-grandfather; and four to an earlier ancestor. In Katakwi, out of thirty-eight informants, ten give precise details of the grandfather; sixteen of the great-grandfather and four of an earlier forbear.

When migration stories are plotted by area and generation, certain patterns emerge. For example, Abela appeared to have been settled in the time of the great-grandfathers, Usuku in the time of the grandfathers and Lale in the time of the fathers. Yet these three are neighbouring areas in northern Usuku. In an area of more ancient settlement, precise dating is impossible. In Toroma, for example, forty out of fifty-six informants had no story of family migration outside southern Usuku. They tended to say, "We have always been here". Furthermore, they had no generalised tradition of where the family originated. When asked, they fell back upon: "We hear that the Iteso came from Karamoja", but were not prepared to commit their own family to a Karamoja origin.[6] Thus

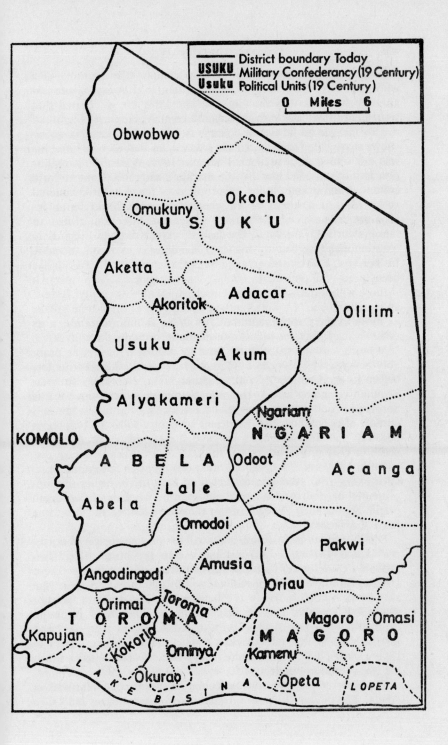

Obwobwo

USUKU

Omukuny   Okocho

Aketta

Akoritok   Adacar

Olilim

Usuku   Akum

Alyakameri

KOMOLO   Ngariam   NGARIAM

Odoot   Acanga

ABELA

Lale

Abela

Omodoi

Pakwi

Amusia

Angodingodi   Oriau

Orimai   Toroma

TOROMA   Magoro   Omasi

Kapujan   MAGORO

Kokorio   Ominya   Kamenu

Okurao   Opeta   L OPETA

LAKE BISINA

District boundary Today
USUKU Military Confederancy (19 Century)
Usuku Political Units (19 Century)

0   Miles   6

generalisations from even a very large sampling in one area to a whole county can be misleading. For example, Lawrance, presumably on the basis of a sample in northern Usuku, discovered that settlement took place in the nineteenth century. He then generalised this to include all of Usuku county. A more widespread sampling shows that while Magoro probably was being settled by 1600, Lale was not settled until between 1880 and 1900. A further complication is that those areas which lie astride a migration route have a continual inflow and outflow of people over possibly three hundred years. Migration stories of the present inhabitants will be an inaccurate reflection of the earliest settlement. Migration stories of families further west whose forefathers passed through the area in question may give better evidence of the dates of earliest settlement. In Toroma, besides the great numbers who say they have always been there—one informant going back ten generations to prove it —those who did settle sorted themselves out almost evenly. Almost an equal number of families settled in the time of their great-greats, as those in the great-grandfathers, as those in the grandfathers, as those in the fathers as even those of the informants themselves.

Magoro was the gateway to Teso for the Iseera and was probably being settled between c. 1550 and 1600. From Magoro, settlers began to pioneer the Toroma-Kapujan area. For long Toroma-Kapujan remained astride the migration route which went west to Soroti and south to Ngora, so that there was a continual inflow and outflow of population. In the nineteenth century when the Iworopom began to pour into Magoro a few settled in Toroma, but most went north to Usuku or south across the lake to Bukedea. The clan distribution of Toroma reflects this story of migration. Out of fifty-one informants, four belonged to a clan of Luo origin, thirty-four represented original Ateker clans and six were of clans of Iworopom origin. Significantly enough, almost the oldest settlement story came from the Ikomolo clan of probable Luo origin.[7]

Possibly because the Imiro[8] were already in occupation of northern Usuku, the Iseera did not move into the north. The Imiro probably came out of Labwor into Amuria and east into northern Usuku. Dating of this movement is difficult, but the Imiro were already in occupation by c. 1750 when the first Iseera settlement was about to take place. Esude, of the Imiro clan of Ngariam, claimed that his people "had been settled here long, long ago" and that they spoke the pure Ateker tongue.[9] However, the elders of Usuku claimed that "the Imiro spoke their own language which the Iteso could not understand".[10]

The first settlement of the Ikumama[11] in northern Usuku was in Abela. The earliest pioneer farmers who settled among the Imiro appear to have been from Toroma in the late eighteenth century. They were possibly of the Irarak clan, who adopted the *etem* name of "Igetoma" meaning "the people of Getom", a long established settlement in Abela. As a result the Itoroma tended to call all the people of Abela and even all of northern Usuku, "Igetoma". The earliest settlers may have been fleeing justice and seeking refuge among the Imiro. The earliest recorded settler, "Oocooco came from Toroma because he killed a man who had committed adultery with his wife . . . He feared that he might be killed in Toroma."[12]

The main settlement period was between *c.* 1783 and 1835. Mostly the settlers were from Malera in Bukedea and most were of the Irarak clan, Imalera *etem*.[13] Some may have come directly from Woropom. One family which claimed to come direct from Woropom said their great-grandfather "came direct from Woropom. He spoke Ateso. He was in the Iworopom clan when he came, but became friendly to people here and changed to Irarak and took up the *etem* name, Imalera." Another member of the same family confirmed this, except that his great-grandfathers "when they came . . . were not speaking Ateso".[14]

The main settlers appear to have been part of the back movement of the Ateker from Bukedea, which included a few Iworopom who may or may not have spoken Ateso but who assimilated into the main clan—the Irarak—of Abela.[15]

Two of the earliest leaders to emerge among the new settlers were Etesot, who may have given his name to the village of Teso in Abela, and Abila, who was from Woropom and after whom Abela was named. Etesot apparently was senior to Abila. The elders of Usuku recount a story of the early pioneer days.

> Prior to the coming of our ancestors, Moro Abela, also called Teso, had been settled by Ateso-speaking people. A second group (of settlers) came and asked the first for food. They refused and they again begged for just dry potatoes. On the third occasion they begged saying "Can't you even break pieces of the dry potatoes for us?" "Teso" comes from the soft sound "tes tes" of the dry potatoes being broken. . . . Teso does not originate from "atesin" meaning graves.[16]

Etesot and Abila were the military leaders of the first group of settlers who originally refused to part with their food. It would be tempting to adjust this story slightly to see Etesot as leader of the first Ikumama settlers and Abila of the second Iworopom settlers and the soft sound "Tes Tes" as the symbolism of the pact worked out between the two groups, whereby the Ikumama accepted the Iworopom as brothers after a period of initial suspicion and in return the Iworopom joined the Irarak clan, the place

names "Teso" and "Abela" commemorating the great leaders of
this pact of amity.

The elders of Usuku county see conflict in the two possible
origins of the word "Teso". In southern Usuku it is believed that
it comes from the Karimojong sending forth messengers to look
for the *atesin*—graves—of their children who had gone forth to
pioneer the wilderness. The most likely explanation is that the
"graves" story was applicable to the Irarak migrants and thus
referred mainly to the people of southern Usuku. In Abela and in
northern Usuku generally, the settlers were not predominantly
from the Karimojong. Not one informant in Abela mentioned his
family origin as in Karamoja, and it seems unlikely, given the feelings of the Karimojong for the Iworopom, that they would refer to
them as their children or bother to look for them. Lawrance adds
to the confusion by appearing to suggest that northern Usuku was
the earliest area of Iteso settlement and further suggesting that the
migration route may have been via Akisim and Napak mountains.[17]
If this had been the migration route, then northern Usuku rather
than Magoro would have been the oldest area of Iteso settlement
in Teso district, and the "graves" story would have been creditable.
Historically it is almost impossible to link the "graves" story with
Teso village. Rather it seems that "Teso" has two origins, or even
three if one accepts that Etesot may have given his name to the
village.

The confusion was deepened when in the early colonial period
a traditional dancing competition was held by which a name was
to be chosen for all the Iteso people. Since the people of Abela
and specifically of Teso village performed their dance more like
the Karimojong than any other group, and since all Iteso acknowledge a vague Karamoja origin one way or another, the name
"Iteso" was taken to be the most ancient of all and applied to all
the people of Teso district. It is apparent that the people of Teso
village danced more like the Karimojong or Iworopom than most
others for precisely the opposite reason: that they had left
Karamoja more recently than most others; one might say they
were the least Iteso of all, judged by length of residence in Teso.
However, historically "Iteso", even if accidental, was probably the
most sensible choice, especially if one accepts the possible dual
origin of the word, for it would mean that "Teso" was applied at
one time or another to the ancestors of all the modern Iteso people.

The new pioneers very soon came into conflict with the Imiro.
Etesot and Abila joined with Celi of Ngariam to fight against the
Imiro, who were led by Oyur, Abwal and Kagai. Some of the
Imiro probably were absorbed into Ikumama society, as the Imiro

clan of Amuria and northern Usuku suggests. However, tradition is silent on this; it rather emphasises the conflict.

Etesot and Abila raided the Imiro who gradually fell back (or were chased back) to Acwa and Obalanga. But the people of Abela did not colonise or settle the area. As the area became vacant it once again became bushy thus when the second (third) group of Iteso came (our ancestors) people of Usuku Sub-county, they found it uninhabited and bushy... Usuku people used to meet the Imiro when hunting in Acwa and Obalanga. . . .

The Ingariama allied with the people of Abela to fight against the Imiro. They were smeared by the same *emuron*. The Abela people needed the services of the *emuron* in Ngariam. [Since Abela had no *emuron* (foreteller) of its own.][18]

It was typical that hostility began over quarrels while hunting. Most settlements seemed to want a hunting grounds over which they felt they possessed rights. Quarrels during the hunt were common. Once open hostility began, the aim seemed to be to drive the enemy from the hunting grounds. Whichever side was getting the worst of it tended to draw back, the settlers slowly withdrawing to greater security, the area being left for hunting, the stronger side not necessarily beginning settlement. It was not until the new wave of settlers came pouring in after the destruction of Woropom in *c.* 1830 that they took up land where the Imiro had once lived (in Usuku subcounty).[19] Thus elders in Usuku tend to say that the land was uninhabited when their forefathers arrived. Informants in Ngariam confirmed this view. Settlement in part of Ngariam had probably begun at the same time as that of Abela. However the main settlement period was, as in Usuku, after the destruction of Woropom in the period *c.* 1821 to 1873. By this time the Imiro had either been assimilated or driven back. The elders of Olilim, Ngariam, reported that while the land was uninhabited when their grandfathers arrived, there were signs of recent habitation.

A number of wells from which their grandfathers got water had been cleared by the Imiro. There are remains today of Imiro buildings in Palam and other remains in Oseomit, both in Olilim *eitela*. Enosi Okiroro says he remembers his grandfather saying that the Imiro moved away; there was no war.[20]

On the other hand, there are many Imiro clansmen in Ngariam but neither they nor others, at least officially, relate them to the Imiro against whom they fought or who "moved away". The evidence of Esude of the Imiro clan of Acanga, Ngariam, suggests both conflict and assimilation. Esude's grandfather, Dokotum, left Ngariam and went to Lango just about the time of the heaviest influx of Ikumama settlers into Ngariam.

Dokotum left Ngariam and went to Miroi (Lango). People were dying there so he returned to Acanga where many of his relatives were. There are very many Imiro in Acanga... Iteseo were then settled here. The section of the relatives who stayed behind in Acanga had been settled here long, long ago. Dokotum spoke Ateso.[21]

Following the final destruction of Woropom in c. 1830, large numbers of settlers began to pour into northern Usuku. It was in the age of the grandfathers, c. 1821 to 1873, that the largest influx of settlers came into Ngariam. This was also the period of settlement of Usuku subcounty as well as Katakwi-Alyakameri. Like the earlier settlers of Abela, these pioneers claim to have come either directly from Woropom or from the Tororo-Bukedea area and especially from Malera. The common historical experiences may account for the close political and military co-operation which developed among Usuku, Abela, Kataki and Ngariam. There was no tradition of war between these military confederacies. They co-operated against outsiders, fighting under a common military commander and coming under the jurisdiction of the same *emuron* (foreteller).

However, there was a certain distinction. The early settlers of Abela and the later settlers of Katakwi appeared to have been part of the back flow of migrants from the Tororo-Bukedea area. They appear to have been largely Ikumama, while the settlers of Usuku and Ngariam on the other hand seemed to have been more Iworopom than Ikumama, either direct from Woropom or returning from Bukedea. New clans predominated, with unusual names seldom found anywhere else in Teso.

Lale appears to have been the last area of northern Usuku to be settled. Settlement probably was taking place in the 1880s by pioneers from Amusia. Amusia is in southern Usuku in the border lands between Magoro and Toroma. Large areas of Amusia have poor and shallow soil, the rock being close to the surface. Even today much of Amusia is almost uninhabited, while a few pockets of good soil are intensely cultivated and densely populated. As settlers poured into Magoro, where open land was scarce, they tended to settle in Amusia, being deceived by the large amount of free land available. But they soon moved on. Given the small area of Amusia, it is surprising the number of people from all over Teso who list it on the migration route of their forefathers. There is even a section of the Atekok clan in Kumi called the Imusiatok (the people of Amusia).[22] Amusia must have attracted and then repelled more pioneers than any other area of Usuku county.

Most of the settlers of Lale were also from Amusia. They appear to have been largely of Woropom origin who moved through Magoro and settled in Amusia; then, disappointed like many before them, they re-settled in Lale. While the Ikarebwok of Iseera origin is larger than any other clan, the new clans of Iworopom origin appear to predominate in Lale.[23]

The new pioneers had barely settled down in their new homes in northern Usuku than they began to undertake wars and raids of revenge against the Karimojong. With time a northern military alliance under Celi of Ngariam and a southern alliance under Oleumo at Magoro were leading regular expeditions against the Karimojong. In the south, most of the conflict took place in Angisa, an attractive hunting area used by both the Imagoro and the Karimojong. The wars drove all settlement out of the Angisa area. Interestingly enough, the northern and southern military alliances never co-ordinated their efforts against the Karimojong. There was a slight dialectical distinction between north and south, a wide difference in historical experiences and certain cultural differences which prevented co-operation and led in the future to conflict. However, as long as the Karimojong menace lasted, the potential rift between north and south did not become actual. While in the north the wars were looked upon as revenge,[24] in the south they were blamed upon famines and droughts in Karamoja which sent the Karimojong against Magoro in search of food and cattle. From the Iteso side, women and children appeared to be the main war prize. An informant in Amusia said:

There was a famine in Karamoja but not in Teso; that was why Karimojong came to Teso to fight. Usuku, Katakwi and Adacar (Ngariam) formed another alliance to fight the Karimojong. . . . The informant (Okedi) heard all of this from his father who secured a Karimojong girl and a boy who is his brother. (Penekasi Inya who was present at the interview). The Iteso never captured Karimojong cattle because they were far away. The Karimojong came with their families to look for food and this was when the Iteso captured them. If a captured girl was very young she could be brought up as a daughter but if she was older she could be taken as a wife. There are many people here today who are offspring of Karimojong. If a small boy were captured he could be brought up as a son particularly if the man had no sons of his own. If a man had sons he was likely to sell the Karimojong boy for he would likely fight with the man's sons when he became older. (Obviously in his own family this had not happened.)[25]

OKADARO'S FAMINE AND THE GENESIS OF CIVIL WAR

The southern alliance did not appear to possess the cohesion of
the northern alliance. This was related to the fact that there were
at least three independent *emurons* in the south. The northern
alliance was under the influence of one *emuron*, the earliest the
elders remember, being a man called Okadaro. Okadaro may have
been the first *emuron* in the area and from Woropom. It is significant that the settlers in Abela, all Ikumama, did not possess an
emuron. Okadaro lived in Adacar, Ngariam, and had messengers
all over the north. He foretold success or failure in war, possibly
advised on tactics and provided the soil with which the soldiers
smeared themselves before setting off for war. Surprisingly enough,
Okadaro, who lived close to the Usuku-Karamoja border, also
made predictions for the Karimojong. He had Karimojong wives
and numbers of Karimojong around his home. This may indicate
that, at least at the beginning of the war, the Ateker were not
clearly distinguishing between who were Karimojong and who were
Iteso, that ethnic feeling between the two had not yet emerged. It
may also indicate that the *emuron* was not yet a widespread institution among the Karimojong. However, if Okadaro was Iworopom,
his behaviour appears to contradict the idea that the war was motivated solely by revenge.

Okadaro, however, may have merely been an opportunist who
was prepared to predict for whoever was ready to pay. The *emuron*
received payment in labour and in cattle. Okadaro was later destroyed by the Iteso because they came to see him as a greedy
opportunist prepared to deal with both sides in the war. Okadaro
fell from influence during the great famine of *c.* 1894–96, after he
had repeatedly performed *elelekeja*, the rain-making ceremony,
and failed. Okadaro and his lay friend, Olokotum, had their homes
destroyed because they were amassing wealth as a result of the
famine and because they continued to foretell for the Karimojong.
The elders of Usuku tell the story:

> The famine lasted three years. *Elelekeja* was performed many
> times. It was after *elelekeja* in the third year of the famine that
> Okadaro's and Olokotum's homes were destroyed. Once their homes
> were destroyed it rained. Okadaro was accused of bewitching the
> rain, that he was using a certain charm which brought drought. No
> rain helped to improve the hunting from which he received a
> share. . . . The Imurwok used to make people work in their gardens
> while they carried on the practice of Amurwonok. The people who
> came were those desiring a foretelling and his messengers. This
> was in the nature of a reward for the *emuron's* foretelling.

Hunters also brought back a portion of dried meat from their kill
for the *emuron* as a payment for his assistance in foretelling what
they would kill. If people went to fight they went to the *emuron* for
a prediction. When they returned from war with cattle as booty,
the *emuron* was rewarded with a lion's share, the war leader and
the soldiers taking the rest. The *emuron* was the controller of the
looted cattle and instructed the military leader how they should
be divided.

Okadaro was in the habit of sending some of the people who
went to his home for a prediction, to work in the fields of his
friend, Olokotum. Olokotum was not an *emuron* but just a wealthy
man. When the famine came, both Olokotum and Okadaro possessed large stores of food from the previous years when they had
many people working for them. Okadaro and Olokotum now
became very rich by selling their food to people who were starving.
People became jealous of this surplus of food which they had
worked to produce, so they destroyed the homes of the two men
in order to seize "their" food. Since Okadaro's *elelekeja* repeatedly
failed to bring rain, the people believed that he was purposely killing the rain in order that he and his friend might amass wealth.

> Orwatum had begun as an independent *emuron* before the famine.
> He also led *elelekeja* unsuccessfully but his home was not destroyed
> because it was believed that Okadaro was bringing the drought.
> Furthermore Orwatum was not getting wealthy as a result of the
> famine.
>   Another reason for the popular dislike of Okadaro was that he
> was very friendly with the Karimojong. He had married some
> Karimojong girls and there were many Karimojong around his
> home. They came to him for foretelling and this annoyed the
> Iteso who were enemies of the Karimojong.[26]

The Karimojong war seems to have broken the family feeling
among the Ateker. The Iteso were beginning to feel themselves to
be a distinct people. Possibly the word Karimojong began to fall
into disuse and be replaced by "Ilok", meaning "hunters of small
animals". The raids and hostility between the Iteso and Ilok dragged on almost to the coming of the Baganda, but the great famine
of 1894–96 appears to have triggered a civil war within Usuku
itself. Thereafter the Karimojong war became very much subsidiary
to the major civil conflict.

The great famine or *ebeli*[27] of 1894–96 (occasionally called
Okadaro's Famine) was a disastrous experience for the Iteso if not
as bad, as Lawrance reports, for the Karimojong, where, as a
result, two thirds of the Karimojong perished or were scattered.[28]
In Teso the network of swamps probably prevented this kind of

devastation. It was the root of a certain lily which grew in the swamps which saved many Iteso lives. However, death from starvation was widespread. It was not uncommon to hear of ten people dying in one family or for an elder to say that he lost both of his parents, that one might go away looking for food and return to find within the homesteads the corpses of relatives which had not been buried or even pulled into the bush because of the weakness of the living.

In Teso apparently the drought came first, followed by a cattle disease, followed yet by swarms of locusts. The rain-making ceremonies were performed in greater and greater panic and the ritual murder of suspected rain-killers or bewitchers reached purge proportions. In certain areas the cattle population was almost wiped out and ravenous people ate the diseased carcasses. Desperate men fought each other over the small water holes in the swamps. The pillaging of granaries and the stealing of children for sale for food turned society into almost total anarchy. Many families had to sell their sons and mortgage their girls for food. Goats, boys and girls were sold into southern Teso, where the famine appears to have been neither as severe, nor as prolonged. It seemed that only the hardy goat survived the torture and many more Iteso would probably have died had it not been for this little-respected animal. Wana Elem of Amusia reported:

> During the famine he was about fourteen years old. Many people died, including his father's younger wife, Ikulumet, and her child. Children and even wives were sold to Ngora and Gweri. If anyone had granaries of food, they were moved into the centre of the home and well guarded. People ate various kinds of leaves and *ikorom* (water lilies). All chickens were eaten up. The cattle disease even killed the wild animals. The informant ate the meat of the dead animals. Once when he went to look for food he returned home to find that some of his people had died. Crops failed completely for three seasons.[29]

> He remembers the great famine. He was about ten years old. *Omilimil* (fly) came before the famine, then famine and then locusts. His mother, two sisters and two half-sisters died of hunger. His step-mother died as well. He was the only child to survive. He fed on roots called *eturai*. He was taken to his father's brother, Celi in Ngariam.[30]

The civil war developed as a three-sided affair. On the one side was the northern alliance led first by Ocilaje and then by Ocopo of Abela. On the opposite side was the Itoroma military confederacy led by Abonya of Angodingodi, allied with the Ikomolo of Amuria led by Omiat. The Ikomolo were named after their leader's clan, but they were in no way restricted to one clan, any more than were the other combatants. It was significant that Abela and Angodingodi, which provided the supreme war leaders, were both the most heavily populated units of their respective military alliances.[31]

In the incident which triggered the conflict, the elders of Angodingodi in the south blamed themselves. The story is a comedy of errors involving the Ikomolo, the peoples of Angodingodi and Abela. The incident involved the abduction of a beautiful girl, Apoo, the stealing, retrieving and restealing of a herd of cattle with no one in the triangle sure as to who had carried out the abduction or the stealing. Finally the people of Angodingodi discovered their cattle in a kraal in Abela. The owners of the kraal said: "Have you found your cattle in our kraal? Go into the kraal and ask the cattle whether they belong to you or not." The people of Angodingodi stole the cattle, which were not theirs in the first place, and when the men from Abela appeared before their kraal they retorted in exactly the same words, "Go into the kraal...." However, the people of Abela stole the cattle again and the war was on. The cattle in question belonged neither to Angodingodi nor to Abela. They had been stolen originally by Angodingodi from their allies, the Ikomolo, Omiat's people. While the Ikomolo lost their cattle, they apparently secured the girl Apoo.[32] Angodingodi brought the Toroma military confederacy plus Omiat's Ikomolo to her side, while Abela rallied the confederacies of the north: Katakwi, Usuku and Ngariam. All of Usuku county became involved in the war, except the Magoro confederacy, which remained neutral.[33]

Omiat had been born and had grown to manhood in a very poor home in Kapujan. He was born into the Ikarebwok clan and there were rumours that he had been illegitimate; however, this may only have meant that the younger brother "cheated" on the older (Omiat's legal father). The legal father died and Maala, the younger brother, took over Amir, Omiat's mother. Having quarrelled with his elder brother, Omiat and some of his younger brothers moved to Getem in Abela. He was expelled from Abela—rumour has it for womanising—and he moved west to Komolo near Wera in Amusia where he joined the Ikomolo clan and built himself into an influential territorial chief. Some say that he was a cousin to Ocilaje, the commander of the Abela forces. There are certain Shakan elements in Omiat's career, youthful poverty and rejection, coupled with scandal in maturity—an autocrat with tendencies to eroticism. Komolo became a new frontier area for a flow of pioneers from Kapujan and Toroma. Ties of kinship, if nothing else, drew Toroma and Komolo together against Abela.[34]

The civil war between northern and southern Usuku probably began originally as a fight over water holes in the swamps which form political boundaries. It probably began during the *ebeli*, but it was not until after the famine that it developed into full scale war rather than minor border raids for cattle. In the north the elders claimed that the basic aim of the war was to re-stock the herds of cattle, for when the rains returned "there were few cows left in the homes of the [military leaders] but ordinary people didn't have any at all".[35] It is significant that the north should turn to war for this purpose, while in southern Usuku and southern Teso generally, cattle depopulation and famine were major reasons which caused people to turn to more intensive cultivation. However, by the 1890s in northern Usuku the iron hoe was not in use as it was in the south.[36] The iron hoe must have produced something of an agricultural revolution which had not reached the north. The iron hoe, or rather the lack of it, may help to explain why the north turned to war.

Furthermore, in the borderland between the two combatants lay an area called Angorom which contained a particular red soil— of the same name—which possessed an important ritual significance for both sides in the war. Both Okolimong and Odokomeri, *emurons* of north and south respectively, used the soil of Angorom for smearing the soldiers before they went to war. It was also used in other rituals connected with the *emuron*'s work. Since Angorom actually lay within the jurisdiction of Abela, the Itoroma either had to secure the soil surreptitiously, or organise military expeditions to seize it. Frequently the Itoroma failed and ultimately had to use other kinds of soil found locally. The elders of Usuku are vague about what powers were connected with the soil. Elders from both sides of the civil conflict claimed that the soil did not give any special power to the warriors, nor did the side which failed to secure it operate under any disadvantage. This, however, seems doubtful, given the strenuous military efforts undertaken to secure it. The prestige of Angorom may have pre-dated the institution of the *emuron*. The Itoroma later used white soil in order to distinguish themselves from the northern warriors. Presumably identification in battle had become a problem. In any case the problem of identification provided an excuse for abandoning the red soil of Angorom, which often was not available.[37]

It seemed highly probable that the people of Usuku county had used the services of the same *emuron*, or else the same *emuron* network had spread throughout the area before the civil war.[38]

Furthermore, it had been traditional that the *emuron* was not consulted, nor did he preside over the smearing of soldiers in a civil or inter-Iteso conflict. If there was a central *emuron* he was probably located in the north, where Okolimong inherited a well organised system (discussed below). In Toroma, Odokomeri had nothing like the same prestige and influence over his area. In some *eitela* he had messengers, but in others independent *emurons* existed. However many of these *emurons*, while making their own predictions, did secure the red soil from Odokomeri.

Oral tradition is silent on how the *emurons* were persuaded to break tradition and begin smearing Iteso warriors to kill other Iteso. The two sides, however, may have for long looked upon each other as semi-foreigners. Iworopom influence was strong in the north and had perhaps produced cultural differences between the two sides. Certainly the Itoroma and Ikomolo were of quite different historical origins and migrations from those of the north. Both may have resented the new settlers of northern Usuku. Whether it was so before the civil war is not clear, but during it, each side began to talk of its opponent as foreign. The people of the northern alliance came to be known by both the Ikomolo and Itoroma as "Iteso", a term of disgust, while both sides called each other "Imo" meaning "foreigners, not of the ethnic group".[39]

The civil war seems to have caused a crisis of loyalty for the people of the Magoro confederacy and Amusia. Magoro as the gateway to Teso was a mixture of all kinds of Ateker as well as Iworopom. The people of Magoro were closely related both to the Itoroma and to the northerners. The result was that Magoro remained neutral in the civil war and continued throughout to direct its main military attention to the Karimojong war. However, the period of the Usuku civil war seems to have been one of strife and raids with spears, not only within the Magoro confederacy but even within individual *eitela* of the confederacy.[40] Oral tradition does not reveal the causes of this internal strife, but it may well have arisen as a result of the civil war creating hostility among Magoro's mixed population. For Amusia the problem was more complex. Amusia was a part of the Toroma military confederacy and, against the wishes of many of its inhabitants, found itself at war with the north. As noted earlier, many had migrated north from Amusia and presumably kinship ties were very close. There may have been a similar lack of enthusiasm for the war in some areas of the north, particularly Katakwi and Lale where settlers had recently moved in from the south. Odeng points out that even families were divided over the war in the south.

In the fighting between the Iteso and the people to the south, Apuda (my grandfather) decided to move to the stronger side. (He) moved here (Abela) with his brother; both of them were married. The two of them started the Ideren ateker (clan) in Abela ... and no relatives followed them at a later time.[41]

In Omodi—part of Amusia—the Ilogir clan (possibly of Iworopom origin) left the area for Usuku. "They left because of the Iteso war since their closer relatives were in Usuku."[42] Generally in Toroma there was an effort by elders to belittle Okolimong, the *emuron* of the north. One said Okolimong "didn't foretell the coming of the Baganda. This foretelling was by Odokomeri [*emuron*] of Toroma; Okolimong was not known well until after his death."[43] In Katakwi, on the other hand, one informant tried to make Okolimong the "king of all Usuku" county.[44] These attitudes are what one would expect from different sides in a civil war. However, the elders of Omodoi, Amusia, tried to claim that Okolimong supported the south rather than the north, and that he even smeared the southern soldiers and not the northern.[45] This merely demonstrated the crisis of loyalty even among those who remained in Amusia during the civil war. Not only was there a general close kinship relationship between the people of Amusia and the north, but Okolimong himself had lived in Amusia and had probably married his first wife from there before he left to pioneer the Usuku area. Furthermore, it seems possible that Amusia possessed at least two messengers who throughout the civil war visited Okolimong for predictions and obtained the soil for smearing even though their soldiers fought on the side of Toroma.

Initially, Amusia seems to have tried to remain neutral like Magoro, but ultimately was brought into the conflict by a northern raid led by Ocopo, aiming to seize the cattle of a very rich man in Amusia. The raid was disastrous, Ocopo's warriors being almost wiped out, Ocopo himself barely escaping.[46] From then on Amusia was drawn fully into the war.

Local skirmishing or feuds appeared customary in Usuku and probably generally in Teso. Feuds might occur between neighbouring *eitelas* or even between clans in one *eitela*. Feuds might occur when judicial procedures broke down, or they might be almost in the nature of sport. In local skirmishes wooden sticks rather than spears were used. "In these fights they used wooden spears; the metal spears were reserved for the Karimojong for the idea was to kill them completely. They [the Iteso] didn't like killing themselves."[47] Women and children were neither captured nor killed in such wars. Occasionally two neighbouring groups would arrange a feud, agreeing to pit two similar age sets against each other.

Sometimes these engagements became heated and metal spears were used. A third group normally intervened as arbiters in such a case. Furthermore, there was never any approach to the *emuron*, nor were the combatants smeared. Other than this, wars between Iteso groups were rare. It would appear that the Usuku civil war was almost unique in that it was deadly serious. Apparently women and children were not captured, but they were killed if they got in the line of battle. The *emurons* smeared their respective soldiers, the aim being to kill the warriors of the opposite side. The struggle was just as fierce as anything undertaken against the Karimojong.

OKOLIMONG

As noted above, the *emuron* Okadaro had been discredited during the great famine c. 1894–96. He was succeeded by one of his messengers, Orwatum, who died shortly after the famine. Orwatum was in turn succeeded by Okolimong. Okolimong had been born at Aarapamu,[48] probably in Old Woropom, possibly between the years 1821 and 1831. His family moved to Magoro and from Magoro to Amusia. Okolimong and his younger brother, Agwari, both of whom were married with young children, migrated from Amusia to Usuku c. 1851 to 1861. Thus they were among the early pioneers of Usuku. They belonged to a new clan, the Ikolituko, referring to the zebra-like colour of their cattle.

Surprisingly Okolimong had not been initiated either through *Asapan* or *Abwaton*, although married when he arrived in Usuku. He did his *asapan* in the home of Orwatum, the messenger of Okadaro, following which he took one of Orwatum's daughters as his second wife. He completed his *abwaton* initiation, took the name Ituko (zebra) and was the leader of his age set.[49] It is believed that he fought under Okadaro against the Karimojong and under Etesot and Abila against the Imiro.[50] Etesot and Abila died of old age during the Imiro wars, and Okolimong took over as military leader and was credited with the final throwing back of the Imiro to Obalanga. He probably was a warrior until c. 1871–81. He was heavily scarred. Okolimong was probably a messenger to Okadaro while he was a warrior. After he grew too old to fight he remained a messenger. At Orwatum's death (c. 1897) Okolimong became the *emuron* serving Abela, Usuku, Katakwi and Ngariam and with considerable influence over individuals in the Magoro—Amusia area.[51] By 1897, when he became *emuron* he had three wives. When the Baganda arrived in 1908 Okolimong was a very old man, too old for a Baganda-style chieftaincy which was given to his son. A description follows of Okolimong in his old age.

> Okolimong wore an ekwaro skin falling from his neck at the back, an akale skin over his chest and a calf skin around the upper arms. He wore an etimat combined with very long hair but he didn't use mud. He had a very long beard falling almost to the belly with a bell tied in it. He wore an iron ring in his nose, a plug in his tongue and ear rings. . . .
>
> Okolimong was very rich in cattle. He would lie at the gate of his kraal and all the cattle would come out without stepping on him. This was done to prevent the cattle from being stolen.[52]

When Okolimong became *emuron*, the northern Usuku alliance was still engaged in its normal struggle with the Karimojong. Despite what had happened to Okadaro for treating with the Karimojong, the rumour spread that Okolimong also dealt with them. Tradition seeks to justify or defend Okolimong for his action. While admitting the rumour, the elders say that this consultation "was only at night and not seen by the Iteso".[53]

> The Karimojong visited Okolimong at night; sometimes he told them the truth, sometimes not, particularly as they continued to kill the Iteso.[54]
>
> The Karimojong also came to Okolimong for foretelling but Okolimong was not sincere with them.[55]

The civil war between Toroma and northern Usuku had just begun prior to Okolimong becoming *emuron*. There is no hint in the evidence as to what his attitude was to this war or whether he ever tried to stop it. As noted above, it was not usual for the *emuron* to foretell or smear soldiers in a war between two Iteso factions. Thus the Usuku civil war was a distinct break with tradition. There is evidence from both sides in the war that Okolimong was prepared to foretell for either side.[56] However, for most people in the south, he was identified with the northern forces.

Like his predecessors, Okolimong controlled a number of messengers—fifteen or more—located throughout the northern area and possibly two in Amusia in the south. The role of the *emuron*'s messenger was explained by the elders of Lale, Katakwi.

> Ailet, the father of Erobot Yowani (who was present) was Okolimong's messenger here. Ailet would go to Okolimong for smearing the soldiers before going to war. Okolimong would foretell their chances of success and Ailet would pass the message to the soldiers. Usually there was a general foretelling for the group as a whole followed by foretelling of the success of particular individuals; occasionally leaves (as charms) were sent to particular people for good luck.

After the battle each man who had killed produced a bull and was smeared with the dung of his own bull. This smearing was in the form of an honour, to encourage others to do better next time. Okolimong had nothing to do with this ceremony. The bulls were eaten to celebrate the victory in battle. It was reported to Okolimong how successful the war had been and a gift of one side or half of a bull plus the skin were sent to him if they had been successful. . . .

Following a successful battle when cattle were taken (as loot), if many taken, each soldier might get one. If less, two men might have to share one. Those who had killed would get a larger share than those who had not. If there were many cattle they might get two each. The military leader—*emuron*—gets only meat. Ailet would get much the same as Okolimong.

Ailet was naked, wore a skin over his chest with many *ilitia* (charms) hanging around his neck. He didn't cut his hair and muddied it to make it long. . . .

Ailet would go to Okolimong for the red earth for barren women. . . . Okolimong might foretell that some enemy of the family was making the woman barren. He would say that the enemy had dug *ilitia* into the earth somewhere and he would send Ailet to dig them out. . . . Okolimong never came here to settle disputes or for any other reason; Ailet would go to Okolimong and be given instructions. . . .

Ailet and his assistant, Ongon, would go to Okolimong for the earth and the drugs for the rain-making ceremony. Ailet conducted the ceremony. Ongon took over as *emuron* when Ailet died. They were from different clans. Ailet was Itikokin, Ongon was Ikarebwok. (Okolimong was Ikolituko.)

Neither Okolimong nor Ailet had anything to do with the detection of *achudans*. (Witches, even those suspected of killing the rain). . . .

Neither Okolimong nor Ailet had anything to do with murder cases. (That) had nothing to do with foretelling. . . .[57]

Most of this information was corroborated elsewhere, with the exception of the share of the spoils of war which the *emuron* received. The weight of evidence supports the elders of Lale; however, the elders of Usuku in discussing Okadaro, whom they obviously disliked, said "The *emuron* was rewarded with the lion's share. . . . [He] was the controller of the looted cattle."[58] Since *emurons* inevitably seemed to be wealthy men with many cattle, the latter view is tempting even if it was supported by minority opinion. The elders of Teso generally look back upon the *emurons* with sympathy and kindness because they were not connected with colonial rule. They were much more critical of the military leaders, who are remembered mainly in their role as colonial chiefs. For example, the great military leader of Abela during the *asonya* was the terror of his enemies, but in Abela itself he was described as a coward, presumably because he became an arrogant and oppressive colonial chief.[59] Because of his colonial behaviour the people could not give the credit due him during the *asonya*. In contrast was the benevolent view of Okolimong held by all groups in northern Usuku.

THE COMING OF THE BAGANDA

During the civil war it seemed as if Toroma was frequently on the offensive, raiding as far as Ngariam. The northern alliance had greater success against Omiat's Ikomolo. They raided deep into Amuria as far as Dakabala, Gweri, Asamuk and Wera swamps. Omiat had virtually been driven out of his home area, which was at the mercy of the northern armies. It was therefore hardly surprising that it was Omiat who petitioned the Baganda in 1901, and twice in 1904, to come to his assistance.[60] Omiat's motives at the initial stage seem to have been more to save himself than to carve out a kingdom. However, once he secured Baganda assistance, his ambitions may easily have grown.

The Baganda arrived at the climax of the civil war in 1907 and began their approach to Usuku as supporters of the Toroma-Ikomolo alliance. Omiat at the same time was busy visiting the military leaders of Toroma to secure their acquiescence in the military arrival of the Baganda. In this he was successful, and there was virtually no resistance in Toroma to the Baganda military columns coming from the south across the lake. Initially it looked as if the Baganda would approach northern Usuku from the south through Toroma and from the west through Komolo. For some reason the southern forces did not take part in the initial move and the invasion came only from Komolo.

Severe resistance might well have been expected from northern Usuku. Omiat was known to be behind the new innovation and, except for the guns and a few officers, the Baganda presence was negligible. The invasion from Komolo was by an Ateso-speaking army led by Baganda and some of Omiat's officers. In northern Usuku this must have appeared as not much more than another action in the civil war. However, resistance was weak. The reason seems to lie in the influence of Okolimong, and Omiat's diplomacy.[61]

Okolimong, like the *emurons* of Toroma and all over Teso—with one exception—advised the people not to resist the "butter-flies" and foretold disaster for those who did. He was undoubtedly aware of the Baganda victories in southern Teso and may have believed that resistance was likely to be futile and disastrous. On the other hand he may have seen the coming of the Baganda as an opportunity to end the civil war of which he may never have fully approved. Whatever his motives, his foretelling produced confusion within the northern alliance and effectively weakened its will to resist.

The initial invasion of the Baganda-led forces from Komolo, led by Enosi Kagwa, was seeking to establish a barracks at Katakwi.[62] The most serious battle took place at Obore Otelu in 1907 in Alyakameri, where five Baganda officers were killed. Otelu, military leader of Alyakameri, led the Iteso army. However, this must have been a remnant Iteso force. Part of Abela sent no warriors to the battle. Katakwi did not take part at all. While the military leader of Lale wished to resist, he could not muster his men.[63] In Usuku, where Okolimong's influence was strongest, the contingent sent to Obore Otelu must have been very small. Despite the confusion in the ranks of the Iteso, they won the battle and the Baganda-led forces fell back to Komolo. For those who fought, the rationalisation was that they were not fighting the Baganda but Omiat. Thus they were not disobeying Okolimong.

Given the victory at Obore Otelu, one might expect that Iteso resistance would have been even stronger when the Baganda returned the following year. By then, however, it had collapsed entirely, and the Baganda established their barracks at Abela and their headquarters at Usuku. Leading Iteso military leaders were given chieftaincies—notably Ocopo, supreme military commander of the northern alliance. Katakwi sent two messengers[64] to Omiat at Komolo and to the Baganda at Usuku, offering to lead their askaris into Katakwi.

Rujumba, the Muganda county chief at Usuku, failed through diplomacy to secure acceptance of Baganda-led forces into Ngariam. One battle took place at Kai Kamosing in Acanga, the Ngariam forces being led by Alileng. After the battle Alileng was offered the chieftaincy of Acanga; he refused and the Baganda struck him so hard that he died. His sub-commander was offered and accepted the chieftancy.[65] In old Ngariam, resistance did not appear likely until the Baganda, probably by accident, seized military leader Ojenatum's favourite bull, Abworongor. This made the people angry and they rose against the invaders. The Ingariama were defeated, and Abworongor was returned to Ojenatum who was offered and accepted a chieftaincy.[66] Northern Usuku was conquered by 1910. By almost any standard, resistance was extremely weak. The elders explained this in terms of the influence of Okolimong and the fear of Baganda guns. Since Okolimong had foretold that the Baganda possessed something dangerous and that resistance would bring disaster, both reasons come back to the powerful influence of Okolimong over the military generals, who were eager to fight. It must have been obvious to the Baganda that while Omiat's troops had been a necessity, Omiat himself was a liability. Omiat seems to have developed the ambition to rule over a vast area including Amuria and Usuku. This was denied him, at least in part, because the people of northern Usuku would not have accepted it. Omiat had to be content with the chieftaincy of a subcounty in Amuria.

When the British took over from the Baganda in 1908, they recognised the influence of Okolimong. Ormsby, the District Officer, visited Usuku in 1908 and reported:

> Kolimong the chief of this part is very old and blind, but I understand that at one time he had considerable power in the tribe and was a friend of Kabarega. He asked that an agent be sent to build at his village and agreed to carry out the work involved. I have therefore arranged to send him our agent at Komolo, who has done excellent work there and had been in touch with Kolimong's people for some time.[67]

In summary, this article seeks to show how the civil war in Usuku in the 1890s was related to the settlement pattern: how the different origins, migrations and other historical experience between north and south were potential sources of hostility. However, these differences were probably not enough to lead to war except for the devastation of the *ebeli* and the destitution of the people in its aftermath. The fact that the north was more prepared to resort to war than the south may be related to the different stages of agriculural development in which the two peoples found themselves. The article also seeks to discuss the role of the *emuron* in the society generally and particularly in relation to war. Finally it shows how Omiat and the Baganda exploited the various factions in the civil war to facilitate their own conquest in the early twentieth century.

NOTES

1. In an earlier article, "Pioneers of Teso", in *Tarikh,* Vol. 3, No. 2 (1970), I used the word Itunga (meaning "people") to describe the Ateker people. This followed the example of A. C. A. Wright. Iteso students in the research team objected to the use of the word in this way and the elders of Usuku also disapproved. They suggested "Ateker" which means those peoples who understand the language. Ateker also

means "clan"—either the enlarged group such as Atekok or the smaller group which observe similar taboos and do not intermarry.

2. J. B. Webster, "A Tentative Chronology for the Lwo", Makerere History Seminar Paper (1971).

3. I am immensely grateful to John Lamphear for his generosity in sharing with me his knowledge about the movements of people in Karamoja. I hope that he does not feel that I have stolen any of his important information and apologise for the simplistic statements which follow. See also J. Lamphear, "Jie Genesis", Makerere History Paper (1970).

4. In this article Karamoja is used to describe the north-central part of the Karamoja district of Uganda. Until the nineteenth century the area south of Moroto is more accurately referred to as Woropom. For a fuller discussion of the Iworopom see John Wilson, "Preliminary Observations on the Oropom People of Karamoja . . .", *Uganda Journal,* Vol. 34, No. 2 (1970).

5. From this point forward this article was first presented as a seminar paper in the Department of History Makerere in September 1969. In an amended form it was read at the East Africa Social Sciences Conference at Nairobi in December 1969. It is to form part of a book *The Iteso during the Asonya,* to be published by E.A.P.H., which will also include the research of N. Egimu-Okuda, C. P. Emudong and D. Okalany.

6. The statistics indicate the difference between Toroma and a more recently settled area in Kumi.

Toroma, 56 informants	Nyero, 30 informants
40 no migration outside southern Usuku	7 no migration outside Kumi
7 from Tororo-Bukedea	10 from Karamoja
3 from Woropom	5 from Magoro-Tisai
4 elsewhere in Teso	3 from Ngora
2 no migration story	2 elsewhere in Teso
	3 no migration story

7. Seven were Igoria whose origin is uncertain. For the Ikomolo, see Teso Historical Texts, No. 7. The oldest settlement story came from the Isorimana who 10 generations ago (early 17th century) lived in Toroma. The origin of the Isorimana is unknown, but they used to be called Isuguro, often an *etem* name of the Ikarebwok, one of the original Iseera clans. T.H.T., No. 6. (Oral interviews are designated Teso Historical Texts.)

8. The Imiro was that migration out of Karamoja which passed through Labwor. The main group moved into Lango to become the modern Langi. However at Wila in Labwor the modern Langi claim to have separated from the Iteso. This Ateker group moved south into Amuria and Usuku, becoming known as the Imiro clan which is widespread at the present time in these two counties.

9. Acanga, Ngariam, T.H.T., No. 27.

10. Usuku, T.H.T., No. 25. Possibly the Imiro, like the modern Labwor, spoke the Ateker and Langi languages.

11. Ikumama is the Karimojong word to refer to the Iteso. I use it here to refer to the Iseera—Karimojong fusion which made up the proto—Iteso.

12. Tomasi Egasu, Abela, T.H.T., No. 22.

13. "Etem" in Usuku roughly means "the name of the clan meeting" and identifies more or less the effective clan unit. In southern Teso,

clans do not possess an *etem* name and tend to talk of "branches" of the clan.

14. Mariko Okiror and Paulo Ekwaro, Abela, T.H.T., No. 22.

15. The correlation of dates is important. The Laparanat famine c. 1785–92 was probably even more disastrous than the Ebeli of 1894–6 and caused mass movements of people in the inter-lacustrine area. One result was the Karimojong-Iworopom wars, the latter being destroyed c. 1830. It was significant that the Irarak followed by the Iworopom were settling northern Usuku c. 1783–1835.

16. T.H.T., No. 25.

17. J. C. D. Lawrance says the genealogical trees of the Iteso show the tribe established in Usuku 120 years ago. He admits that southern Usuku was settled about 100 years earlier. *The Iteso* (O.U.P., 1965), pp. 9–12. The "graves" interpretation was repeated to me by Symon Olinga of Toroma, T.H.T., No. 2. After hearing the "Tes Tes" interpretation in Usuka, the county chief of Usuku arranged another interview with a man from Toroma to correct the mistaken view I had heard in Usuku. The arranged interview was with Matayo Akileng who repeated the "graves" story. Katakwi, T.H.T., No. 28.

18. Elders of Usuku, T.H.T., No. 25. Further field interviews revealed the following: "Abila fought against the Imiro under Abwal. They moved (or were chased away) to Nyakwai beyond Obalanga. They had originally come from Lango direction near Nyakwai.... Abwal's son stayed behind and Abwal's sister was married to Kere, an Etesot and an ejakait (chief) ... of Abwanget.... Abwal's son was called Ogwal and his sister, Akwi, who was born in Teso and given an Iteso name ... Ogwal eventually married an Atesot, Inemi, from Abwanget.... They feel that the (Ogwal) began the Imiro clan.... The Imiro spoke both Ateso and Acholi". Elders of Abwanget, Katakwi, T.H.T., No. 146. The major details of the above were confirmed in a second interview in Abela, Katakwi, T.H.T., No. 147.

19. The reader may be confused because "Usuku" may refer to the entire county as in "The Civil War in Usuku" or to the subcounty which is being discussed here or to Usuku village. Many of the names in Teso refer to more than one geographical unit.

20. T.H.T., No. 26. *Eitela* is today translated as parish and refers to the pre-colonial political unit.

21. T.H.T., No. 27. When questioning about the Imiro was the only time when I felt that we came up against nervousness among the elders that our research had political overtones. Today among the Iteso "Imiro" means "Langi". Since the president of Uganda at the time of our field research was "Imiro" I had the feeling that questioning about an earlier Imiro population created fear that we had been sent to establish Langi claims to the land. In Magoro, for example, the elders denied that there were any Imiro clansmen there until a young man spoke up and said there were many of them and that, he, in fact, was married to a woman from that clan. Thereafter the elders said, "There is a clan called Imiro here today. But the Langi never lived here. There is also a small village called Miroi (Lango) which is partly in Omasia. They don't like to hear that the Imiro were here". T.H.T., No. 150.

22. Information from C. P. Emudong.

23. Among fifteen informants in Lale, six were Ikarebwok (Iseera origin);

one Irarak (Karimojong origin); eight were new clans of possible Woropom origin.

24. Elders of Lale, T.H.T., No. 24. The Ingariama were probably a separate Iseera group living in Karamoja in the eighteenth century. They were defeated and some absorbed by the Karimojong (see Dyson-Hudson, p. 89) while others moved away to the Ngariam area of Usuku. Their defeat and absorption probably took place in the early nineteenth century and for them the wars against the Karimojong were motivated by revenge.

25. Okedi of Amusia, T.H.T., No. 10.

26. This and the quotation above from T.H.T., No. 25.

27. It was explained that *Ebeli* was a severe and widespread famine while *itengi* (hunger) referred to a shorter and localised famine. However, many elders used the two words interchangeably. Among the Jie and in Usuku, *Ebeli* can also mean a famine caused by a witch or rain killer.

28. Lawrance, pp. 9–12.

29. T.H.T., No. 11.

30. T.H.T., No. 16.

31. Today both Abela and Angodingodi have the largest number of tax-payers in their respective subcounties. There is little reason to believe that this is significantly different from during the *asonya* or pre-colonial period. The only factor which might upset the percentages of population among the *eitela* is the location of subcounty headquarters, which have tended to draw an administrative and mercantile community. Yet despite this, Angodingodi has a heavier population than its subcounty headquarters Toroma. Abela has a greater population than Katakwi, which is not only a subcounty but also a county headquarters. The balance of population in favour of Abela and Angodingodi was probably even greater in the *asonya*. Getom, a major settlement of Abela, means "full stomach", suggesting a fertile agricultural area. During the *asonya*, what is today the subcounty of Katakwi consisted of three political units, each of which was broken into two *eitelas* or parishes in the colonial period. Taxpayers as of 1969 are indicated in brackets after each political unit. 1. Abela-Abwanget (1,224). 2. Alyakameri-Katakwi (978). 3. Dadas-Aleles (873). The pioneer settling of Dadas-Aleles (called Lale during the *asonya*) had only just got under way by the time of the outbreak of the civil war.

32. Elders of Angodingodi-Angodingodi, T.H.T., No. 12 and Elders of Aparisia-Angodingodi, T.H.T., No. 14.

33. The effective political unit among the Iteso was the *eitela* which was usually about the size of a modern parish or occasionally two parishes. A number of *eitela* were united in what I call a military confederacy. There were five military confederacies in Usuku county: Magoro and Toroma in the south; Katakwi, Usuku and Ngariam in the north. Wars were never fought among the *eitela* within one confederacy although feuds might occur. *Eitela* within a confederacy were expected —but not obliged—to go to war in support of its partners within the confederacy. A discussion of the political and military system appears in *The Iteso During the Asonya*. The Ikomolo military confederacy led by Omiat is today within the county of Amuria and historically it belongs to Amuria rather than Usuku.

34. I have not really sought here to sort out the mass of contradictory and confused evidence about the early life of Omiat, collected both by myself and by N. Egimu-Okuda, who was carrying out research on "The History of Amuria and the Rise of Omiat". My information comes mainly from Toroma, T.H.T., No. 6, Abwanget, T.H.T., No. 146, Abela, T.H.T., No. 147, Orimai, T.H.T., No. 148.

35. Elders of Usuku, T.H.T., No. 25.

36. This information was originally given to me by the elders of Katakwi, T.H.T., No. 23. Mr. N. Nagashima, University of Tokyo, who had been doing research in Usuku for eight months, disputed that the people of northern Usuku did not have the iron hoe until the Baganda military occupation. Nagashima claimed that Banyoro traders had brought iron hoes to the home of Okolimong during the *asonya*. However in a further interview, the elders of Abela supported those of Katakwi and said that the "Baganda brought the first real hoes. This was after the Baganda conquest. They gave some hoes to Okolimong to show him that they intended peace not destruction." The son of one of the early blacksmiths who made spears but not hoes was present at this interview. His grandfather had also been a blacksmith. See Ideet, son of Opolot, son of Ejoropet, Abela, T.H.T., No. 147. The elders of Abwanget reported: "One says the Baganda (another the Banyoro) traders first brought iron hoes. These were not brought until the Baganda came as conquerors. The Baganda, for example, gave Okolimong a number of hoes to convince him of their good intentions. They used the *akuta* (of wood) until the Baganda came." Informant David Onyait says "the Baganda and Banyoro came together. He knows the difference in language between the two." T.H.T., No. 146.

37. Wana Elem of Amusia, T.H.T., No. 11; Nasanari Olaki of Abwanget, T.H.T., No. 146; Orimai, T.H.T., No. 148; Kapujan, T.H.T., No. 149.

38. T.H.T., No. 146.

39. *Imo* was often used during the colonial period to refer to the Baganda. "The Abela people called the Toroma people 'Imo' not 'Iseera'. They were called Imo because they were enemies and because they were not from here (also known as Teso). Long ago the Toroma dialect was different." Odeng of Abela, T.H.T., No. 22. During the civil war Orikimo, military leader of Amusia, thought he had killed Alikileng, military leader of Ngariam. He came home with a large number of captured cattle, singing, "I killed the big or mature Imo and brought the young ones home." Okedi and his brother Penekasi Inya of Amusia, T.H.T., No. 10.

40. For civil strife in Magoro see Omasia, T.H.T., No. 152.

41. T.H.T., No. 22.

42. Daudi Madudu, Omodoi, T.H.T., No. 16.

43. Symon Olinga, Toroma, T.H.T., No. 2.

44. Matayo Akileng, Katakwi, T.H.T., No. 28.

45. T.H.T., No. 16.

46. Okedi and his brother Penekasi Inya, Amusia, T.H.T., No. 10.

47. *Ibid.*

48. Lawrance, p. 9.

49. Elders of Usuku including Samwiri Pilang a relative of Okolimong, T.H.T., No. 25.

50. Elders of Abela, T.H.T., No. 22. and Elders of Usuku, T.H.T., No. 25.

51. Elders of Abela, T.H.T., No. 22 and Okedi and his brother Penekasi Inya of Amusia, T.H.T., No. 10.
52. Elders of Lale, T.H.T., No. 24.
53. Elders of Olilim, Ngariam, T.H.T., No. 26.
54. Elders of Acanga, Ngariam, T.H.T., No. 27.
55. Okedi and his brother Penekasi Inya, Amusia, T.H.T., No. 10. The elders of Abela claimed that one of Okolimong's wives, Ajenga, was a Karimojong. T.H.T., No. 147.
56. T.H.T., Nos. 10, 16 and 22.
57. T.H.T., No. 24.
58. T.H.T., No. 25.
59. T.H.T., No. 22.
60. G. Emwanu, "The Reception of Alien Rule in Teso 1896–1927", Uganda Journal, 31/2 (1967), p. 172.
61. "... and Omiat's diplomacy" was added here after reading the first draft of N. Egimu-Okuda's, "The History of Amusia and the Rise of Omiat", which appears in The Iteso during the Asonya.
62. The best account of the conquest is by Emwanu, ibid. Lawrance has a small section in Chapter III, pp. 23–25.
63. T.H.T., Nos. 22, 23, 24.
64. Okwanga and Ongimatem interviewed at Katakwi, T.H.T., No. 23.
65. Elders of Acanga, Ngariam, T.H.T., No. 27.
66. Elders of Olilim, Ngariam, T.H.T., No. 26.
67. Ormsby to Jinja, 20 October 1908, Entebbe Archives, SMP 241/08. I am indebted to Dr. M. Twaddle for this reference and for turning over to me all of his notes on pre-colonial Teso from the Entebbe and Soroti archives. Such generosity is unusual. I am very grateful.

SOURCE MATERIAL

PRIMARY—ORAL

The field work for this article was carried out in April, May and September 1969. Thirty-seven interviews, mainly group interviews, were conducted and 245 elders questioned. Four Makerere history undergraduates of Iteso origin were interviewing elsewhere in Teso during the same period. For ease in footnoting and indexing all interviews were numbered as Teso Historical Texts and are available in the Department of History, Makerere. The full series of Texts are as follows; those collected by myself, Nos. 1–30 and 146–52; those by David Okalany in Pallisa and southern Kumi, Nos. 31–76; by N. Egimu-Okuda in Amuria, Nos. 77–112; by C. P. Emudong in Kumi, Nos. 113–38; and by Miss E. Tino, Nos. 139–45. My own interviews may be classed by county and subcounty as follows:

Usuku County

Toromo subcounty T.H.T., Nos. 2–16.
Magoro subcounty T.H.T., Nos. 17, 150, 152.
Kapujan subcounty T.H.T., Nos. 148, 149, 151.
Katakwi subcounty T.H.T., Nos. 22–24, 28, 146, 147.
Usuku subcounty T.H.T., No. 25.
Ngariam subcounty T.H.T., Nos. 26–27.

Kumi County
T.H.T., Nos. 1, 20, 21, 30.

Budedea County
T.H.T., Nos. 18–19.

Soroti County
T.H.T., No. 29.

PRIMARY—WRITTEN

Soroti District Archives, courtesy of Dr. M. Twaddle. Adams, 1912 Anthropological Notes, NYIS/6/X/1911.
Father Kuyer, c. 1920, Notes on the Teso Tribe, XMIS/6/66/35.
F. R. Kennedy, 1933, Teso District, compiled for the Uganda Handbook, XCST/1.
Amooti Ka Etesot Association, n.d., Transcript Notes (mostly on age sets) XMIS/6/66/35.

SECONDARY—PUBLISHED

F. G. Burke, *Local Government and Politics in Uganda* (Syracuse, 1964).
N. Dyson-Hudson, *Karimojong Politics* (Clarendon, 1966).
G. Emwanu, "The Reception of Alien Rule in Teso, 1896–1927", *Uganda Journal*, Vol. 31, No. 2 (1967).
P. H. Gulliver, "The Teso and the Karimojong Cluster", *Uganda Journal*, Vol. 20 (1955).
P. and P. H. Gulliver, *The Central Nilo-Hamites*, I.A.I. (1953).
B. M. Kagola, "Tribal Names and Customs in Teso District," *Uganda Journal*, Vol. 19 (1955).
F. R. Kennedy, "Teso Clans", *Uganda Journal*, Vol. 5 (1937).
J. C. D. Lawrance, *The Iteso* (O.U.P., 1957).
——, "A History of Teso to 1937", *Uganda Journal*, Vol. 19 (1955).
B. A. Ogot, *History of the Southern Lwo*, Vol. 1 (E.A.P.H., 1967).
C. I. Walshe, "Notes on the Kumam", *Uganda Journal*, Vol. 11 (1947).
J. B. Webster, "Research Methods in Teso", *East Africa Journal* (February 1970).
——, "Pioneers of Teso", *Tarikh*, Vol. 3, No. 2 (1970).
J. B. Webster, D. Okalany, C. P. Emudong and N. Egimu-Okuda, *The Iteso during the Asonya* (E.A.P.H., 1972).
F. L. Williams, "Teso Clans", *Uganda Journal*, Vol. 4 (1937).
A. C. A. Wright, "Notes on the Iteso Social Organisation", *Uganda Journal*, Vol. 9 (1942).

SECONDARY—UNPUBLISHED MAKERERE HISTORY SEMINAR PAPERS

J. Lamphear, "Jie Genesis", November 1970.
N. Nagashima, "Traditional Social Institutions among the Iteso of the Present Usuku Subcounty", September 1969.
J. B. Webster, "A Tentative Chronology for the Lwo", August 1971.

3

THE VIOLENCE OF TEWODROS*

Donald Crummey

It may be, as Lenin remarked, that violence is a characteristic of all forms of the state.[1] But some forms are more violent than others; and some practitioners of statecraft are more violent than others. Within the Ethiopian state tradition, Tewodros is one of the most violent of all monarchs—probably *the* most violent. Indeed, violence is one of the most essential keys to an understanding of his personality, and his failing as a ruler. It is not that the Ethiopian tradition is a notably pacific one—quite the reverse. A number of Tewodros's predecessors and successors had been celebrated for their activities as warriors—Amda Seyon (1314–44), Sarsa Dengel (1563–97), Yohannes IV (1872–89)—but their fame came from essentially foreign wars, in which the violence they perpetrated was contained within the accepted conventions of warfare, and in which the monarchs represented the values of the Christian Semitic tradition against Muslims, Falashas, or pagans. The violence of Tewodros is unique because it was directed against his own people. Indeed, within the Ethiopian tradition only two parallels come to mind—the religious terrorism of Zar'a Ya'qob (1434–68) and the civil wars of Susenyos (1607–32); and, in neither case, did the policy of royal violence sink to such a level of arbitrary and indiscriminate terrorism as that which characterised the later years of Tewodros, roughly from 1864 to 1868. So intensive, indeed, were the civil wars of Tewodros, and so heavy did his terrorism lie on the land, that it can be seen as a turning point in Ethiopian history.

Beginning with the reign of Sarsa Dengel, in the late sixteenth century, the centre of the kingdom had come to be the region of Bagemder and Dambeya—the areas north and north-east of Lake Tana. Here we find the principal royal sites of the period—Enfraz, Danqaz, Gorgora, Arengo, and finally Gondar. Through

* A copy of this paper has appeared in the *Journal of Ethiopian Studies*, IX No. 2. For comments and suggestions I am especially indebted to Dr. H. Marcus of Michigan State University, and to my two colleagues, Prof. S. Rubenson, and Dr. R. Caulk.

the succeeding two and a half centuries power shifted round this centre—the power of the lords of Amhara giving way to that of the lords of Qwara and Gojjam in the first half of the eighteenth century, and then late in the second half to that of the Galla of Yajju and Wallo—with a brief Tegrean interlude. Effectively, however, power was held within the modern provinces of Bagemder, Wallo, and Gojjam. It was the reign of Tewodros which ended this. He, too, was absorbed within the now traditional framework, and, contrary to what Dr. Darkwah seems to suggest in an article in the *Journal of African History*,[2] it was not the resistance which Shawa offered to Tewodros which provided the inspiration for its later rise to pre-eminence. Quite the reverse. The later pre-eminence of Tegre, and subsequently of Shawa, partly stemmed from their refusal to resist renewed imperial rule, which enabled them to thus escape the devastation which followed the resistence of Semen, Wallo and Gojjam. The reign of Tewodros marks the end of the era of Bagemder as imperial centre, and it does so, in part, because Tewodros exhausted it, and its adjacent areas. There are other important factors—the coherent, integrated state structure of Shawa—and the more advantageous positions of Tegre and Shawa for controlling renewed international trade[3] and contacts with the outside world. But it is not unfair to say that the violence of Tewodros dealt the *coup de grace* to the central provinces.

Tewodros is well known in both the foreign and Ethiopian sources for the violence of his personality. The manner in which he could fly into a temper, the way in which suspicion could lead him into vindictive abuse, and his acute sensitivity over any slights to his personal sovereignty—these are traits noted by a number of early observers.[4] The Ethopian sources are more vivid. "The fire of Qwara", "The entire person of Tewodros is simply fire"; "Did you see the lion die down there?" "He will roar like a lion".[5] And within his own lifetime, his violence was a byword: "May God deliver you to the wrath of Tewodros."[6] Well known are the atrocities and terrorism of his later years from the various accounts of the Abyssinian captives.[7]

What connection then, if any, is there between the celebrated personality and the policy of terrorism; and what relationship, if any, is there between the terrorism and the failure? These, briefly, are the questions which this paper attempts to investigate and answer. Its argument is that from the beginning of his reign Tewodros's tendency to violence was evident. This, however, was counter-balanced by a sweeping desire to reform and a sympathy for the lot of the common people.[8] As his reign progressed, and as his goals of reform, national re-unification, and modernisation continued to elude him, unable either to modify the objectives, or create a new strategy for their attainment, he had recourse to terrorism which exacerbated the problems he sought to solve. A vicious circle was created: increased terrorism produced increased resistance. The circle turned into a spiral, and its course was relentlessly downward. During the last five years of his reign, the territory which Tewodros controlled shrank progressively, until at the end he held only the mountain top upon which he committed suicide. The key to his failure was the instinctive recourse to violence, and the inability to temper ambition. Thus the personality led to the policy—and the policy to the failure.

Tewodros was formed in the harsh environment of the late Zamana Masafent (the Era of the Princes), the period of national disintegration and feuding war lords.[9] Ambition, survival even, demanded a mastery of the arts of war, and it was as a warrior attached to several different courts that Tewodros began his career. Independent activity first expressed itself in banditry in the lowlands along what is now the Sudan border. Already contradictory tendencies began to reveal themselves. On the one hand, Kasa (as he then was) felt no hesitation at disrupting legitimate trade, or at delivering a substantial number of captives—evidently common folk—to be executed by a fellow bandit. His fury at the defiance of a pact expressed itself in mutilations. On the other hand, he used his position to improve the lot of the peasants by giving them money and by using his men to help them extend the area under cultivation.[10]

The period of Kasa's rise to power—the late 1840s and early 1850s—reveals a consummate generalship and an increasingly powerful personality, which, within a few years, made itself the focus of discontent and of aspirations for national renewal. So awesome, and charismatic, had his reputation become that on one occasion an army is said to have laid down its arms in front of him.[11] At this stage, strict control over his army, and a clear, popular policy gained for him widespread support. Although in 1851, the unruliness of his troops brought him into conflict with the clerical authorities of Gondar,[12] in a little over a year his earliest chronicler could remark that Dajjach Kasa was merciful and gentle and that God had endowed him with the facility to be thoughtful of others.[13] Kasa's policy seems to have been an appeal to Christian Amhara resentment against the effete rule of the last of the Yajju dynasty—Ras Ali II and his mother Wayzaro Manan[14]—and his treatment of prisoners at this stage was strikingly clement, a fact which doubtelessly increased his popularity.

By 1855 he had defeated the rulers of Bagemder and Gojjam, and following his victory over Dajjach Webe of Semen, he was crowned emperor.[15] In defeating Webe, Tewodros had also conquered the ruler of Tegre. However, he did not feel it necessary to conquer Wallo and Shawo before claiming the Imperial crown, nor did he enter Tegre before turning his attention to the southern and eastern provinces. In a major campaign from April 1855 to March 1856 he sought to incorporate these provinces which had fallen off from imperial control. They presented two quite distinct problems, and Tewodros approached them differently. Wallo had been the bastion of Muslim Galla power throughout the Zamana Masafent, only loosely controlled by the Yajju Rases whom it supported. Shawa, on the other hand, had long been remote from Gondar politics, and had preserved the Christian Semitic tradition. Tewodros needed to incorporate Shawa to claim an authentic restoration of the Imperial tradition, and to defeat Wallo to confirm the end of the divisive past. From the beginning, Tewodros's treatment of the Galla in general and the Wallo in particular, differed from his treatment of the Amhara.

In Zanab's chronicle we hear of two incidents in the year 1854–55 in which Tewodros severely punished, by mutilation, several soldiers who had murdered or plundered Amhara peasants.[16] And again, in the case of his entry into Shawa, he mutilated those of his troops who maltreated the peasants.[17] His defence of the rights of the poor was clearly articulated: "Soldiers; how is it that you have butchered that which belongs to the poor —in this way God will be against you."[18] On the other hand, Tewodros's very real concern with the rights of the poor had definite limits, and partly stemmed from his attempt to rally the support of all of Christian Ethiopia.

By contrast, towards Wallo, from the beginning, his policy was one of greater severity, although it was not without its subtlety and flexibility. From the accounts of the first Wallo campaign of mid-1855 came the first reports of terrorism; both by the mutilation of prisoners of war and by the destruction of property. During this campaign Tewodros prophesied that before the advent of the Ethiopian New Year in September, he would cause Gallas and Amharas to eat from the same table, thus claiming both victory[19] and subsequent reconciliation. But the price of triumph proved to be terrorism. On several occasions the Emperor had the hands and feet of prisoners amputated and then sent his victims back to their families, while Plowden reported: "The King is now, I hear, wasting Warrahimand (a Walla district) with fire and sword."[20] The prophecy was fulfilled, but the banquet was not to last long. However, Tewodros's policy towards Wallo was by no means wholly negative. His initial arrangements there were very generous, and his most important political appointment was an impeccable one—Imam Liban, a Wallo of high standing.

In Shawa things went rather differently. The Shawas did not resist as the Wallo had, and Tewodros seriously attempted to *win* their allegiance. He did this by stringently disciplining his troops—and by appointing a popular and reputable governor—Hayla Mika'el, son of the famed King Sahela Selasse.[21] On the other hand, his treatment of the Shawan Galla revealed his capacity for extreme measures. Tewodros decimated the Galla living between Dabra Berhan and Angolala, after they had offered resistance scarcely distinguishable from that of the Shawan royal house.[22]

A final incident during the Shawan campaign of 1855–56 revealed an aspect of Tewodros's personality which was significant for the future. Plowden had noted: "He is peculiarly jealous . . . of his sovereign rights";[23] and while the context referred to Tewodros's dealings with foreign powers, it applied equally to his own people. Tewodros's army had now been campaigning for a comparatively long time and some soldiers, men of Damot, a district of Gojjam, began to preach sedition. Tewodros's reaction was swift. The culprits were seized and mutilated, while the ringleaders were carried to their home district to be executed there as a public warning.[24]

The severity towards sedition, first revealed in Shawa, was repeated in Gojjam after the King entered that province in March 1856. Here a number of rebels had arisen—principally Tadla Gwalu who was to be a thorn in Tewodros's side throughout his reign. Those rebels whom he could seize he executed, and those districts which he suspected of harbouring rebels he plundered—particularly Mechcha, a district to the south of Lake Tana, which now began a long and unhappy period.[25]

However, we should not consider that, on balance, Tewodros had proved himself oppressive at this stage. Far from it. His appointees were generally local men of real standing, while the broad lines of his policy were enlightened and progressive, and brought peace and prosperity to significant parts of the country. Equally, his violence was controlled. At this stage, and for the following four or five years, the balance of Tewodros's record continued to show either considerable achievement, or continuing promise. The watershed seems to have been the years 1859–61.

None the less, there is continuity between the early discriminate terrorism and the subsequent degeneration which is revealed in his dealings with religious questions, as well as political ones. In September 1856 there broke out the first of the King's controversies with the Church, in the course of which he revealed a considerable capacity for invective and insult. Even though there was a genuine conflict of interests at stake between Church and State, it must be noted that Tewodros's verbal violence was brought into play at the beginning of the dispute, and undoubtedly made the problem more difficult to resolve. One chronicler felt compelled to record that, in the course of the argument, Tewodros had gathered his troops, although to what end he did not presume to judge.[27]. Tewodros went so far as to accuse the clergy of contemplating murder. Injudicious behaviour served to erode what support the Emperor had gained from the Church by restoring its natural position. Further religious incidents revealing an erratic and intemperate personality were not wanting in the early days of Tewodros's reign.

In one case, Abba Gabra Mika'el, a distinguished elderly convert to Catholicism, was harried to death, not so much for his acceptance of a foreign creed, as for his defiance of the sovereignty of Tewodros.[28] On another occasion, the Coptic Patriarch was subjected to personal abuse, temporary imprisonment, and the plundering of his personal property (subsequently restored).[29] Now in all these cases some form of genuine reconciliation was brought about. The conflict with the clergy was resolved, if temporarily. Abba Gabra Mika'el was dead, but the Catholic communities of Northern Ethiopia did not suffer continued persecution. And the Patriarch parted on reasonably good terms.

Although the tendency to violence was clear at this stage, what was even clearer was the variability of the Emperor's moods. Flad, in his account of the sacking of the Patriarch's goods, makes the point that only very strong pressure from his court prevented Tewodros from instantly distributing the plunder to the poor. He goes on to tell how the abuse of the Patriarch was followed by an abject apology from the Emperor, and a fervent professions of faith and submission. Finally, Tewodros was capable of acts of great generosity. Flad also recounts how, on one occasion, the King himself went among a multitude of poor, diseased, and disabled, distributing alms. He continued: "He is so great a benefactor to the poor, that his army is often without food in consequence of his lavish generosity." Abuna Salama told of an occasion on which Tewodros ran out of money and persuaded the Queen to give up her personal jewellery as gifts for the poor.[30]

The period from 1857 to 1861 is dominated by Tewodros's relationship with three rebellious provinces:[31] Gojjam, led by Tadla Gwalu; Wallo, whose principal rebel was Amade Bashir; and the north (Semen, Wagara and adjacent areas, and parts of Tegre) where two Agaw brothers, Tasamma and Neguse, held sway, supported by Garad, son of Tewodros's half-brother. It was Tewodros's inability to suppress these rebellions, and others which grew up in their shadow, which drove him to increasingly violent and drastic measures. While his difficulties deserve considerable sympathy, they were exacerbated by errors in strategy and judgement.

In comparison to his opponents, Tewodros represented a much more progressive position. His vision of national re-unification, modernisation, and renewed national purpose, contrasts sharply with the apparently particularist views of his opponents. Although it is only for the northerners that we have any substantial material, there is no reason to suppose that any of the rebels represented anything other than the essentially reactionary response of provincialism to the centralising ambitions of the Emperor, or that any of them could remotely rival him in terms of personal gifts. However, having said this, we must note that Tewodros failed to develop a strategy to cope with the situation. Superb tactician that he was, he never rose above successive personal confrontations with his opponents, and Zanab's Chronicle, the only one to deal with the years 1856 to 1860 in any detail, is little more than a record of marches and counter-marches through Begemder, Wallo, and Gojjam.[33]

Plowden pointed out that Tewodros found it impossible to split his army.[34] Thus the rebels were able to co-ordinate their activities. When the king marched to pacify one area, the rebels there would retire, while other insurgents rose to threaten the imperial army's rear.[35] Plowden believed that Ethiopia's recent divisiveness and its continuing particularism made treachery and insecurity commonplace, and required the constant presence of the Emperor with his troops. Plowden's analysis is correct in part, but it is also a notable fact that Tewodros trusted and confided in no one. Indeed, it is striking that in all the chronicle literature, no other figure appears in Tewodros's court who can be considered a really substantial, independent figure.[36] Thus the Emperor compounded his difficulties by his failure to delegate, and by his ability to alienate even the most loyally-inclined by his suspicious nature.

Equally, he contributed to his difficulties by not developing a coherent set of priorities for consolidating his rule. He became obsessed with Wallo, a province of limited strategic value, and paid an unjustifiably high price in trying to pacify it. Beginning early in 1857, and reaching an apogee of devastation at the end of 1859, there took place a series of descents upon Wallo, which distracted the Emperor's attention from more substantial targets. Already at the time of his first Wallo-Shawa campaign, rebels had come forth in Gojjam, Wagara and Semen; the latter, not the Wallo, constituted the major threat of Tewodros's policy of rallying the Christian Semitic speakers. Particularly serious were the activities of Garad, who constantly threatened Gondar, and who spread sedition in the rich province of Dambeya; and of Neguse and Tasamma who kept the north in a state of unrest, and who intrigued for French involvement blocking Tewodros's access to the Red Sea.[37] Garad helped to erode one of Tewodros's most substantial bases of support,[38] while the Agaw brothers for some time prevented him from realising much cherished closer relations with Europe in the interests of Ethiopian development. Had the Emperor been content to secure Bagemder, Semen, Tegre and Gojjam and to extend his rule into Wallo and Shawa from this base, he might have met with success. After all, despite their very high nuisance value, Garad, Tasamma and Neguse were swept aside quickly enough when Tewodros confronted them. Equally, even through Tadla Gwalu was repeatedly defeated in the field, the King never found the time, nor made the effort to seize his stronghold, because his presence was always required elsewhere. Had Tewodros solidified his authority in the north, he might have been able to develop an opening on the Red Sea into a profitable avenue of intercourse with Europe. But here again he lacked the time and patience, and instead resorted to repression and terrorism.

The escalation of violence was slow, but relentless. Following his unsuccessful attempts to capture Amade Bashir in Wallo in 1857, Tewodros entered Gojjam, and, in the course of a campaign that lasted until early 1858, the wives of two rebel chieftains were executed for their husbands' activities, and a number of prisoners were executed, after they had abused the King's clemency.[39] In March 1858 more rebels were delivered into the King's hands, this time by popular action. Wagshum Gabra Madhen, who had been confirmed in his position by Tewodros, and who had subsequently rebelled, along with Betwaddad Berru, who had defected from the King's service, and others, were seized by the peasants of Lasta and brought to Tewodros: " . . . who hacked the hands and feet from the two alike, as far as their knees and elbows, and then had all nine hung from a tree."[40] Finding leniency and the acceptance of local power structures an ineffective policy, the King turned to an equally ineffective repression. It was not long before Gabra Madhen's son Gobaze had arisen to replace him. And Tewodros never caught up with him.

Towards the beginning of June 1858 the King entered Wallo, remaining there for most of the next fifteen months. At first his policy was a mixture of controlled terrorism, and generosity; but slowly the situation got out of hand. Restlessness, and a desire for plunder amongst his soldiers increased the pressures driving Tewodros to acts of violence. Initially, a pattern of seizing Galla property, but of clemency towards Galla prisoners of war, was established.[42] However, peasants who transferred their allegiance to Amade Bashir, were, in the words of Zanab, "exterminated". The contradictions of this policy were considerable, and Tewodros lacked the ability, and possibly by now the control over his troops, to maintain a policy of discriminating violence. In February 1859 Plowden remarked: "I must confess . . . that he has so entangled himself in this part of the country that it is almost impossible for him to abandon it."[43] The Wallo campaign was building to a war of extermination.[44] In September 1858 Kienzlen, an observer stationed at Magdala, in the heart of the Galla country, remarked on the King's personality: "In justice he is terrible. The Abyssinians fear him more than 50,000 soldiers. He is just and merciful. When his worst enemy begs for forgiveness he gives it in passing, but even his closest Minister, his friend, when he least suspects it, he will instantly have hanged, as he recently did."[45] And Kienzlen went on to remark that Gondar was greatly threatened by the Tegre rebels, "But the Wallo Gallas are still worse, for they want to make all Abyssinia Muhammadan, as the King well knows, hence the present campaign."

Here we have the heart of Tewodros's difficulties: the obsession with Wallo, to the exclusion of more serious problems; the strange combinations of mercy and severity which precluded a carefully calculated campaign, and the suspicion of even his closest associates which forbade a rational strategy. Following the urging of Plowden, in February 1859, Tewodros moved his camp near to Wadla, a district of Bagemder, more strategically placed to deal both with the Wallo and the Tegre rebels.[46] But before long he was back in Wallo, and this time his campaign was really terrible. As his army advanced it looted, burned and killed prisoners,[47] while Wallo resistance took the form of retreat. What the king did not demolish the Wallo themselves destroyed in a scorched earth policy, effectively designed to deprive the royal army of food and fodder. Mass mutilations took place,[48] while many children were seized and forcibly removed from their homes. The Protestant missionaries whom the King had temporarily lodged on Maqdala for security, closely reflected his thinking on the barbaric Wallo campaign. Its justification was three-fold: Tewodros had given the Wallo every possible chance, over a period of five years (actually four); the law code, the Fetha Nagast, prescribed death for rebellion;[50] and the Wallo were the spearhead of a Muslim attempt to take over Ethiopia. Zanab reflects the same reasoning when he recounts that the King had returned a full seven times and had issued a proclamation: "Submit—I beg you—leave me in peace, do not rebel."[52]

However, only the first reason, Tewodros's exasperation with Wallo, had much substance, and this reflects the failing of the King, as much as it reflects the intransigence of the Wallo. As far as the question of Islam is concerned, it has recently been shown how closely connected the rule of the Yajju had become with the rise of Egyptian power in the Red Sea in the early 1840s.[53] However, the threat of a link-up between indigenous and foreign Islam had sharply receded with Tewodros's victory over Ras Ali in 1853, and it is a measure of the Emperor's distorted strategic views that he allowed such a factor to distract him from the broader questions at hand. Moreover, his Wallo policy failed. He never controlled Wallo closely, or even seriously threatened the activities of the rebels there. Indeed, his campaigns probably only reinforced the link between the rebel chiefs and the local people.[54] By 1862 he may have resorted to mass deportations of the Wallo to western Ethiopia, still without significantly resolving the problem.[55] Above all, the Wallo campaign established terrorism as a major instrument of control. Thus, when rebellion became established in Shawa under Sayfu, a member of the traditional ruling house, Tewodros reacted harshly. Although he still severely punished his troops for maltreating the peasants, he now mutilated a large number of his opponent's soldiers, and sacked the important town of Ankobar, during which a number of clergy were killed.[56] Despite this extreme severity, which was to increase, Tewodros's European friends still placed great hopes on him, and found many good qualities to praise. Waldmeier, who had entered the country as late as May 1859, found him to be a model prince, raised up by God, gifted with compassion, piety, and concern for the poor.[57] None the less, Saalmuller, one of the missionaries closest to Tewodros, who had arrived in Ethiopia with Waldmeier, retrospectively found the Wallo and Shawan campaigns of late 1859 to have been a turning point for the Emperor.[58] Saalmuller reports that, on his return from Shawa, Tewodros was extremely arrogant, and began to beat the common people who came to seek his justice. He was now bent on the destruction of the northern rebels, although he still sought a political solution. After the death of his beloved wife Tawabach, Tewodros became betrothed to Terunash the daughter of Dajjach Webe of Semen and thus a relative of the rebel Neguse. The Emperor appealed to Neguse to surrender, promising him amnesty, as they were now related by marriage.[59] On receiving the rebel's refusal in January 1860 Tewodros flew into a rage, and stormed after him. Neguse, however, eluded the imperial forces. With the rainy season imminent, Tewodros moved on Gondar, where he executed several clerical supporters of Neguse's ally Garad. Following the rains he marched north to confront Garad, whom he finally forced into a bloody battle, during which both Garad, and John Bell, an intimate of the King's, were killed. Then the prisoners were taken to Dabareq market place, the nearest centre of importance, and massacred. Garad was fortunate to have died in battle. Neguse and Tasamma did not. In January 1861, Tewodros caught up with them in Tegree, and condemned them to a hideous lingering death.[62] (According to Walda Maryam), the King proclaimed: "I will consider as my enemies everyone who does not rejoice on my behalf." Everyone rejoiced.[63] But, if Saalmuller is to be believed, the increasing harshness and severity of the Emperor had already cost them considerable support, both at the popular level, and with the army command.[64] This analysis gains weight from the fact that Saalmuller, despite his negative opinions about Tewodros's moral state, was still overwhelmingly sympathetic to him, and believed that the primary cause of the general disaffection with him was not so much due to his methods, as to his primary end—the restoration of centralised monarchy.[65] Thus Tewodros's enemies were particularists. While this is undoubtedly true, it was surely a political failing that, six years after his advent to the throne, Tewodros was not significantly further ahead in finding a basic *political* solution to the question of national unity. Within three years of his victory over Neguse, precisely the same areas were disaffected—Lasta, and much of the north, under Wagshum Gobaze; Walgayt, and large parts of the northwest, under Teso Gobaze; Wallo was still very restive despite the death of Amade Bashir in October 1861.[66] Shawa was now almost completely alienated under Tewodros's former governor, Bazabeh, and Tadla Gwalu's position in Gojjam was scarcely affected, despite one of the King's biggest and bloodiest victories there, at Enjabara in 1863.[67] By 1865, Tewodros controlled only a very small part of the country—basically the eastern part of Bagemder, and adjacent districts.

Without knowing much more about the government and administration of Tewodros than we now know, it is impossible to make any final judgement about the degree of his political failure. His violence and his inability to delegate authority clearly were major factors, particularly so in the light of the activities of Tewodros's successors. Although Yohannes IV, Menilik II, and Hayla Selasse I had strikingly different personalities, each enjoyed much greater success in dealing with the regional nobility and in moving towards a centralised government. The example of Yohannes is most instructive, for he is closest in time to Tewodros. The former's essentially federalist approach was successful, and he became the first Emperor in modern times to rule the whole of the country as it then was, and in the face of significant political rivals. Both Menilek of Shawa and Ras Adal (later Negus Takla Haymanot) of Gojjam were formidable rivals by any standard, yet Yohannes (by granting them a certain autonomy) brought them under his sway. The reign of Yohannes was therefore freer of fundamentally disruptive internal conflict than that of Tewodros. Wallo was still a problem, but it was never allowed to distract Yohannes from more important, more basic issues; and, with the conversion of the Wallo nobility in the early 1880s, a major step had been taken towards a political resolution of the problem.[68]

As suggested, Tewodros may have contributed to Yohannes' success by exhausting the central provinces, now in a much worse state than in the early 1850s. They were torn apart by even more deeply established provincial elites, and large areas had been devastated. Gondar, the jewel of the national revival of the seventeenth and early eighteenth centuries, had been devastated. The rich lands of Dambeya, Gojjam, Wallo, and Bagemder had been sacked and plundered. Power thus began to pass from the central provinces, but no tangible contribution had been made to finding a new political basis for national revival. Yohannes had to begin anew.

The later years of Tewodros, considered from the standpoint of internal politics, are a distressing period. They are a story of the progressive isolation of the King from all but a tiny group of loyal followers, and of increasing, and increasingly erratic, oppression. Even his faithful and devoted missionary friends became the object of suspicion and abuse. Towards the end of 1861 when several missionaries left Gafat to visit Flad in Gondar, the King had them pursued, their goods seized, and their servants beaten.[69] Although the question was quickly smoothed over, it was symptomatic of Tewodros's increasing suspicion and eccentric violence—characteristics which also revealed themselves in his handling of foreign relations.

In October 1862 Tewodros finally had launched his long awaited diplomatic offensive with letters to Britain, France, and other European powers. The intent of these letters was to establish closer relations with the Christian powers in order to strengthen Ethiopia against a seemingly increasing threat from Turkish aggression, and to provide Tewodros with the technology and advice for the modernisation of his country.[70] They were reasonable and laudable objectives, and the refusal of the powers to treat them seriously was unreasonable and deplorable. After all, the requests were minimal. However, the British incompetently did not reply at all, and the French insisted on conditions, principally the right of Catholic proselytism.[71] Having received only a minimum of attention from the French, who at least deigned to answer his letter, Tewodros permitted the French consul Lejean to depart, although not without having had him chained briefly.

With the British representatives, official and unofficial, it was a different affair. The King had been led to expect great things from Britain, initially by Abuna Salama,[73] and then by Plowden, and by John Bell. Also, the fact that his missionary artisans were rather tenuously under British protection probably further increased his anticipation. After it became clear that no letter was coming, in a series of incidents from late 1863 to early 1864, the principal representatives of British influence were seized and imprisoned:[74] first the missionary to the Falashas, Henry Stern; then the British consul, Cameron; and finally Abuna Salama. In the case of both Salama and Stern other factors were at work.

Salama of course personalised the King's conflict with the Church, while towards Stern Tewodros felt a profound personal antipathy. Their offences were intimately linked to the insulting British inaction, and the frustration which Tewodros felt in the continuing defiance of his sovereignty, not only by his own people, but now also by foreign powers. Thus, as Professor Rubenson has pointed out, Tewodros's reaction to foreign insolence was the same as his reaction to internal resistance—the use of force. Stern and his associate Rosenthal were subjected to humiliating abuse, and over four years' imprisonment, some of it in chains.[75] Cameron and Salama were similarly imprisoned, although so far as we know, Salama was never shackled. Such incarceration was an arbitrary act of violence, by no means carefully calculated to achieve Tewodros's long-term ends. Indeed by so acting the Emperor had probably destroyed the possibility of fruitful relations with Europe, just as his deeds within Ethiopia had ruined his policy of internal reconstruction.

Internally, as well as externally, the years 1864–65 mark an important turning point. Towards the end of 1864 Tewodros sacked parts of Dambeya and Gondar; while in July 1865, following the escape of Menilek from Maqdala, horrible reprisals took place against hostages at the royal prison.[77] (In Menilek, recognised heir of the last Shawan King, Hayla Malakot, Tewodros had lost a vital hostage, and gained a rival for control of Wallo.) By sacking Dambeya and Gondar, Tewodros had decisively turned on the areas which had been most likely to support him, and the devastation was repeated two years later.[78]

As depicted in the chronicle of Walda Maryam, the picture of the last few years of Tewodros is one of mounting atrocity. Reflecting the insecurity of the clergy and captives on Maqdala, of whom he was one, the chronicler quotes a current saying: "How are we to live in security? With King Tewodros that which ought to irritate him disposes him to pity, and that which ought to dispose him to pity provokes his fits of anger."[79] As defections amongst his troops increased, the Emperor replied with repression and large-scale executions.[80] Faithful allies were alienated and massacred.[81] With the royal army melting away, the peasants organised resistance, precisely in those areas in which, for so long, no sedition had appeared—the Dabra Tabor region, Balassa, Dalanta, Wadla and Dawnt.[82] And the arbitrary violence which characterised Tewodros's behaviour in these last two years or so is reflected at the personal level in a story found both in foreign and indigenous sources. Appealing for mercy and compassion a poor person cried out "Getoch" (master, lord). The Emperor interpreted this as another abuse of his sovereignty and, in a fury, had him beaten to death.[83]

Yet, to the very end, he retained qualities of awe and charisma. It is a striking fact that none of the rebels, now grown so powerful, dared face him, although the prize would have been a leading claim for the succession. Thus both Wagshum Gobaze and Menilek approached Maqdala, but retired without attempting to seize it. Equally, as late as the end of 1866, Rassam could exclaim, "How affectionate he is!" although the context does suggest irony.[84] Amongst the artisans, Waldmeier retained his loyalty to the end, at the price of considerable suspicion on the part of his fellows. And Henry Dufton, who wrote in 1867, with some of the captives accounts before him, told sentimentally of how in 1863 he had witnessed the tenderness of Tewodros towards little children:

When I behold the arms of this warrior-king—this man who had slain his thousands and tens of thousands—thrown, in a fond caress, round the little child of the white man, I felt that Theodore must have tenderness lying in him somewhere. His passion for children was confirmed to me by several testimonies. I was told that he has always adopted, as a kind of King's Own, all children born during a campaign, and has charged himself with their education and bringing up.[85]

Any summing up of Tewodros's personality must take account of such testimony, and the numerous other accounts of his generosity, compassion, and identification with the poor. Equally relevant are the accounts of his high political objectives: national renewal, modernisation, reform, and his concern for Christian morality. Yet, for the more limited purpose at hand—an investigation of his violence, and the connection between that personal trait and his ultimate political collapse—it seems clear that, perhaps in a tragic sense (which would have appealed to him), there was a fatal flaw which marred his claim to lasting greatness, and which led to his utter failure. And this flaw, again in tragic terms, was a kind of pride—an overbearing personality which made him impatient of subordinates, a suspicion which made him distrustful of them, and a confidence in his own might which led him to an instinctive recourse to violence. In the end the violence proved an end in itself, engulfing the nobility and compassion. It is a fitting reflection of the basic contradictions of his character that Walda Maryam should thus depict Tewodros's reaction to the sufferings which he had brought on his people:

O my Creator! Look what you have done to me!
Let me die quickly that your creatures will
finally have some rest![86]

NOTES

1. In "State and Revolution"; A. Fried and R. Sanders (eds.), *Socialist Thought. A Documentary History*, 477.
2. "Emperor Theodore II and the kingdom of Shoa, 1855–1865", *Journal of African History* (X, 1969), 105–15.
3. M. Abir, *Ethiopia. The Era of the Princes. The Challence of Islam and the Re-Unification of the Christian Empire 1769–1855* (London; Longmans Green, 1968), Chapter VIII.
4. Principally the British consul Walter Plowden. See especially his famous "Report" in the Public Records Office, FO 401/1, No. 477; 25. VI. 1855. This was reprinted, in part, in his *Travels in Abyssinia and the Galla Country with an Account of a Mission to Ras Ali in 1848* (London, 1868), 456.
5. I. Guidi, *Proberbi, Strofe e Racconti Abissini* (Roma, 1894), 122–3;

C. Mondon-Vidailhet, *Chronique de Theodoros II Roi des Rois d'Ethiopia* (EBLA–EBPB) *d'Après un Manuscrit Original* (Paris, n.d.), 73, 76—this is the chronicle of Walda Maryam, and will henceforth be referred to as Walda Maryam; Alemayehu Moges, *Ityopyawi Qine* 22, quoted in S. Rubenson, *King of Kings: Tewodros of Ethiopia* (Addis Ababa, Nairobi 1966), 32, n. 59. I am deeply indebted to Professor Rubenson's book and to a number of insights which he has shared with me. He is in no way, however, responsible for the opinions put forward in this paper.

6. Walda Maryam, *Chronique*, 51. Note the identical phrase in the anony-mous letter from one of the Chrischona missionaries published in *Magazin fur die neueste Geschichte der evangelischen Missions—und Bibelgesellschaften*, VIII (Basel, 1864), 518—and note also the date of publication, suggesting that the letter may have been written as early as late 1863.

7. For example—H. A. Stern, *The Captive Missionary; being an Account of the Country and People of Abyssinia, Embracing a Narrative of King Theodore's life, and His Treatment of Political and Religious Missions* (London, n.d.); H. Rassam, *Narrative of the British Mission to Theodore, King of Abyssinia, with notices of the countries traversed from Massowah through the Soodan, the Amhara, and back to Annesley Bay from Magdala* (London; 2 vols. 1869); and H. Blanc, *A Narrative of Captivity in Abyssinia, with some account of the late Emperor Theodore, his Country and People* (London, 1868; reprinted Frank Cass, London, 1970).

8. For a discussion of this question see Rubenson, *King of Kings*, and my article "Tewodros as Reformer and Modernizer"; *Journal of African History*, X (1969), No. 3.

9. For which see Abir, *The Era of the Princes*. Especially Chapters II, VI, and VII; and Rubenson, *King of Kings*, Chapters II and III.

10. M. M. Moreno, "La cronaca di re Teodoro attribuita al dabtara 'Zanab'" *Rassegna di Studi Etiopici*, II (1942), 152–5. Hereafter refer-ences are to Zanab, *Cronaca*. The disruption of trade is particularly notable in the light of his later efforts, largely successful, to suppress banditry in the interests of trade.

11. The army of Dajjach Beru in Gojjam, in 1854—Zanab, *Cronaca*, 159.

12. C. Conti Rossini, "Nuovi Documenti per la storia d'Abyssinia nel secolo XIX, *Rendiconti della Reale Accademia dei Lincei*, S8, II (1947), 403.

13. *Ibid.*, 407.

14. This emerges explicitly only in the latest of the chronicles, a rather problematic one, written many years after the death of Tewodros. How-ever, as we will see with regard to the first Wallo campaign of 1855, there are definite signs of a pro-Christian Amhara, anti-Muslim Galla policy evident from the earlier sources. L. Fusella, "La cronaca dell Imperatore Teodore II di Etiopia in un manoscritto amarico", *Annali dell'Instituto, Universitario Orientale di Napoli*, NS, VI (1954–56), 67, 73. This chron-icle is quite anonymous and will be referred to as Fusella, *Cronaca*.

15. For these campaigns see Rubenson, *King of Kings*, Chapter III.

16. 160–1.

17. Zanab, *Cronaca*, 163.

18. *Ibid.*, 160-1. See also the famous statement to the missionary J. L. Krapf —"If I do not help the poor, they will complain of me with God, I have been poor myself"—*Travels, Researches and Missionary Labours During an Eighteen Years' Residence in Eastern Africa* (London, 2nd ed., with a

new introduction by R. C. Bridges, Frank Cass, London, 1968), 458. This is only slightly altered from the manuscript account in the Church Missionary Society Archives, CA5/016, 178, from which I quote.

19. Zanab, *Cronaca*, 162.
20. Zanab, *Cronaca*, 162–3; Walda Maryam, *Chronique*, 9–10; Fusella, Cronaca, 79:, PRO, FO 401/I, No. 447, p. 254; Plowden's Report, 25. VI. 1855).
21. Darkwah, "Theodore II and Shoa", 110–11.
22. Zanab, *Cronaca*, 163 PRO, FO 401/I, No. 469; Plowden to Clarendon, Gondar 22. XII. 1855: Darkwah, 108–11.
23. PRO, FO 401/I, No. 447; Plowden, "Report", 25. VI. 1855, p. 254.
24. Walda Maryam, *Chronique*, 16–17, 19: Zanab, *Cronaca*, 164–5; Gabra Selasse, *Chronique du Règne de Menelik II Roi des Rois d'Ethiopie. Traduite de l'amharique par Tesfa Selassie. Publiée et annotée par Maurice de Coppet.* (Paris; 2 vols. 1930–2), I, 90–1. (Hereafter Gabra Selasse, Menilek.)
25. Zanab, *Cronaca*, 165–7; Walda Maryam, *Chronique*, 19.
26. See Rubenson, *King of Kings*, 53–66; and my article "Tewodros as Reformer and Modernizer", *Journal of African History*, x (1969), No. 3.
27. Conti Rossini, "Nuovi Documenti", 412. Zanab, *Cronaca*, 166–7; in Zanab, Tewodros used the feminine form of address as a sign of contempt, Cf. Rubenson, *King of Kings*, 68ff.
28. C. Conti Rossini, "Vicende dell'Etiopia e delle missioni cattolich ai tempi di Ras Ali, Deggiac Ubie e Re Teodore, secondo un documento abissino", *RRAL*, S5, XXV (1916), 523–5; Takla Haymanot, *Episodi della vita Apostolica di Abuna Yacob ossia il venerabile Padre Giustino De Jacobis* (Asmara, 1915), 238–9; PRO, FO 401/I, No. 447, Plowden "Report", 25, VI. 1855, pp. 254–5; and No. 448, Plowden to de Jacobis, Gondar, 27. VI. 1855. Abba Takla Haymanot is the author of the first as well as the second document.
29. J. M. Flad, Notes from the Journal of F. (sic) M. Flad one of Bishop Gobat's Pilgrim Missionaries in Abyssinia ... (London, 1860), 47–51; PRO, FO 401/I, Plowden to Clarendon, Dabra Tabor, 15. I. 1857: Zanab, *Cronaca*, 167–8.
30. Flad, *Notes*, 74–5. For other instances of generosity, see: Krapf, *Travels, Researches etc.*, 457; Th. Waldmeier, *The Autobiography of Theophilus Waldmeier, Missionary: Being an Account of Ten Years' Life in Abyssinia; and Sixteen Years in Syria* (London, 1889), 17, 73–4; Zanab, *Cronaca*, 158; H. Dufton, *Narrative of Journey through Abyssinia in 1862–63. With an appendix on "The Abyssinian Captives Question"* (London, 1867). 140–1.
31. As indeed is the succeeding period, 1861–68. However, by then, especially by 1864, the question of Europe had become important.
32. The attitudes and foreign policy of Neguse have been dealt with in my *European Religious Missions in Ethiopia, 1830–68*, unpublished Ph.D. thesis (University of London, 1967).
33. 170–80.
34. PRO, FO 401/I, No. 595; Plowden to Malmesbury, Camp., Ein Amba, II. 1859.
35. *Ibid;* see also FO 401/I, No. 568; Plowden to Clarendon, Worrahaimano, 5. VII. 1858. Staats-archiv des Kantons' Basel Stadt, C. F. Spittler Privat-Archiv 653, D3/9; Saalmuller to Schneller, Magdala, 12. X (?), 1859, p. 25 The Basel material is hereafter referred to as *Spittler-Archiv*.

36. See for example the case of Ras Engeda, imprisoned for a time. Zanab, *Cronaca*, 168.

37. L. Fusella, "L'ambasciata francese a Neguse", *Rassegna de Studi Etiopici*, VII (1948), 176–91; G. Lejean, *Theodore II et le Nouvel Empire d'Abyssinie*, S. Russel, *Une Mission en Abyssinie et dans la Mer Rouge, 23 Octobre 1859—7 Mai 1860* (Paris, 1884).

38. *Spittler Archiv* D3/9 Saalmuller to Schneller, Gaffat, 13. I. 1861.

39. Zanab, *Cronaca*, 169.

40. *Spittler Archv* D3/5; Kienzlen to Flad, Suramba, 3. VI. 1858. See also Zanab, *Cronaca*, 170–1.

41. Although as late as 1860, the missionary Stern met Gobaze at Tewodros's court, his disaffection must have occurred shortly afterwards. H. Stern, *Wanderings among the Falashas in Abyssinia Together with a Description of the Country and Its Various Inhabitants* (London; 2nd ed., with a new introduction by Robert Hess, Frank Cass, London, 1968), 57.

42. Zanab, *Cronaca*, 172.

43. PRO, FO 401/I, No. 595; Plowden to Malmesbury, Camp, Ein Amba, 1. II. 1859.

44. PRO, FO 401/I, No. 613; Plowden to Malmesbury, Begemder, 20. IX. 1859: *Spittler Archiv* D2/3; Kienzlen to Parents, Magdala, 10. X. 1859, p. 15–16: Zanab, *Cronaca*, 177.

45. *Spittler Archiv* D3/5; Kienzlen to Spittler, Magdala, 30. IX. 1858. The "closest Minister" to whom Kienzlen refers is unknown to me.

46. PRO, FO 401/1, No. 595, Plowden to Malmesbury, Camp, Ein Amba, 1. II. 1859; No. 598, Plowden to Malmesbury, Begember, 10. III. 1859.

47. *Spittler Archiv*, D3/9; Saalmuller to Schneller, Magdala, 12. X (?). 1859, p. 26.

48. Zanab, *Cronaca*, 179: Spittler; D3/2, Flad to Krapf, Magdala, 3. X. 1959; D2/3, Kienzlen to Parents, Magdala, 10. X. 1859, pp. 14–15; D3/9, Saalmuller to Schneller, Magdala, 12. X. (?), 1859, pp. 24ff. Zanab gives 1000 for the whole campaign; while Flad gives 300 for one incident for which Zanab gives 777. The numbers were undoubtedly high.

49. See my article "Reformer and Modernizer".

50. See The Fetha Nagast. *The Law of the Kings. Translated from the Ge'ez by Abba Paulos Tsadua.* Edited by Peter L. Strauss (Addis Ababa; The Faculty of Law, Haile Sellassie I University, 1968). The relevant positions appear to be pp. 271–2, 274, and 295.

51. See the references in footnote 48. See also *Spittler Archiv* D3/2; Martin and Paulina Flad to Spittler, Makdela, 7. X. 1859.

52. 179.

53. M. Abir, *Era of the Princes*, 112–16. See also M. Abir, "The Origins of the Ethiopian-Egyptian border problems in the nineteenth century", *J.A.H.*, VIII (1967), 443–61.

54. Rubenson, *King of Kings*, 80, with references. The Wallo traditions collected by Isreilli, as published and annotated by Conti Rossini, are particularly unhelpful here. See D. Brielli, "Ricordi Storia dei Vollo", in C. Conti Rossini, (ed.), *Studi Etiopia* (Roma 1965a), 105–106. I am grateful to Dr. Caulk for this reference.

55. London Society for Promoting Christianity Amongst the Jews, *Jewish Records*, NS, Nos. 28 and 29, April and May 1863, 19; Journal of Flad, 4. X. 1862.

56. At the end of 1859. Walda Maryam, *Chronique*, 26: Gabra Selasse,

Menilek, I, 96: Zanab, *Cronaca*, 179–80: *Spittler Archiv* D3/9; Saalmuller to Schneller, Magdala, 12. X. (?), 1859, p. 39.
57. See my article, "Reformer and Modernizer"; and Waldmeier's *Autobiography*. See Also PRO, FO 401/I, No. 601, Plowden to Malmesbury, Gondar, 27. V. 1859.
58. *Spittler Archiv* D3/9, Saalmuller to Schneller, Gaffat, 13. I. 1861, p. 8. See also "Reformer and Modernizer".
59. *Ibid.*, p. 6. There are some difficulties in the chronology of this letter. Saalmuller clearly dates the Tewodros-Terunash marriage to 1859, whereas it took place *after* the northern campaign. A betrothal in late 1859 which is purely surmise, makes sense of the chronology.
60. For which see Stern, *Wanderings*, 228–9.
61. *Spittler Archiv* D3/9, Saalmuller to Schneller, Gaffat, 13. I. 1861. pp. 10–14; D3/1, Bender to Family, Gaffat, 15. I. 1861, Fusella, *Cronaca*, 88–9: Walda Maryam places the number at 500 although this is certainly much too high.
62. Walda Maryam, *Chronique*, 29: Fusella, *Cronaca*, 90–4, PRO, FO 401/1; No. 684, Inc. 2, Theodore to Barroni, n.d.; No. 692, Inc. 11, Playfair to Anderson, Aden, 5. II. 1861; No. 692, Inc. 12, Playfair to Anderson, Aden, 13, II. 1851.
63. *Chronique*, 29–30.
64. *Spittler Archiv*, D3/9; Saalmuller to Schneller, Gaffat, 13. I. 1861, pp. 7–8, 10, 15.
65. *Ibid.*, 10.
66. *Ibid.*, D3/1; Bender to Gobat, Dschadschaho, 20. XI. 1861. For the progress of the rebellions in general see, L. Fusella, "Le lettere del Debtara Assaggakhan", *R.S.E.*, XII (1953), 80–96.
67. See Rubenson, *King of Kings*, 79–81. For the battle of Enjabara see Rassam, *British Mission*, I, 238; Walda Maryam, *Chronique*.
68. There is no reliable modern study of the reign of Yohannes. I am deeply indebted to conversations with my colleagues Dr. R. Caulk, who is in no way responsible for my abuse of his knowledge.
69. *Spittler Archiv* D3/1, Bender to Gobat, Dschadaschaho, 20. XI. 1861; D3/11, Schimperto Gobat, Adoa, 6, II. 1862; D3/12, Waldmeier to Committee, Gaffat, 24. XI. 1862.
70. See the most recent account in Rubenson, *King of Kings*, 84ff, with references.
71. See Rubenson, *op. cit.*, and my thesis, "European Religious Missions".
72. Lejean, *Theodore II et le Nouvel Empire d'Abyssinia*.
73. See my thesis, "European Religious Missions", and Plowden, PRO, FO 401/1, No. 447; "Report", 25. 1855, p. 255.
74. Rubenson, *King of Kings*, 85–6.
75. Stern, *Captive Missionary. The Church of Scotland Home and Foreign Missionary Records*, NS, III (Edinburgh, 1864–65), 225: PRO, FO 401/II, No. 17, Inc. 2, Haussmann to Petherick, Khartoum, 4. I. 1864, No. 35, Inc. 2, Haussmann to Petherick, Matemma, 14. II. 1864; No. 93, Ayrton to Russell Cairo, 19. IX, 1864; No. 145, Flad to Rassam, Gaffat, 26. I, 1865, No. 189, Inc. 5, Stern to Wife, Amba Magdala, IV, 1865; No. 189, Inc. 4, Rosenthal to Goodhart, n.d.; and No. 225, Inc. 3, Cameron to Shaw, Magdala Prison, 28. V. 1865.
76. PRO, FO 401/II, No. 105, Inc. 2; Rassam to Mereweather, Massowah, 12. X. 1864: J. M. Flad, *The Falashas (Jews) of Abyssinia, with a Preface*

by Dr. Krapf (London, 1869), 10–11: Fusella, "Lettre Assaggakhan", 81–2 Walda Maryam, *Chronique,* 48–50.

77. Walda Maryam, *Chronique,* 40–41: Gabra Selasse, Menilek, 100: Fusella, "Lettere Assaggakhan", 83: PRO, FO 401/II; No. iii, Rassam to Badgar, Massowah, 20. I. 1865, No. 317, Inc. 12, Stern to Rassam, Amba Magdala, 9. VII, 1865, No. 266, Inc. 11, Stern to Wife, Amba Magdala, 13, VII, 1865; No. 266, Inc. 7, Cameron to Shaw, Magdala Prison, 14. VII. 1865.

78. See Walda Maryam, *Chronique,* 48–50; Fusella, "Lettere Assaggakhan", 88–9.

79. See note 59 above.

80. Walda Maryam, *Chronique,* 43: Fusella, "Lettere Assaggakhan, 90–91: *Jewish Intelligence,* NS, VII (1867); 229–30; Rosenthal, Magdala, 10. VI. 1867, India Office Archives, *Abyssinian Original Correspondence,* I, 361–2.

81. Rassam, *British Mission I,* 238; Walda Maryam, 44–50.

82. Walda Maryam, *Chronique,* 42–3: Fusella, "Lettere Assaggakhan", 90–91: 10 A, *Ab. Or Corr.,* I; 314–5, Blancto Merewether, Magdala, 30. IV. 1867; 295–6, Merewether, Aden, 15. VI. 1867, enclosing Rassam to Merewether, Magdala, Ca. 3. V. 1867; and the references in footnote 80.

83. Blanc, *Narrative of Captivity,* 174; Walda Maryam, *Chronique,* 64–5. The stories vary so utterly in their circumstantial details that they may refer ot two quite distinct occasions.

84. 10A, *Letters Received (Various).* Letters from Aden, XLIII, 466–7; Rassam to Merewether, Magdala, 5. XI. 1866. But see also *ibid.,* 449–51; Rassam, Magdala, 26. VIII. 1866 and the various accounts of Rassam's encounters with Tewodros from January to July 1866, in *British Mission,* and FO 401/II.

85. Dufton. *Narrative of a Journey,* 1867, 106.

86. See Note 24 above.

4

WAR AND LAND IN RHODESIA IN THE 1890s[1]

Robin H. Palmer

*"You will give us land in our own country! That's good
of you!" Ndebele induna to Rhodes, Matopos Hills,
28 August 1896.*[2]

The 1890s, like the 1960s, was a decade of great turbulence in
Rhodesia. The initial confrontation between black and white
was exceptionally violent, with murder, looting and rape almost
commonplace activities. Attempts to tax the unconquered Shona
produced a series of armed clashes; the Ndebele state was destroyed in a crudely imperialist war; post-war pillaging provoked
ChiMurenga, the spectacular risings of 1896–97 which so nearly
threw off European rule; and finally the savage suppression of the
Shona rising was followed by a most uneasy peace, punctured
abruptly by the heroic Mapondera until his resistance too was
finally brought to an end in the early years of the twentieth century.[3] This decade of violent "pacification" greatly conditioned
the subsequent racial and political attitudes of both Africans and
Europeans.[4]

The problem raised in this paper is that of the interconnection
between early land policies and the war of 1893 and the risings
of 1896–97. Since land and its apportionment have subsequently
proved to be the most significant of the many racially divisive
features imposed over the years by white Rhodesian governments,
it may prove rewarding to look at the way in which early land
policies were evolved, to ascertain the extent to which they were
moulded by the violence of the period, and to discuss their
immediate impact upon the African peoples of Rhodesia. The
question is by no means merely academic, since so much of what
subsequently happened was clearly foreshadowed in the 1890s,
when some five thousand Europeans arrived, looking for gold,
and seeking to realise that most chimerical of fantasies, a "white
man's country".

The Europeans entered a country where two different state

systems co-existed, though not in peace. In the northern, eastern and central parts of the country lived the indigenous Shona-speaking peoples, while in the south and west the newly arrived Ndebele had created a military state which was feared and respected throughout Southern Africa by Africans and Europeans alike.

The great days of Shona history had long since passed. Towards the end of the fifteenth century the Empire of Mwene Mutapa had stretched from north of the Zambezi to the Limpopo, and from the Kalahari almost to the Indian Ocean, while in the seventeenth century the armies of the Rozvi Empire had defeated Portuguese forces on three occasions. But in the early nineteenth century, the *Mfecane* brutally shattered Shona independence. In the 1820s the Shona were obliged to endure the destructive passage of Zwangendaba and Nxaba and the regular raiding of Soshangane, while in the late 1830s Mzilikazi's Ndebele finally came to rest at Bulawayo and began to assert their dominance over the surrounding country.

The result of all this upheaval was that by 1890 the agricultural Shona peoples possessed no centralised authority, and were scattered throughout Mashonaland and part of Matabeleland, living in small, and often rival, chiefdoms (*nyika*), in which coherent decision making was rendered difficult by a complex collateral system of succession. Subjected in the south and west to Ndebele attacks, and in the east and north to periodic Gaza and Portuguese *prazo* raids, the Shona tended to avoid the open country and to confine their settlement to the rugged, granite *kopje* regions,[5] though this "stronghold complex" may well have pre-dated the *Mfecane* and existed in the last, and far from tranquil, days of the Rozvi Empire. By 1880, however, a massive influx of guns had so strengthened the Shona that their capacity to resist the Ndebele had greatly increased, though this tendency continued to be offset by their lack of political unity. It may well have been the desire to compensate for this disunity which encouraged a number of paramounts in northern and eastern Mashonaland to enter a series of alliances with the Portuguese in 1889–90, designed to block Ndebele power. These alliances naturally fell away when the British took control of "Mashonaland" late in 1890. But though politically fragmented, the Shona retained, in the Mwari cult and through their spirit mediums, a degree of religious cohesion which was to prove of crucial significance during their rising of 1896–97.[6] In European eyes, however, the Shona were a cowardly, degenerate people who clearly welcomed the British as protectors. They were natural "loyalists", whose feelings did not need to be taken into consideration.

The small and highly centralised military state of the Ndebele was situated on the Matabeleland highveld within an approximate sixty-mile radius of Bulawayo. The state was ruled by an absolute monarch, subject only to advice, and not direction, from the three great councillors and the two councils, the *izikulu* and the *umpakaiti*. Beneath the king was the aristocracy or *zansi*, comprising the "pure" Ndebele who had set off on the long march from Zululand. They occupied almost all the important offices of state and positions of command in the army, and they manned the leading regiments. Below them were the "middle class", the *enhla*, who were mostly Sotho and Tswana captives incorporated into the "snowball" state in the course of its wanderings south of the Limpopo. They were obliged to swear an oath of personal allegiance to the king, and very quickly came to regard themselves as true Ndebele. They tended to despise the serf class, the *holi*, consisting mostly of Shona peoples captured after the final settlement at Bulawayo. The *holi* performed most of the menial work, but even they felt a degree of loyalty to the state which had so abruptly adopted them, and some at least joined the Ndebele rising of 1896. In this rigidly hierarchical society, a person was not allowed to marry someone from another caste.

The Ndebele state was organised on a military basis and was littered with army barracks. There were five large provinces, each ruled by a senior *induna*, in which the top regiments occupied provincial towns and the lesser ones regimental towns. Compulsory military service began at the age of fifteen. Unlike the Shona, the Ndebele were pastoralists. They made relatively little attempt to cultivate, but raided the neighbouring peoples annually for food and cattle, as well as captives. This helps to explain their preference for the Matabeleland highveld, which was free of tsetse fly and was ideal cattle country. By 1890 the Ndebele had acquired an enormous herd of somewhere in the region of a quarter of a million, which attracted the envious attention of many would-be European ranchers. Europeans also coveted the rich red and black soils of the highveld. The Ndebele were feared and respected for their military prowess, they basked briefly in the high esteem widely exhibited towards pastoralists, and acquired something of the mystique reserved in Kenya for the Maasai— a mystique which betrays unmistakable signs of racialism.[7]

The essential motive behind the European occupation of Mashonaland in 1890 was the possibility of discovering a "second Rand". The pioneers who trekked up from South Africa came in search of a quick fortune, but Rhodes was dreaming of much wider horizons. He envisaged a rich Mashonaland acting as a counterweight to the Transvaal and thus reasserting British supremacy in South Africa. The British Government, reluctant as ever to spend money, was prepared to grant him what amounted to a free hand; it stationed no official in Salisbury, and its High Commissioner resided in Cape Town, some 1,600 miles away. Thus Rhodes' nominee, Jameson, was permitted to rule Rhodesia in a highly idiosyncratic manner. He was, as a subsequent Chief Justice admitted somewhat wryly, "admirably fitted for the period in which rough justice was appropriate."[8] Yet despite the fact that the Company was given a free rein, the early expectations of boundless wealth proved to be totally ill-founded. With Chartered shares falling fast on the London market, the Company close to exhausting its capital, and many pioneers returning disgruntled to South Africa, Rhodes turned his acquisitive eye towards Matabeleland, whose mineral wealth was believed to be at least the equal of Mashonaland, and where the fertile, well-stocked highveld was an added inducement. Accordingly, Jameson, "the instinctive surgeon," who "could operate, with a few swift cuts, not only on people, but on history,"[9] seized the opportunity afforded by the Victoria Incident of July 1893 to push matters to a head. "We have the excuse for a row over murdered women and children now," he wired Harris, the Company's Cape Town Secretary,[10] "and the getting Matabeleland open would give us a tremendous lift in shares and everything else."[11] Hence the Matabele War and the absurdly easy Company victory, aided considerably by "abominably bad" Ndebele generalship.[12] The victory had obvious political repercussions, but it was also important psychologically, for it left the Europeans with a dangerous belief in their invincibility and a conviction that Africans were not a factor meriting serious consideration.

The impact of the war on future land problems was also immense. Even before battle had been joined, the economic future of Matabeleland was largely predetermined by a unilateral act on the part of the settlers. In August 1893 the Europeans in Fort Victoria refused to fight for the Company, though they were under a legal obligation to do so, until they had been granted certain concessions. Jameson had no option but to meet their demands, which were incorporated into the Victoria Agreement. This agreement, which applied both to the 414 men who invaded Matabeleland from Fort Victoria and to the 258 men of the Salisbury column, stipulated that everyone taking up arms was to be entitled to a free farm of 3,000 morgen (6,350 acres) any-where in Matabeleland with no obligation to occupy the land. Each man was also granted fifteen reef and five alluvial claims, while the Ndebele cattle, the "loot", was to be shared: half going direct to the Company, and the remaining half being divided equally among the officers and men. The British Government was not informed of the terms of the agreement.

"Within a few months of the European occupation," noted a senior official of the Rhodesian Native Department, "practically the whole of their most valued region ceased to be their patrimony and passed into the private estate of individuals and the commer-cial property of companies. The whole of what their term *nga pakati kwe lizwe* (the midst of the land) conveyed became meta-morphosed . . . into alien soil and passed out of the direct control even of the Government."[13] The settlers immediately began to enjoy the spoils of victory; "before many weeks had passed the country for sixty miles and more around Bulawayo was located as farms,"[14] and by January 1894 over 900 farm rights had been issued and half of them pegged out.[15] The lands of the Ndebele, situated within this sixty-mile radius, had been expropriated vir-tually *in toto*. H. J. Taylor, who as Chief Native Commissioner for Matabeleland was subsequently confronted with the problems posed by this wholesale expropriation of land, observed with monumental understatement, and without punctuation, that "the policy of the Government in throwing Matabeleland open for the acquisition of farms without first having studied the native side of the question as affecting their tribal lands did create diffi-culties".[16]

In an attempt to combat these difficulties, a Land Commission was appointed in 1894, empowered to make a final settlement for the Africans of Matabeleland. The Commission was appointed on 10 September, and, with a haste typical of the period, produced its report by 29 October. It took the line of least resistance, turned away from the highveld, which by now was virtually a huge European reserve, and assigned two large, remote and virtually uninhabited areas, the Gwaai and Shangani Reserves, estimated to be 3,500 and 3,000 square miles respectively.[17] The commissioners were unable to hazard a guess as to the African population of Matabeleland; they made no provision for those who found themselves living on European farms; and they were able to inspect for themselves only a small portion of the Shangani Reserve. Much of the evidence given to the Commission by the Ndebele *indunas*, which apparently indicated that the reserves were of good quality, was in fact so vague that it is impossible to determine whether they were actually referring to land situated within the reserves.

The British Government, which had briefly but unsuccessfully attempted to take charge of the post-war settlement, took no exception to the Commission's Report, which the Colonial Secretary approved in January 1895, noting that the commissioners "appear to have given their best attention to the questions and arrived at well-considered conclusions".[18] In reality, as Jameson's successor Grey admitted, the Ndebele regarded the two reserves as "*cemeteries* not homes",[19] and the Colonial Office, after a later enquiry, came to regret its earlier approval, one official writing bluntly that "the proceedings of the Land Commission were a farce".[20]

Before assessing the immediate effects of this conquest settlement, it will be helpful to look at what was happening in Mashonaland during this time. The 1890 pioneers were each entitled to a free farm of 1,500 morgen (3,175 acres), but it was gold rather than land which had brought them to Mashonaland, and many therefore sold their land rights to speculators while still on the march to Salisbury. An immediate attempt was made to avoid conflict with the Shona by confining provisional land grants to a relatively uninhabited area between the Umfuli and Hunyani rivers, roughly between present Hartley and Norton. The architect of this scheme was Archibald Colquhoun, recently Deputy Commissioner for Upper Burma, a civil servant with a love of ordered administration, who was very much out of place in Rhodesia, and who subsequently admitted having felt "an utter distaste for the atmosphere of mining speculation and company promoting which pervaded the country".[21] Such squeamishness soon earned the displeasure of Rhodes, who at the end of 1890 promoted the swashbuckling Jameson over Colquhoun's head. Jameson exhibited no such regard for Shona land rights and allowed the settlers to peg their farms where they pleased, though they were told that "no land was to be taken which was used by the natives for their villages and gardens."[22] In practice this proviso was almost universally ignored, especially by the missionaries who made a point of selecting land adjacent to, and sometimes including, African villages. Land was alienated principally around the main centres of Salisbury, Umtali and Fort Victoria at Enkeldoorn, where a large number of Transvaallers settled; and in the Melsetter district after the 1893 Moodie Trek, where Europeans "were allowed to peg off farms whenever they chose, and apparently without respect to the rights of the Natives. In fact, the very spots on which the Natives were most thickly situated, were, to a great extent, selected as farms."[23] In this district the Free State trekkers were rewarded with farms of 6,350 acres, while their leader, Dunbar Moodie, carved out for himself a huge estate of over 60,000 acres and appeared "entirely to have studied his own interests at the expense of those of the country."[24] Melsetter is thus in many ways comparable to central Matabeleland, and it is interesting to note that early in 1896 the local Native Commissioner responded to this situation by asking on his own initiative for the establishment of native reserves, to protect Africans in the likely event of their being evicted from European farms in the future.[25] His colleague at Chibi-Chilimanzi, near Fort Victoria, facing a similar though less pressing problem, made an almost identical plea at the same time.[26]

What were the practical effects of Jameson's lavish liberality? In the short term they were in fact rather less than might be supposed, principally because much of the so-called "European land" remained unoccupied, as the settlers in both Mashonaland and Matabeleland had obtained the "right" of not having to occupy their farms. By October 1892, for example, only an estimated 300 farms in Mashonaland were said to be occupied.[27] This is almost certainly an over-estimate and the word "occupation" is somewhat misleading, since "one owner would 'oversee' several farms if they were relatively close together," and "In the case of the great land companies, one 'ranger' sufficed to 'occupy' an area of up to 170,000 morgen, when such a large area had been alienated in a single grant".[28] Hence those few Shona who found themselves living on the 300 occupied farms were rarely displaced, since very little active farming was undertaken. Without adequate equipment or supplies of labour, and lacking both a railway and a mining boom, the European farmers were obliged to work on a very small scale, much in the African manner, and they frequently purchased food from their African neighbours. Around Enkeldoorn, a few farmers "had some lands planted before the rising, but many more were content to grow just enough to keep themselves for the near future, and some . . . left their farms and took up transport-riding".[29] Such "farmers" had no reason to compel Africans to move, and in any event there was ample room for movement on a farm of 3,000 acres or more.

Whilst it is certainly true, therefore, that the future tenure of the Shona was prejudiced by such alienation, their immediate tenure was very largely undisturbed. There was also something of a fortunate difference of soil preference which allowed the Shona to avoid by and large the fate of the Ndebele, since in general the Europeans took up land on the heavy red soils of the highveld, which the Shona tended to ignore in favour of the lighter, and more easily manageable sandy soils.[30] Moreover, the Shona were far more widely dispersed than the centralised Ndebele, and their *kraals* were of a more temporary nature and were rebuilt much more frequently than the large Ndebele military settlements. This much looser pattern worked to their advantage, as did the fact that after 1893 many Europeans deserted Mashonaland for the seemingly greener pastures of Matabeleland. Even in the case of the Ndebele one must not forget that European absentee landlordism was the rule rather than the exception, so that by March 1895 a mere 900 acres were claimed to be under cultivation.[31] Moreover, no attempt was ever made to force the Ndebele to move into the Gwaai and Shangani Reserves; they were far too highly prized as a potential labour force for such a scheme to be contemplated.[32] Of course, the Ndebele had numerous grievances at this time, but the loss of land was generally not immediately felt, though the long-term effects of the conquest settlement of 1893 were to prove colossal.

Evidence that the immediate effects of land alienation were not deeply felt comes from the fact that no direct correlation can be drawn between the extent of land alienated and the outbreak of resistance in 1896, since some paramounts who had suffered great loss of land did not join the rising, while others who had lost no land came out in revolt. In Melsetter, surprisingly, there was no rising; in Fort Victoria Chiefs Zimuto and Chikwanda, whose lands had been alienated, did not rise;[33] while at Enkeldoorn Chief Chirumanzu, who had lost land, stayed out, and Chief Mutekedza, who had not, became a leading "rebel".[34]

Land grievances were not, therefore, a major factor in bringing the African peoples of Rhodesia out into armed revolt in 1896. There were instead a number of much more potent pressures. The Ndebele, after the war of 1893, were treated very much as a conquered people. Perhaps as much as 80 per cent of their cattle was first looted by Company and Shona freebooters and then decimated by the rinderpest; forced labour was widespread and much resented by the aristocratic *zansi*; while the African police acted with great brutality and paid off a number of old scores.[35] For the Shona, who had not been defeated and had ceded no sovereignty, the demand for a ten shilling hut tax was bitterly resented and provoked widespread resistance. Forced labour was common, the N/C Hartley observing late in 1895, that "I am at present forcing the natives of this district to work surely against their will, using such measures as I think desirable."[36] Conditions of work were generally appalling. Not only was there widespread recourse to the *sjambok*, both by employers and by the young, inexperienced Native Commissioners—the N/C Mazoe "had a reputation for flogging indiscriminately"[37]—and numerous fatalities in the primitive mines, but many employers were not above picking quarrels with their workers towards the end of the month, with the predictable and intended result that workers left their employment unpaid. In the circumstances it is scarcely surprising that Africans ultimately broke out in armed revolt.

At the end of 1895 Jameson invaded the Transvaal in an attempt to overthrow the Kruger government. The raid was a complete fiasco, which gave the Ndebele the opportunity to rise in March 1896, and the Shona followed suit in June. Professor Ranger's invaluable pioneering study of the risings[38] is at last undergoing some modification. In particular, it is argued, Ranger paid insufficient attention to those who did not resist an important omission, since the "collaborators" were ultimately responsible for the failure of the risings. In Matabeleland for example, the Ndebele under the *induna* Gambo, influenced by the attitude of the Mwari shrine at "Umkombo", remained "loyal" and refused to cut the vital road to the south, with the result that supplies and reinforcements were able to reach the besieged *laager* in Bulawayo. In Mashonaland too, collaborators played a vital role, for they greatly influenced the spatial expansion of the rising and also limited the possibilities of combined "rebel" military operations. Dr. Beach, in his local study of South West Mashonaland, has revealed a complex pattern of resistance, collaboration and neutrality, in which traditional Shona politics, fears of a Ndebele resurgence and realistic assessments of the likely outcome of the fighting all played their part.[39] The politics of resistance and collaboration were also to play an important role in the post-war land settlement.

The Jameson Raid and the risings at last goaded the British Government into action. With the morale of the Company at its lowest ebb, the British were able to take control of military operations against the "rebels"; to dominate, though not always intelligently, the subsequent political settlement; and to place a permanent resident in Rhodesia. With regard to land policy, the Imperial Government had two major objectives: first, to ensure that adequate "native reserves" were established throughout the country, and second, to protect as far as possible those Africans who found themselves living on land owned by the Europeans. The Company agreed to meet these demands, and so in 1897 Native Commissioners in Matabeleland began the difficult task of demarcating reserves; while their colleagues in Mashonaland, where the rising took much longer to subdue, followed suit in 1898. But the surveys took time, the South African War intervened, and the reserves were not formally passed by the Executive Council until the end of 1902. Thereafter they were subjected to close Imperial scrutiny and were finally approved in July 1908, with the important proviso that they were to be regarded as provisional and subject to possible future consideration.[40] Outside the reserves, a proclamation, drafted by Imperial and Company officials, and modelled on Cape legislation, was issued in October 1896, initiating a system of locations on European farms. Before discussing the effects of these policies, it is worth noting that they were based upon two very serious misapprehensions: first, that the native reserves were simply a temporary, emergency expedient which would be abolished as the country became more economically developed; second, that there would be no widespread eviction of Africans from European farms in the foreseeable future.[41]

The Company bowed to Imperial pressures, though it realised quite clearly that if it did not rapidly put its house in order, it might either lose its Charter or be confronted by continued African resistance. With Jameson on his travels between Pretoria Jail, Wormwood Scrubs and Holloway, the Company appointed Grey, one of its well-connected directors, and Milton, a senior civil servant seconded from the Cape, to take his place. Both were horrified at the legacy of the Jamesonian era. Milton, on arrival, noted that "Everything here is in an absolutely rotten condition," and he stressed the need to "clear out the Honourable and military elements which are rampant everywhere" and in whose interests the country had been run.[42] Grey lamented that "Land is our great difficulty. It has all been given away."[43] Together they determined on a three-fold programme of reform. Firstly the Native Department was placed on a rather more regular footing than hitherto, and Milton managed to recruit a number of tolerably well-qualified officials from Natal and the Cape. Secondly they attacked absentee landlordism by attempting to impose a policy of "beneficial occupation or surrender". But, as in Malawi, the attempt foundered on the rock of settler opposition, expressed in the new Legislative Council.[44] A compromise was eventually reached in 1903, but it was one which favoured the settlers, and it was by then too late to use any of the surrendered land for the native reserves. Finally, Grey and Milton entrusted the task of establishing native reserves throughout the country to the new Native Commissioners. How they went about their task and to what extent they were influenced by the risings will be examined presently.

The two risings came to an end in markedly different ways. Whereas, in the face of strong settler opposition, Rhodes and the leading Ndebele *indunas* made a peace treaty as between equals, the Shona paramounts were ruthlessly hunted down and had their caves, full of people, blasted with dynamite until the last pockets of resistance were utterly crushed. No peace treaty was signed in Mashonaland.

By the middle of 1896, Rhodes recognised that it would require much time and money, and cost a great many white lives, before the Ndebele "rebels" could be driven from the virtually impregnable Matopos. He therefore persuaded them to accept peace terms which stipulated, *inter alia*, that they would be allowed to return to their homes. And so they were. But, as the Chief Native Commissioner for Matabeleland admitted, "it was natural for the Matabele to assume they would be secure in regard to their tribal lands. On this assumption they surrendered and returned to their homes."[45] The assumption was ill-founded, for as a result of the 1893 war their homes had become European property. It is true that the Company might have attempted to expropriate this land or buy it back from the settlers, but neither action was really within the bounds of political or economic feasibility. Expropriation, in Rhodesia, was something that happened to Africans but not to Europeans.

Grey and Milton did make some attempt to alleviate immediate hardship by using three blocks of farms as reserves: Sauerdale, 81,000 acres, in the Bulawayo district; Insangu, 33,000 acres, in Bubi; and De Beers, 200,000 acres, in Insiza-Belingwe. But Sauerdale was Rhodes' personal farm and so could not become an official reserve, though it was used "to settle a good many former rebel chiefs . . . so that they might be securely watched and controlled."[46] De Beers and Insangu were only leased for five years, the cost of outright purchase proving too high for the Company, and as a result they offered only temporary security. Elsewhere, undisturbed tenure could only be guaranteed for two years; thereafter, the Ndeble were at the mercy of their European landlords. To this day the Ndebele believe that a solemn promise was broken; as late as 1931 Chief Mdala of Insiza was complaining that "After the rebellion when we were in the 'Gusu' [rocky country] we were told to return, as we would be given land. This promise has not been carried out. The Government has sold the land to Europeans."[47]

Many of the Ndebele who returned to their homes after the

rising, only to find themselves living on European farms, were obliged to enter agreements with their landlords, resident or absentee. This was done under the terms of the High Commissioner's Proclamation No. 19 of 14 October 1896, which, in order to diminish the prospect of an immediate recurrence of violence, allowed the Ndebele a two-year period of grace, during which time no rents were to be charged and no tenants could be evicted. Thereafter rents were to be fixed between landlords and tenants and approved by the Chief Native Commissioner, who was to act as arbiter in the event of disputes. Where labour agreements were imposed, these too had to receive the sanction of the CNC and were not to last for more than one year at a time. Finally, at the suggestion of Grey, who believed that the Ndebele should not be permitted to gather in numbers large enough to threaten the peace,[48] the number of tenants was to be limited to seven heads of families to each farm of 1,500 morgen. In practice, this last stipulation came increasingly to be ignored, and by the end of 1907 as many as 40,000 Africans in Matabeleland had come under the terms of the Proclamation.[49]

The 1896 Proclamation was an attempt to meet the immediate post-rising situation. It endeavoured on the one hand to encourage the Ndebele to return to their homes and start planting their crops, thereby avoiding a famine the following year, while at the same time providing those few Europeans who were actually farming with a readily available supply of labour. But at the end of 1898 the period of grace came to an end, and landowners began to demand rents. This closely followed the imposition, for the first time in Matabeleland, of a hut tax of ten shillings per annum. The Ndebele bitterly resented paying rent, generally one pound per adult male but sometimes as much as two or three pounds in Umzingwane, near Bulawayo, for the privilege of remaining on their own land, though the vast majority preferred to stay rather than move into the reserves, which were situated mostly in unfamiliar and inhospitable country.

The Company, prompted by the Imperial Government, had made its gesture of reform, and the fact that rent and labour agreements were in theory controlled by the CNC gave the Ndebele some slight degree of protection; but in general they were totally at the mercy of the white farmers, who could evict them at will, even against the wishes of the administration. Thus the Jamesonian legacy continued to dominate the affairs of Matabeleland.

In Mashonaland the situation was rather different. A much smaller proportion of the population found themselves living outside the reserves, which, when defined, were generally much larger

and more accessible than in Matabeleland. Much less use was
made of the High Commissioner's Proclamation, which in any
case was drawn up before the Shona rising had been put down, and
a mere 705 Shona, in the Chilimanzi, Gutu, Makoni and Melsetter
districts, came under its terms.[50] Unwritten agreements tended to
be the norm, and while these allowed farmers greater freedom of
action, tenants did have the security of knowing that a reserve was
usually available within easy reach. This also meant that European
farmers in Mashonaland wishing to retain Africans on their farms
as labourers, were obliged to treat them with rather more deference
than was the case in Matabeleland, where the Ndeble tended to
cling to their traditional homeland no matter what burdens were
imposed on them.

As peace was slowly restored to Mashonaland, it became Company policy to move the Shona into reserves, where this was prac-
ticable. It was also decided that they should be moved away from
their inaccessible *kopjes* into more open country and settled in
much larger *kraals* than hitherto—thereby, it was hoped, reducing
the chances of a further rising and making it easier for Native Commissioners and chiefs to exercise control.[51] This policy provoked
strong reactions, for the Native Commissioners of Chibi, Marandellas, Mrewa and Ndanga all admitted that force was necessary
to make the Shona comply with these instructions. In fact the
scheme was partly abandoned after a few years, when it was found
that the larger *kraals*, while easier to administer, tended to produce
problems of erosion and sanitation.[52] But the implementation of
the policy in the first place left little doubt that ruthless pacification
was being followed up by very firm direct rule.

The most positive result of the armed resistance of 1896–97 was
the creation of native reserves throughout the country after the
restoration of the *Pax Rhodesiana*. The risings on the one hand
convinced administrators of the urgent need to assign land for
African use, and on the other they helped to mould the shape of
the reserves settlement to a considerable extent. Thus whilst the
Africans of Rhodesia lost the war, they at least achieved some
tangible gains from the peace. Hitherto, with the exception of the
grossly inadequate Gwaai and Shangani Reserves, there was no
land in Rhodesia which was free from the threat of instant expropriation. One might argue that the sheer impact of white settlement
would ultimately have compelled the Company to assign reserves
of some sort, as happened subsequently in Kenya and Zambia, but
it was the risings which made their provision an absolute necessity;
and without violence, the reserves might not have been established

until much later, by which time considerably more land would have been taken up by the Europeans.

The reserves created at the turn of the century are important because they have survived, with a good deal of amendment but recognisably in the same pattern, down to the present. This was not foreseen at the time. H. J. Taylor, the CNC Matabeleland, was by no means alone when in 1904 he expressed the view that reserves "involve the negation of all progress, and should be regarded only as a temporary makeshift".[53] The reserves were therefore not initially designed to be the Africans' share of the land; they were essentially *ad hoc* creations intended to solve the post-rising refugee problem, to cushion somewhat the impact of alien rule, and to provide respite for those who found the exactions of white landlords too great. In the circumstances, one cannot criticise the early Native Commissioners for failing to realise that they were establishing the basis of a land division which has remained fundamentally unaltered ever since, and which subsequent administrators attempted to enforce with increasing rigidity when segregation became the official policy.

The manner in which the reserves were created reveals the futility of attempting to erect a simple stereotype which views all colonial administrations as totally monolithic. This is no more valid than the old imperial stereotype which saw "the Africans" as an undifferentiated mass. In this particular case in Rhodesia, there were enormous differences of approach among the Native Commissioners, to whom the task of demarcating reserves was entrusted, and there were also conflicts between the Native Commissioners, the two Chief Native Commissioners and Administrator Milton. On the whole, the Native Commissioners tried to obtain as much good land as possible, and were even on occasion prepared to recommend the expropriation of European land to meet African needs,[54] while the CNCs attempted to "balance" the respective demands of Africans and Europeans; and Milton always tended, in cases of conflict, to back the settlers and point out that Africans who found difficulty obtaining land could always move to other districts where there was a great abundance.

In many ways the task of the Native Commissioners was an unenviable one. Dr. Beach has pointed out that in Charter the reserves were demarcated as early as 1896 "by a harassed Native Commissioner and his assistant, faced with the problem of a fragmented society in his area, while the rest of Mashonaland was still fighting".[55] This state of political uncertainty was matched by an astounding degree of administrative chaos. The Native Commissioners were not supplied with criteria on which to base their selection of land; they were left to fend for themselves and do the best they could in the conditions obtaining in their districts. Moreover, they did not appear to be aware of the desirability of working in concert with their colleagues in neighbouring districts, and their interpretations of what was required tended as a result to differ most markedly. The N/C Hartley, for example, made his reserves "large enough for all purposes", on the grounds that they would be easier to reduce than increase in the future,[56] while the N/C Lower Gwelo decided, for reasons unstated, that his reserves should be "as small as possible".[67] Some, like "Wiri" Edwards at Mrewa, paid careful attention to tribal boundaries and to the needs of shifting cultivators,[58] while others failed, or were unable, to make such provision. A confused pattern therefore emerged, in which individual inclinations were allowed to run riot.

Inclinations had to be tempered however by a solid core of reality, for it was clearly understood that certain definite categories of land could under no circumstance be selected for a reserve. Foremost among these were the land already alienated to Europeans, land on the goldbelt,[59] land near existing or projected railways,[60] and, in districts such as Salisbury, land which could easily be defended in the event of another rising.[61] Thus the extensive vested interests built up during the Jamesonian era were left untouched. The 15,762,364 acres granted to Europeans by March 1899,[62] representing one-sixth of the total area of Rhodesia, and, quite literally, the Europeans' pick of the country, and including virtually the entire Ndebele homeland, could not be considered for African use, though some Native Commissioners were extremely reluctant to concede this point. But it was not quite as simple as that, for the Survey Department, responsible for assigning European land, and the Native Department, which demarcated the reserves, did not work hand in hand. The result was that most Native Commissioners had no idea what land had been granted to Europeans, since so much of it was lying unoccupied. They wrote in to headquarters, but the CNCs were unable to enlighten them.[63] Often therefore they inadvertently included European farms within the boundaries of their reserves; such farms subsequently had to be excised from the reserves, rendering them totally inadequate in many cases.[64]

It must be remembered too that the creation of the reserves was intimately linked with the suppression of the risings, especially in Mashonaland. Towards the end of the risings the most urgent priorities facing the Native Commissioners were first to get people to surrender, then to disarm them, and finally to settle them in the new reserves. As a general rule, "rebels" were rounded up first, and then, when the district was felt to be secure, "neutrals" and "collaborators" were attended to. One might logically expect that the collaborators would have been singled out for generous treatment, but in fact nowhere in the written records is there any mention of a Native Commissioner specifically rewarding a paramount for his "loyalty" by assigning him a generous reserve. In part this can be explained by the fact that the settlement was already prejudiced by the amount of land given away to Europeans before the risings, and, irrespective of the intricacies of Shona and Ndebele attitudes during the fighting, such land could not be expropriated and made available for African use. On the other hand it is reasonable to suppose that some Native Commissioners—and nearly all of them were involved in the fighting—may have decided, without mentioning the fact, to reward collaborators, so far as it was in their power to do so. In this category might be placed paramounts Chirumanzu, where the situation was somewhat complicated by Native Commissioner Weale's marriage to the chief's daughter, Chibi, Zimuto, Matibi and Gutu, all of whom were rewarded for their "loyalty" with subsidies in 1897,[65] and subsequently received generous treatment in the allocation of reserves. But whilst in some instances the "rebels" were rounded up into small, condensed areas, and the "loyalists" were left with the pick of the land when the Native Commissioner was free to attend to them in a more leisurely fashion, this was not always the case. In Mazoe, where the rising involved nearly the whole district, Chief Chiweshe was the first to surrender, and as a result found himself located on an extensive reserve, named after him, and rewarded with the nominal paramountcy.[66] Similarly in Charter, the "rebels" were situated on what became the Narira and Mangene reserves, while "collaborators" such as Gunguwo and Huchu, the brother of Chiramanzu, were left stranded and subsequently had their land occupied by European farmers.[67] Thus no uniform pattern emerged, and much was left to the fortunes of war and the personal inclinations of the Native Commissioners. This is perhaps best illustrated in Marandellas, where pacification took the form of clearing the road between Salisbury and Umtali and driving Africans away from their homes along the road into the neighbouring hills. When the Native Commissioner subsequently came to assign reserves, he did so in the areas into which Africans had been pushed, mistaking them for their traditional homes.[68]

In the light of all this complexity, it is scarcely surprising that the quality and extent of the reserves varied greatly from district to district. In Matabeleland, where land was generally more arid and thus had a smaller carrying capacity than in Mashonaland, the area of the reserves was estimated to be 7,753,140 acres, or a mere

17 per cent of the total area of the province, of which 5,293,466 acres comprised the remote, waterless and largely uninhabited Gwaii, Shangani and Nata Reserves. As High Commissioner Milner confessed, "The selection of the additional reserves has been a matter of no small difficulty owing to the fact that so large an amount of the best land in the country was, in the first days of the occupation, alienated to syndicates and private individuals."[69] Hence no reserve could be assigned in the Bulawayo district, and only a small one of under 5,000 acres in Umzingwane, where over half of the district was in the hands of a single company. Similarly, in Insiza and southern Bubi the Native Commissioners were able to make only very limited and inadequate provision for Africans. The N/C Insiza's suggestion that the Company expropriate some European land was flatly rejected.[70] In Matobo a reserve was selected in the Matopos by the first Native Commissioner, but his successor was unable to find it, and it was eventually abandoned when found to conflict with the peace terms issued at the end of the rising.[71] This left the district without a reserve. The general pattern in Matabeleland then, was that practically the whole of the central highveld around Bulawayo was in European hands and hence only grossly inadequate provision could be made for the Ndebele. The great bulk of the Matebeleland reserves lay in the dry Kalahari soils to the north and north west of Bulawayo, which the Ndebele had never deigned to inhabit.

In Mashonaland, where the reserves totalled an estimated 17,138,560 acres, or 37 per cent of the province, the situation was a little better. This was partly because much less African land had been taken up by Europeans, but an additional factor may have been a highly irregular circular in August 1900 from the CNC Mashonaland, informing Native Commissioners that "It is to be clearly understood that after this no recommendation for the setting aside of any ground for a Native Reserve will be considered by ... [Milton] so that adequate provision for our requirements for all time should now be made."[78] The Imperial authorities were insistent that the provision was certainly not to be a final one, but the circular may have had the effect of making some Native Commissioners assign land generously, though one must remember that by the time it was issued, the vast majority had already made their selection of land.

Even in Mashonaland however, Resident Commissioner Clarke wrote, "In some parts a difficulty in finding suitable land has been experienced ... owing to the large portions of territory alienated to Companies and individuals before the justice of making provision for natives had not (sic) the consideration which it has since received."[73] The CNC, Taberer, also admitted that "In some cases Native Commissioners have been driven to select ground not altogether suitable for Reserves", and that while some reserves were "unnecessarily large", "this is mainly accounted for by the fact that they have had to select ground interspersed with granite and ground unfit for cultivation".[74] This was certainly the case in Inyanga, where the Native Commissioner was forced to disregard the general directive that the Shona be moved from easily defensible *kopjes*, and to assign reserves in precipitous, inaccessible, and badly watered country because all the good land had been taken up by Europeans.[75] In Fort Victoria[76] and Umtali, where land had also been extensively alienated, small scattered reserves were all that could be provided, the N/C Umtali observing that these would afford less danger in the event of another rising and would moreover facilitate the supply of labour.[77] One of his successors was of the opinion that the "loyalty" of the Africans of Umtali during the rising merited a fairer distribution of land than had in fact taken place.[78] The Native Commissioners at Makoni,[79] Mazoe,[80] and Salisbury[81] all experienced great difficulty in selecting suitable reserves, since so much of the best land had been taken by Europeans. At the other extreme, however, in the remote and unhealthy districts on the borders of Rhodesia—Darwin and Mtoko in Mashonaland, Gwanda, Sebungwe and Wankie in Matabeleland—where there had been no European penetration or settlement, it was not felt necessary as yet to assign any reserves. This task was left to the Native Reserves Commission of 1914–15.

In many cases, however, the full repercussions of the reserves settlement did not become apparent for several years; indeed, some Native Commissioners had no wish to disturb Africans by telling them that a division of the land had been made. In 1898 the CNC Matabeleland thought it unwise to mention the matter, as "it would inevitably lead to a good deal of discontent amongst the natives, as they are much too primitive to understand the portioning out of land",[82] while the Native Commissioners at Mazoe and Fort Victoria refrained from pointing out the reserve boundaries until as late as 1908, in order not to "worry the minds of the natives prematurely".[83] But such a fiction could only be maintained for a short period within the reserves, on unalienated land, or where European owners neither occupied the land nor charged Africans rent for living on it. As soon as landlords began to impose rent or labour agreements, Africans were only too aware that a land division had been made. Their awareness spread rapidly after 1908, when, with the introduction of a "white agricultural policy" as a result of the comparative failure of the mining industry, the Company began to charge them rent for living on unalienated land, and to launch an attack on the reserves with a view to reclaiming all the best land for prospective European settlers. Thereafter, land policy was primarily concerned with squeezing Africans out of the "European areas" into the increasingly overcrowded reserves,[84] with the result that political grievances, especially among the Ndebele, were dominated by land issues.[85]

War and land were thus intimately connected during this initial decade of European rule. The pioneer settlers in Mashonaland, who had come prepared to fight but were not called upon to do so, were granted land rights which soon resulted in considerable alienation around the main centres. The white mercenaries who invaded Matabeleland continued this tradition and expropriated the highveld in a manner paralleled only in parts of South Africa. The repercussions of this scramble for land now play their part in the current Rhodesian crisis. They do so because the Company, with its primary obligations towards its shareholders and the white settlers, was unable to break this white stranglehold in any decisive way. Here we can see quite clearly the beginnings of the "settler problem". Finally, the risings of 1896–97 brought some compensation for Africans in the shape of Imperial intervention and the establishment of native reserves throughout the country. Yet the Native Commissioners who assigned these reserves were forced to work within the limits imposed by Jameson's liberality, and their ultimate achievement was shaped, in a complexity of ways, by the risings and their immediate aftermath.

NOTES

Note on sources: unless otherwise stated, archival sources refer either to the National Archives of Rhodesia or to the Public Record Office, London. The PRO files contain the prefix C.O. or D.O., and consist of original correspondence belonging to the Colonial and Dominions Offices.

1. An earlier, and somewhat different, version of this paper has been published as "War and Land in Rhodesia", *Transafrican Journal of History*, 1, ii (1971).
2. V. Stent, *A Personal Record of Some Incidents in the life of Cecil Rhodes* (Cape Town, 1924), 60.
3. T. O. Ranger, *The African Voice in Southern Rhodesia* (London, 1970), 3–7.
4. The normally phlegmatic Selous considered that the "rebels" were "monsters in human shape, that ought to be shot down mercilessly like wild dogs or hyaenas, until they are reduced to a state of abject submission to the white man's rule". F. C. Selous, *Sunshine and Storm in Rhodesia* (London, 1896), 88.
   The brutal suppression of the risings had an intimidating effect upon

subsequent African political activities, for "the collapse of the risings brought greater disunity instead of the greater unity which was its aspiration; a collapse of morale instead of triumphant self assertion.... It was to be a long time before self-confidence returned to the mass of the Shona people." Ranger, *African Voice*, 1–2.

In much the same way, German suppression of Maji Maji meant that TANU recruiting in the affected areas was extremely difficult. G. C. K. Gwassa, public lecture delivered at Makerere, 1969. Cited in D. Denoon and A. Kuper, "Nationalist historians in search of a nation: the 'new historiography' in Dar es Salaam", *African Affairs*, 69 (1970), 343.

5. R. H. Palmer, "Red Soils in Rhodesia", *African Social Research*, 10 (1970), 747–58.
6. D. N. Beach, "The rising in south-western Mashonaland, 1896–97" University of London, Ph.D. thesis (1971); M. L. Daneel, *The Gods of the Matopo Hills* (The Hague, 1970).
7. J. E. G. Sutton, "The Settlement of East Africa", in B. A. Ogot & J. A. Kieran (eds.), *Zamani: A Survey of East African History* (Nairobi, 1968), 97; B. A. Ogot, "The role of the pastoralist and agriculturalist in African History: the case of East Africa", in T. O. Ranger (ed.), *Emerging Themes of African History* (Nairobi, 1968), 126.
8. R. C. Tredgold, *The Rhodesia That was my Life* (London, 1968), 61. For more detail on the attitude of the British Government, see R. H. Palmer, "Aspects of Rhodesian Land Policy, 1890–1936", *Central Africa Historical Association*, Local Series 22 (1968), 10–13.
9. S. G. Millin, *Rhodes* (London, 1937), 258.
10. It is usually assumed that Jameson and Harris were bosom friends, but on one occasion Jameson felt constrained to observe that "Harris means well in Cape Town but is really a muddling ass—on the surface a genius; but under the crust as thick as they are made." Hist. MSS. JA 1/1/1, Jameson to Sam Jameson, 11 August 1892.
11. Rhodes House, Rhodes Papers, MSS. Afr. s.228, C. 3B, Jameson to Harris, 19 July 1893.
12. Hist. MSS. SE 1/1/1, Selous to his mother, 15 November 1893.
13. N 3/16/9, S/N Bulawayo to CNC, 1 June 1920.
14. A. Boggie, *From Ox-Wagon to Railway* (Bulawayo, 1897), 26.
15. C. L. N. Newman, *Matabeleland and how we got it* (London, 1895), 147.
16. D.O. 63/3, Memo by Taylor, February 1927.
17. C. 8130, *Matabeleland, Report of the Land Commission of 1849, and correspondence relating thereto* (London, 1896).
18. C.O. 417/130, Ripon to Loch, 25 January 1895.
19. Rhodes House, Rhodes Papers, MSS. Afr. s.228.1., Grey to Rhodes, 26 May 1897.
20. C.O. 417/219, Minute by Graham, 26 June 1897.
21. A. R. Colquhoun, *Dan to Beersheba* (London, 1908), 294.
22. W. H. Brown, *On the South African Frontier* (New York, 1899), 120.
23. NUE 2/1/2, Report of the N/C Melsetter for the half-year ending September 1897.
24. L 2/2/95/22, Magistrate Melsetter to Acting Administrator, 12 April 1896.
25. NUE 2/1/1, N/C Melsetter to CNC Mashonaland, 2 April 1896.
26. N 9/1/1, Report of the N/C Chilimanzi for the year 1895.
27. British South Africa Company, *Report on the Company's proceedings*

and the condition of the Territories within the sphere of its operations, 1889–92 (London, 1893), 25.

28. D. N. Beach, "Afrikaner and Shona Settlement in the Enkeldoorn Area, 1890–1900", *Zambezia*, 1, 2 (1970), 26.

29. Beach, "Afrikaner and Shona", 28.

30. Palmer, "Red Soils".

31. British South Africa Company, *Report 1894–95*, 67.

32. Immediately after the 1893 war, Frank Johnson lamented the fact that "we have excellent labourers in the Matabele, and from the mining and commercial point of view I regret the loss of the 2,000 odd Matabele killed in the late war very much". In A. R. Colquhoun, "Matabeleland", *Proceedings of the Royal Colonial Institute*, xxv (1893–94), 98.

33. D. N. Beach, "The Politics of Collaboration: South Mashonaland, 1896–97", unpubl. (1969), 9.

34. Beach, "Afrikaner and Shona", 28.

35. Stent, *A Personal Record*, 39–47.

36. N 1/2/2, N/C Hartley to CNC Mashonaland, 30 November 1895.

37. C. G. Chivanda, "The Mashona Rebellion in Oral Tradition: Mazoe District", unpubl. (1966), 7.

38. T. O. Ranger, *Revolt in Southern Rhodesia, 1896–97* (London, 1967).

39. Beach, "The rising".

40. C.O. 417/451, Crewe to Selborne, 11 July 1908.

41. C.O. 417/213, Milner to Martin, 24 August 1897; C.O. 417/392, Minutes by Grindle and Harris, 20 and 22 November 1904.

42. Hist. MSS. MI 1/1/2, Milton to his wife, 25 September 1896.

43. Rhodes House, British South Africa Company Papers, MSS. Afr. s.77, Grey to Cawston, 26 May 1897.

44. Rhodes had pressed for settler representation in the Legislative Council, established in 1898, in an attempt to check Imperial influence, while the British Government had done likewise in the hope of curbing the Company!

45. D.O. 63/3, Memo by Taylor, February 1927.

46. L. H. Gann, *A History of Southern Rhodesia* (London, 1965), 133.

47. D.O. 35/389, Native Board Meeting at Fort Rixon, Insiza, 27 March 1931.

48. C.O. 417/168, Grey to Martin, 29 June 1896.

49. RC 3/7/14, Milton to Chester-Master, 17 December 1907.

50. RC 3/7/14, Milton to Chester-Master, 17 December 1907.

51. N 9/2/2, Report of the CNC Mashonaland for the half-year ending September 1898.

52. Hist. MSS. ED 6/1/1, Reminiscences of "Wiri" Edwards, 102.

53. L 2/1/175, Memo by Taylor, 17 June 1904.

54. NB 6/1/2, Report of the N/C Insiza for the year 1898–99; N 3/1/5, N/C Charter to CNC Mashonaland, 12 November 1900.

55. D. N. Beach, "South Charter: an example of intensive settlement," unpubl. (1968), 20.

56. He added comfortingly that "the soil in question is not such as will be hankered after by European occupants on account of its poorness." N 3/24/11, N/C Hartley to CNC Mashonaland, 7 July 1900.

57. L 2/2/117/10, N/C Lower Gwelo to CNC Matabeleland, 20 May 1899.

58. *African (South) 659*, Acting N/C Mrewa to CNC Mashonaland, 21 May 1901; N 3/24/21, Acting N/C Mrewa to CNC Mashonaland, 29 January 1898.

59. The CNC Mashonaland informed his deputy that "it is not permissible to have a Native Reserve on a Gold Belt." N 3/24/11, CNC Mashonaland to Assistant CNC Mashonaland, 12 March 1900.
60. The N/C Makoni revealed that "Mr. Milton told me that it was not desirable to make a Native Reserve on the railway line." N 3/24/16, N/C Makoni to CNC Mashonaland, 2 December 1899.
   This attitude was still prevalent when "native purchase areas" were established during the 1920s. According to Coghlan, the Rhodesian Premier, "the natives do not want... [land] on the railway; their needs are not connected with the railway. They want land with grass for their cattle and where they can live their usual lives". *Legislative Assembly Debates*, Vol. 3, Col. 734, 21 May 1925.
61. P. S. Garlake, The Mashona Rebellion East of Salisbury", *Rhodesiana*, 14 (1966), 10.
62. Report of the Surveyor General for the two years ending 31st March, 1900. In British South Africa Company, *Reports on the Administration of Rhodesia, 1898–1900* (London, 1901), 175–6.
63. The N/C Umtali asked his chief to "please inform me if there is any ground available for native reserve.... It is impossible for me by looking at the country to tell whether ground is vacant or not, from what I know the whole country is pegged off as farms or for large companies." The CNC commented that "it has been impossible to find out with any accuracy what ground has been alienated or to find beacons of Farms and Concessions granted". N 3/24/32, N/C Umtali to CNC Mashonaland, 28 January 1898; N 3/24/1/1, CNC Mashonaland to Under Secretary, 18 March 1898.
64. Instances of this kind occurred in at least six districts: Charter, Salisbury, Umtali and Fort Victoria in Mashonaland, and Belingwe and Umzingwane in Matabeleland.
65. Beach, "Politics of Collaboration", 30.
66. Chivanda, "The Mashona Rebellion", 13-4.
67. Beach, "Politics of Collaboration," 30; Beach, "Afrikaner and Shona", 31.
68. R. Hodder-Williams, "Marandellas and the Mashona Rebellion", *Rhodesiana*, 16 (1967), 51.
69. C.O. 417/213, Milner to Chamberlain, 31 December 1897.
70. NB 6/1/2, Report of the N/C Insiza for the year 1898–99.
71. NBE 1/1/1, N/C Matobo to CNC Matabeleland, 31 July 1898; C.O. 417/213, Martin to Milner, 18 September 1897. The terms of peace stated that the Ndebele should vacate the easily defensible Matopos.
72. N 4/1/1, CNC Mashonaland to all Native Commissioners, Mashonaland, 26 August 1900.
73. C.O. 417/392, Clarke to Milner, 2 December 1902.
74. N 3/24/1/1, CNC Mashonaland to Under Secretary, 18 March 1898.
75. N 3/24/12, N/C Inyanga to CNC Mashonaland, 12 October 1900.
76. The N/C Victoria reported, "I do not see that Reserves could be formed so as not to cause great dissatisfaction amongst the Natives, if they had to observe them in the near future, as nearly all the land where the Natives are, within a considerable area of the Town is held by Farmers & Companies granted at a time when the Native Department had not been established." N 9/1/4, Report of the N/C Victoria for the year 1897–98.
77. He also felt that it was "particularly unfortunate... that nearly all

the ground had been taken up here before my appointment and those parts which have been unappropriated have been either too small for reserves or not suitable." NUA 2/1/3, Report of the N/C Umtali for the half-year ending March 1900.

78. S 138/21, N/C Umtali to CNC, 12 August 1933.
79. The N/C Makoni lamented, "Of course the best land in the District is occupied by farmers, syndicates and companies, and there is very little now vacant". N 9/4/5, Report of the N/C Makoni for the month November 1899.
80. The Acting N/C Mazoe warned that "Our one great difficulty will arise out of our being in some cases compelled to move Paramounts out of their districts on account of the land being taken up by Coy's & farmers". N 9/1/4, Report of the Acting N/C Mazoe for the year 1897–98.
81. The N/C Salisbury complained that "The Salisbury District is one of the smallest in Mashonaland but has more disadvantages to contend with than any other, owing to its having been nearly all pegged out as farms". N 9/2/1, Report of the N/C Salisbury for the half-year ending September 1897.
82. C.O. 417/320, Memo by CNC Matabeleland, 22 July 1898.
83. ZAD 3/1/1, N/C Mazoe to Secretary, Native Reserves Commission, 29 May 1915.
84. Palmer, "Aspects", 18–54.
85. Ranger, *African Voice*.

5

PARTICIPATION IN THE "BOER WAR": PEOPLE'S WAR, PEOPLE'S NON-WAR, OR NON-PEOPLE'S WAR?

Donald Denoon

Though the South African war of 1899–1902 has been thoroughly examined as an episode in Imperial (and anti-Imperial) history, students of African history have tended to dismiss it as little more than a ruling-class squabble. Judging purely by the colour of most of the active combatants, of course, that point of view is tenable. On the other hand, so restricted a view of the war is somewhat misleading. In Southern African history, in war as in "peace" the communities do not belong to discreet historical compartments. Much may be learned of the nature of Southern African society (and societies), by looking at the effects of war upon it (and upon them). For one thing, the white discouragement of African assistance requires some comment; for another, the role played by some Africans would appear to have had a marginal effect upon the course of the war; and most important, the reasons for the apparent neutrality of most of the African communities require a great deal of explanation. Furthermore, the peculiar circumstance that the majority of affected people were not supposed to take part in hostilities imposed curious constraints and conventions upon the activities of the combatants themselves. Finally, despite the constraints imposed upon the combatants, the South African war was (among other things) a war by a "people" against an Empire, and exhibited interesting symptoms of developing into something like a people's war as presently understood. As African liberation movements and government forces both prepare today to enter another guerilla war on the same terrain, the point is likely to gain in gruesome significance. The present paper proposes to examine the South African war as an African war and as an anti-Imperial war. The questions which excite most interest include: the rationale of the white powers in limiting African participation; the degree to which Africans participated actively despite that discouragement; the reasons for the general failure of African societies to seize the military initiative; the impact of the war upon the African societies themselves; and finally the effect of the war upon the combatants. Tentatively, the conclusion may then be proposed, that the Afrikaners were not only one of the first African nationalist movements, but also one of the first to experiment with the techniques of a "people's war".

White discouragement of African participation may quickly be considered. Both the Afrikaners and the British, as will be seen, had potential African allies even though the potentiality was infrequently tapped. However, British and Afrikaners had passed through a century of sporadic warfare against each other, beginning with the suppression of the Swellendam republic in the late 1790s. During that century the convention had gained force, that African auxiliaries should not be used in such affairs. The Afrikaners, being on the spot and less affected by the discontinuous leadership than the British, were especially involved in that convention. Furthermore, as will be seen, there was reason to believe that a considerable majority of African groups would favour Imperial arms as against Republicans, so that a policy of involving Africans would not make sense even in the short term. But most important, the prime condition for Afrikaner survival—more important even than independence from the Empire—was the constant subordination of the African communities. Without that condition, for example, African labour would not be available at the price (or non-price) which the farmers were willing and able to pay. Further, the military conquest of the Pedi within the borders of the Transvaal was incomplete in 1899; the subordination of the Swazi was a matter of conjecture; and the Sotho neighbours of the Free State were notoriously unconquered. It was too early in the day to take the subordination of the African communities as a matter of course. It would have been suicide for the Afrikaners to permit these communities to bear arms, even as allies.

The Imperial case, however, was rather more complex. If the Afrikaner war-aim was to preserve the status quo, then the Imperial war-aim was to bring about some change. That change was described by Milner as follows: "In order that ... South Africa may be a source of strength, not weakness, to the Empire, it is necessary that the British population should be so increased, and British interests, British ideas, British education, should gain ground to such an extent, that the natural leaning of any federal government of the future will be towards Great Britain and the Imperial connection...."[1] To one of the leading Uitlanders he observed that the "*ultimate* end is a self-governing white community supported by *well-treated* and *justly governed* black labour from Cape Town to Zambesi."[2] In the Imperial scenario, then, Imperial authority was to be sustained by the local English-speaking white community, which would act as a collaborating community. In that scenario, Africans were at least as open as Afrikaners, to the criticism that they were non-Imperial and un-reliable in the long run. They were at the further disadvantage that they no longer had the arms and independent power to offer themselves as an alternative collaborating community. Though patronisingly paternal observations were made by the Imperial authorities, Imperial paternalism was neither very different from Colonist rule, nor relevant to the central Imperial interest in the sub-continent. There was no hesitation, therefore, in declining assistance which was offered by local African communities, by Hausa troops, or even by Indian and Chinese regiments. Imperial war-aims were not compatible with any such enlargement of the scale of military operations, and could in any event be accomplished without that kind of support.

If the Africans were supposed to behave like an animated geographical background, however, they did not always accept that role. When the representatives of the Afrikaner forces still in the field (the bittereinders) in 1902 converged upon Vereeniging, their reports included disturbing comments on African irregular activity.[3] In the south-eastern Transvaal, for example, the security of the Afrikaners to fight the British without African interruption, had depended upon an immobile but secure alliance with the Swazi kingdom. That alliance had developed steadily during the second half of the century, when each partner felt itself threatened by the Zulu state to the south, which might hesitate to attack either ally. As the fortunes of the Afrikaner troops declined, how-ever, the threat implied by the alliance faded away, and the Afri-kaner forces were threatened by various African communities in north-east, east and south-east Transvaal. In one incident, Zulu irregular forces killed fifty-six Afrikaners in Vryheid District (of the Transvaal Republic, transferred by the Imperial Government to Natal). The Pedi were also reputed dangerous in the weakened circumstances of the Afrikaner forces. These episodes, significant in themselves, assumed a much greater importance as well: the guerilla war could continue only so long as the Afrikaners could spread themselves over a large land area, thereby thinning out the superior numbers of Imperial troops. If they were forced to evacuate eastern districts in the face of African attacks, they would be obliged to concentrate to a dangerous extent in the vicinity of British block-houses and columns. The importance of that development was admirably summed up by General du

Toit of Wolmaransstad, who noted that "the eyes of the delegates, while directed towards God, were able also to observe the conditions of the eastern part of the country".

Further south, the crucial relationship was between the Afrikaner commandos of the Orange Free State and the Basotho of Paramount Chief Lerothodi. The Imperial authorities of Basutoland Protectorate, and the Republican authorities in Bloemfontein, both formally advised the Basotho to remain neutral, though it would seem that none of these authorities was quite sure how the Basotho would react.[4] The Free State posted troops to the borders of Basutoland as soon as war broke out, and transferred them to the Natal front only after they were certain that the Basotho were likely to remain largely inactive. Nevertheless on a couple of occasions the rallying of local loyalist levies on the border seems to have prevented the Free Staters from using parts of Basutoland for strategic purposes. During the siege of Wepener, for example, a small village on the Free State bank of the Caledon river border, Lerothodi, led several hundred followers to prevent the Afrikaners from crossing the border so as to enfilade the British troops in the besieged garrison.[5] On the other hand, the Imperial authorities believed that certain Free Staters had stirred up one of the innumerable Basotho factions to defy his rival loyalists, in the belief that Basotho neutrality could be guaranteed only if the Basotho were actually involved in a civil war. In addition, it appears that individual Basotho took the opportunity of the war to indulge in probably a-political looting.

The situation in the Bechuanaland Protectorate was similar. The siege of Mafeking gave Baden-Powell ample rope with which to hang his future military prospects: both his superior officers and his opponents[7] were agreed that he was one of the most incompetent performers in a war characterised by incompetence. One of the things which irritated the Africans of the Protectorate, however, was that he employed some of them as scouts, but afterwards took the lead in punishing his allies for excessive zeal in their engagements with the enemy.[8] The use of African scouts was a marginal case in the unwritten conventional law of white warfare: it was considered not quite fair, and of course extremely unfair if the scouts were given arms, but on the other hand no commander could bring himself to dispense with "tainted" information altogether. Smuts[9] reports an instance in which an Afrikaner general had permitted African scouts to be armed, though he argued that this was an isolated incident, whereas British officers were more widely at fault. Smuts, in the same context, reports the fate of the only Afrikaner attempt to form a stationary refuge for women and children. The problem of non-combatants in the guerilla phase of the war was obviously acute. On this occasion, in the Western Transvaal, a permanent laager of wagons was formed, in which women and children could live, guarded by old men too enfeebled to withstand the rigours of the war of movement. This camp was dispersed by Africans—who are not otherwise specified, and who are not mentioned in the British accounts of the war.[10] It is entirely appropriate that they preserve this anonymity, which accurately reflects their role in white perceptions of the war—a shadowy, generalised threat, seldom realised but always anticipated.

From the historian's point of view, however, such anonymity is unsatisfactory. How did particular communities see their role in South African affairs during the war? The Zulu, having fought unsuccessfully against both the Imperial and the Afrikaner authorities, might have been expected to put a curse on both houses; but in practice they tended to favour the Imperial cause, even though the Natal colonists also favoured that cause. An Afrikaner victory would bring them no advantage, whereas an Imperial victory might conceivably put an end to colonial control over Zululand.[11] The Imperial tide in Zululand, however, was partially mitigated by an anti-Imperial backwash in Swaziland. Before the war the Transvaalers and Swazi had been allies against any threat from Zululand, and the alliance continued in effect during the war.[12] Here, as elsewhere, it was the division of African opinion, rather than its uniform neutrality, which explains the relative unimportance of African attitudes in determining events. In Basutoland, similarly, the factions in power tended to favour the Imperial forces, while the factions out of power therefore tended to side with the Republicans. As in the East, however, the pro-Imperial factions seem to have predominated, and it was the strong who supported the Empire while the weak went into opposition.[13] In Bechuanaland the situation, though more complex, seems to have been similar: most of the tribal groups favoured the Imperial authorities, though some resumed old alliances with the Afrikaners. Tswana intervention was neither encouraged nor influential, and is no more than an index of the peoples' attitudes; but even as an index it is of some significance.[14]

The attitudes in the Eastern Cape are of especial interest, since that area possessed what Mr. Trapido had described as being the most sophisticated political culture in southern Africa. Here again it would seem that on balance a majority of the groups favoured the Imperial authorities. If the Cape official publications and

Stanford's reminiscences are to be trusted, neutrality was moderated by a general partiality for the Imperial troops.[15] Other issues were also involved, however. Jabavu, the editor of *Imvo Zabantsundu*, was a political ally of the Cape Liberal group which included J. X. Merriman. Since he hoped that African political advancement might result from his group returning to power, he was prepared to follow them into alliance with the Afrikaner Bond; and as a result of this alliance he had his paper suppressed for the duration of the war. The rival African newspaper, *Izwi Labantu*, rejoiced in the suppression of a paper which so conspicuously lacked Imperial patriotism.[16] It must be borne in mind that these organs represented the views of an African elite which had accepted the necessity of operating through the Cape political system: they were not necessarily representative of widespread sentiments. Nevertheless it is interesting that the division of opinion expressed in the newspaper columns was not widely different from the attitudes expressed in action by the Zulu, Swazi, Tswana and Sotho peoples outside the Cape political culture; nor did they differ very much from the views reported as being held by the mass of the people in the Eastern Cape itself.

African labourers in the industrial areas of the Transvaal, whose attitudes towards employment after the war proved to be of crucial importance, appear to have reflected this widespread drift of opinion. By the turn of the century, the Witwatersrand goldfields were drawing African labourers from all the neighbouring colonies, and from the southern districts of Portuguese East Africa. The catchment area for industrial labour was substantially smaller than it is now—Northern Mozambique, Malawi, and South West Africa had not yet been included—yet the compounds contained the largest and most varied assembly of southern Africans hitherto assembled. Although they may not fully have understood the network of government incentives, government exhortations and private inducements which drew them to the goldfields, nevertheless their economic and political interests were reasonably clear. The available evidence suggests that the workers in the urban areas of the Transvaal, more coherently than Africans elsewhere, anticipated something of an economic and social revolution as a result of an Imperial victory: and their exuberant attitude suggests that anti-Imperial opinion elsewhere was factional rather than representative of majority opinion. At any rate urban Transvaal attitudes were expressed without ambiguity. When Imperial troops arrived in Johannesburg and Pretoria during 1900, there were mass burnings of Passbooks which, it was believed, would no longer be required. The Imperial military authorities took sharp and swift punitive action to dispel the illusion; but the illusion itself is more important in this context than its suppression.[17] Though the Imperial authorities ignored African support, to their cost, nevertheless in 1900 the tide of approval for Imperial aims flowed quite strongly, particularly in the industrial areas, but also in the country districts as a whole.

In general, it may be said that Africans suffered the effects of the war as severely as did Afrikaners, but had fewer opportunities to recuperate. For that reason it may further be said that the war was a turning point in the relative fortunes of white and black users of the land. What is known about the conditions of African societies in Southern Africa would actually encourage the view that the labour supply should have been larger: the war had certainly made many families less able than before, to withstand the economic pressures which created migrant labour. The argument was often advanced by frustrated employers, that the Africans after the war were "rolling in money", having been paid extravagantly high salaries by the military. That assertion would appear to be the reverse of the truth. The number of Africans employed at relatively good wages was trivial: the fate of the vast majority was simply to suffer the consequences of war without deriving any benefits.[18] In the Transvaal, for instance, Africans were subject to a system of concentration camps. It was the same system which, when applied to Afrikaner families, caused an immense scandal at Westminster. The Africans, however, did not have the ear of British parliamentarians, and their conditions were never the cause of an Imperial commission of enquiry. By the end of the war some 56,000 Transvaal Africans were detained in concentration camps, which were run with a degree of economy which is untypical of the rest of the war effort. The cost to the Imperial authorities was less than a penny per day per inmate: the cost to the inmates included a death rate which at one stage reached 32 per cent per annum.[19] The scorched earth policy also applied to African earth. It is implausible to suppose that the Africans became so affluent during the war, that they could sit back on the scorched earth and wait for a good season.

Nor were they materially assisted by the payment of compensation moneys, for which they were eligible on account of damage done to their property during the war. Milner's statement on the subject requires no further comment. "Compensation to natives must needs be a very rough and ready affair. Great thing is to give something quickly to re-start them as they are fearfully destitute. If the Army was to pay for all it has taken from natives I do not think they would want anything else. But I fear army receipts as regards natives have been so casually given or not given that it is hopeless to expect them to get compensation from that quarter in reasonable time."[20] In due course the Central Judicial Commission set to work in its methodical and unhurried way: they assessed African compensation claim at £661,106, and decided that they would pay £114,000, which sum had still not been paid by the middle of 1904. Nor, by that date, had any of the military receipts been honoured. Meanwhile the black Transvaalers were paying direct taxes of roughly £275,000 p.a.[21] The evidence of African destitution is overwhelming. The W.N.L.A. recruiters, who were certainly not sentimental about their recruits, found it necessary to detain one in eight of all mining recruits, to recuperate their strength before being allowed to attempt mining work. At a time when labour was scarce, the W.N.L.A. would not have detained these recruits unless their physical condition was really poor.[22] Scorched earth and malnourished bodies produced the result which might be expected, namely severe rural destitution: To suggest— as potential employers suggested—that the Africans were "rolling in money", was wishful thinking.

If the war marked an economic turning point in race relations, the peace marked a military turning point. The terms of the Treaty of Vereeniging permitted British officers to leave arms in possession of surrendering Afrikaner soldiers who lived in "border" areas—which meant in practice areas bordering upon concentrated African settlements. That permission was extensively employed. For example, General Walter Kitchener (brother of the man with the squint) at Waterkloof: "Here 765 men gave up 825 rifles, and 374 licences were issued—41 to officers and 333 to border farmers selected by General Celliers [the Afrikaner commander of the detachment]."[23] In the Eastern Transvaal, along the border with Swaziland and Zululand, General Hamilton not only recommended sending in the police to protect the Afrikaners from the erstwhile British allies, but even recommended that the Afrikaner military organisation be kept intact, to act as communicators between government and the white farmers.[24] Conversely, the first efforts of the South African Constabulary, a paramilitary organisation commanded by Baden-Powell to combine the roles of police and garrison in the ex-republics, was to disarm all Africans. Afrikaners had been recruited into this Imperial garrison even before the end of the war; promotion depended partly upon proof of fluency in Dutch; Baden-Powell was overjoyed when the Afrikaner farmers congratulated him on managing to disarm the Africans—some of them for the first time ever.[25] In many respects the war between Boer and Briton marked a truce in the undeclared war between black and white: and the end of the white war was the end of that truce.

Nevertheless the formal war was taken seriously by those involved in it, and before dismissing their opinion as irrelevant, we should look at one curious aspect of that war. It was noticed at the time that the nature of Afrikaner leadership changed: as Merriman put it. "The old Boer—the so-called 'takhaah' [i.e. uncombed hair] of whom Paul Kruger was the idol and the most prominent representative, has practically disappeared as a factor. . . . The soul of the fighting force consisted of young men and progressive farmers many of them well-to-do, in some cases rich men."[26] On closer inspection, however, the shift of power is even more interesting than Merriman supposed. If we may perform a quick "Namier" operation on the "old" and the "new" Afrikaner leadership, the point should emerge quite clearly. In the Transvaal, President Kruger took refuge in Europe in 1900, at the end of the formal war, when the guerilla war had scarcely commenced. The first Commandar-in-Chief, Piet Joubert, who failed to capture Natal when it was undefended, died in 1900. He had been appointed Commander-in-Chief as a consolation for being an unsuccessful political opponent of President Kruger. A. D. W. Wolmarans, member of the Executive Council, accompanied Kruger into exile in 1900. General P. A. Cronje, one of the original voortrekkers, was Commander-General of the Western Transvaal. Having failed to capture Mafeking, he surrendered with 4,000 troops in 1900 and after the war performed in a circus in the United States. Commandant P. D. de Wet (younger and landless brother of C. R. de Wet) surrendered in 1900 and became the leader of one of the pro-British regiments of National Scouts. Smuts provides a large number of instances of government officials (as opposed to military officers, though the distinction is less clear than that) either staying in their posts when the British arrived in 1900, or else joining the British soon after.[27] In the Orange Free State, the bulk of the bureaucracy did stay at its place and resumed office under the British: However, in the Free State a large proportion of the bureaucracy was English-speaking, and in any event Bloemfontein (the capital) fell very early, before anyone suspected that the formal war would be followed by a guerilla phase.[28] Nevertheless it is clear that, by the end of 1900, one way or another the old Transvaal leaders had yielded place. Several had left the country on one pretext or another, a few were dead, some had surrendered, and a depressingly large number had changed sides. By the end of the war, about a thousand Transvaal Afrikaners were bearing arms for the Crown.[29]

Such a mass departure of leaders requires some explanation. Before venturing upon an explanation, however, it is salutary to perform the same Namierian service upon the new leadership. The economic and educational circumstances of acting President Schalk Burger are unknown, save that he had land and little formal education. Louis Botha, who became Commander-in-Chief in 1900, was a very prosperous and progressive farmer, who had entered enthusiastically into the cash economy opened up by the Witwatersrand gold mining community, and later became a company director. Smuts was, of course, a highly educated man and a trained lawyer. De La Rey, Commander-in-Chief in the West, had been in feud with Kruger, to the point of being "accidentally" omitted from the voters' roll. When war broke out he left his farm and joined the army as a very junior officer, rising to the rank of Commander-in-Chief in the Western Transvaal only after guerilla warfare began. General C. F. Beyers was a Cape-educated attorney prior to his rise as the leader of the Afrikaner forces in the Northern Transvaal. He, like another attorney, Ewald Esselen, became a member of the executive of the Nationalist Movement in the Transvaal after the war, having been very obscure hitherto. A similar pattern may be observed in the Orange Free State, where the lawyers Fischer and Hertzog, and the landowner C. R. de Wet, all experienced accelerated eminence on account of the war.

Conversely, the composition of the National Scouts (the Afrikaners fighting for Queen and Empire) largely comprised landless men or holders of minor office, anxious either to obtain land or to retain position.[30] Predominantly they were "bijwoners"—tenants-at-will of landed kinsmen—or ex-bijwoners who had been given trivial bureaucratic appointments in order to conceal from them the fact of their unemployability. We may therefore advance the following social explanation. When war broke out, Afrikaner society was already becoming stratified: a tiny number of western-educated men were capable of holding executive office in the administration, and were beginning to replace the expatriates in those capacities. Of the vast majority, however, who continued to live on (though not always "off") the land, a minority were in extremely reduced circumstances. Constant sub-division of land on the completion of a generation, the closure of the racial frontier, and the incapacity of rural Afrikaners to compete for gainful urban employment, were creating a non-productive class, whose non-productivity was scarcely concealed by the fact that they were often bijwoners. As the relationship between bijwoners and landed kinsmen inevitably increased in distance each generation, so the relationship became increasingly vexatious: to the landowner it seemed wasteful, to the bijwoner it was humiliating. After the discovery of gold, the state could afford to alleviate rural poverty among Afrikaners by inventing posts to be filled by them. The "bijwoner class" therefore included persons who had no direct connection with the country districts at all; particularly the polite, but also the numerous municipal officials. Conversely the "landed class" had links with the new Afrikaner professional people of Pretoria: the latter tended to invest in land; while the former could afford education for their children and thereby place them beyond the reach of the majority of Afrikaner children.

It was precisely the landed/professional class which emerged to direct power in the course of the military campaign; and precisely the bijwoner class which sold out or otherwise failed. Two further factors slightly confuse this essential simplicity. One is that education was partly a function of generation. Before the discovery of gold almost all Transvaal Afrikaners were unable to provide for themselves an adequate education beyond Biblical literacy: after the mineral revolution many could afford to "re-Europeanise" themselves and their families, and did so. In 1900, then, it was almost axiomatic that anyone over the age of thirty who had been born a white Transvaaler was no more than Biblically literate. The generation movement therefore tends to exaggerate the significance of the class movement, since both tended to produce an educated leadership. The second factor is that large numbers of Afrikaners were denied the opportunity to polarise between British Imperialists and determined Republicans, since they had been removed to remote prisoner-of-war camps in different continents at an early stage of the war.

It is impossible to decide whether the nature of the leadership determined the nature of the war, or vice versa, or whether the changes were unrelated directly. At any rate the formal war (from October 1899 to say June 1900) differs from the guerilla phase (from then until May 1902) as much as the early leaders differ from the old. The formal war was fought by the Afrikaners with overwhelming timidity, as the various military leaders allowed themselves to be drawn into protracted, unsuccessful and totally unnecessary siege operations. By besieging Ladysmith, Joubert declined to capture the port of Durban; by besieging Mafeking, Snyman enabled his troops to learn cricket; by besieging Kimberley, the Afrikaners gave the inhabitant Rhodes even greater notoriety, but closed the door to the possibility of a substantial Afrikaner rising in the rest of the Cape Colony. So discredited were the old leaders by the time Pretoria fell to the British, that there was a moment when the war very nearly came to an end before the guerilla phase had begun.[31] The vast majority of Afrikaner soldiers simply went home until such time as the terms of peace were announced, and only returned to action when the hard core of guerilla leaders proved that the war *could* be continued.

Conversely, the war of movement was led by people who had some idea of how to win the war, and therefore took strong objection to Kruger's project for surrendering under protest. The plan was two-fold: to destroy the gold mines, and to raise revolt in the Cape.[32, 33] Had that plan been implemented in 1899, the Afrikaners might have won the war; by 1900 it was too late to hope for a substantial rising in the Cape, and the British had probably too many troops on the spot to make an Afrikaner victory conceivable. Nevertheless the new leadership did have a plan, which is more than can be said for their predecessors. As the delegates argued at Vereeniging before they met the British[34] militarily they were no worse off in 1902 than they had been in 1900; and the consideration which compelled them to come to terms was not a military one in the Boer/British dimension, but the risk of the destruction of the Afrikaners as a people in the concentration camps (a factor in the black/white dimension).

From the preceding discussion, it seems possible to advance the following hypotheses:

(a) That the South African War was a non-war, not only because the vast majority of the people were instructed (by both sides) not to participate, but also because the war could only be fought on condition that the convention was observed. The war was, therefore, fought during a truce in the enduring racial struggle.

(b) That the war came to an end because factors in the black-white dimension intruded upon the white-white dimension— these factors being the growing intervention of Africans in the fighting, and the increasing risk of the destruction of the Afrikaner community.

(c) That Africans appear to be neutral, when in fact they were neutralised by the absorption of potential leaders in the Cape political structure, by hostility between ethnic groups, and by factionalism within these groups.

(d) That the "white community" remained intact during the war, and despite the war.

(e) But that Afrikanerdom's leadership changed drastically during the conflict, with the older generation and the economic incompetents yielding place to a new "class" of leaders recruited from wealthy landowners and professional men. The conduct of the war changed in consequence. It should be noted in passing that the new leaders share many features in common with the "New Men" in East Africa so elegantly described by Dr. Lonsdale and Dr. Iliffe.[35]

NOTES

1. C.O. 417/290. Milner to Chamberlain, 23 May 1900.
2. Headlam, *Milner Papers*, Vol. 2, pp. 35–6. Milner to Fitzpatrick. 28 November 1899.
3. At Vereeniging, the British delegates (Milner and Kitchener) neglected to provide the Imperial Government of a full transcript of proceedings. The most accurate reports are therefore records of discussions prepared by the Afrikaner delegates. Of these, the most reliable is Kestell and van Velden, who published their account as an official one, since they had been the accredited secretaries of the two republican governments. The second, and livelier, account, appears in C. R. de Wet, *Three Years War*. This paragraph is based upon the former, but the quotation is derived from the latter.
4. See especially, G. Y. Lagden, *The Basutos*, Vol. 2. Though Lagden was paranoid and mentally very slow, he was after all the British Resident in Basutoland at the time of the war.
5. *Ibid*, Chapter XXIX.
6. Kitchener Papers, Public Record Office, P.R.O. 30/57. Correspondence between Roberts and Kitchener, 1902 *passim*.
7. C. R. de Wet, *op. cit.* W. K. Hancock and J. Van der Poel, *Smuts Papers*, Vol. 1. Smuts Memoirs of the War, C.U.P., 1966.
8. S. T. Plaatje, *Native Life in South Africa*. Plaatje was later one of the founders of the South African Native National Congress.
9. W. K. Hancock and J. van der Poel, *op. cit.*
10. e.g. the official account, J. F. Maurice et al, *History of the War in South Africa* (4 vols): and L. S. Amery (ed.) *The Times History of the War in South Africa* (7 vols).
11. I am grateful to Dr. Shula Marks, of S.O.A.S., for providing me with this information from her own research work in Zulu History.
12. *Ibid*.
13. G. Y. Lagden, *op. cit.*
14. S. T. Plaatje, *op. cit.* E. E. Reynolds, *Baden-Powell*.
15. S. Trapido, "African Divisional Politics in the Cape Colony 1884–1910", *Journal of African History*, 1968. J. W. Macquarrie (ed.). *Reminiscences of Sir Walter Stanford*, van Riebeck Society.
16. *Inve Zabantsundu*, *passim*, and especially 8 October 1902 when it resumed publication. *Izwe Labantu*, especially 4 June 1901 and 27 August 1901. In January 1903 Izwe published the statement of the South African Native Congress that "the natives of South Africa are naturally Imperialistic in their sympathies."
17. H. J. Batts, *Pretoria from Within*, p. 192. L. S. Amery *op. cit.*, Vol. 6, p. 595.
18. E. P. C. Girouard, *Detailed History of the Railways during the War* . . . , Vol. 1, p. 257 et seq.
19. C.O. 291/55. Report upon Native Refugee Department.

20. C.O. 291/40. Milner to Chamberlain, 21 July 1902.
21. Transvaal Government, Native African Affairs Department report for 1903–04.
22. South African Native Affairs Commission, evidence, Vol. 4; Mac-Farlane General Manager of the W.N.L.A., p. 735.
23. 1902 (lxix), 988. Appendix to Commander-in-Chief Kitchener's despatch of 19 June 1902.
24. *Ibid.*
25. E. E. Reynolds, *op. cit.* Transvaal archives, *Notes and Instructions to South African Command.*
26. Merriman to Bryce, 21 July 1902, quoted G. H. L. Le May, *British Supremacy in South Africa*, p. 214.
27. W. K. Hancock and van der Peel, *op. cit.* substantiated by C. R. de Wet, *op. cit.*
28. This is well and conveniently explained in L. S. Amery, *op. cit.*
29. J. F. Maurice *et al., op. cit.*
30. C.O. 291/43. Intermediate report on resettlement of National Scouts, 15 September 1902.
31. W. K. Hancock and van der Peel, *op. cit.* L. S. Amery, *op. cit.* C. R. de Wet, *op. cit.*
32. N. J. van der Merwe, *Martinus Theunis Steyn.*
33. W. K. Hancock and van der Peel, *op. cit.*
34. Kestell and van Veldem, *op. cit.* W. K. Hancock and van der Peel, *op. cit.*
35. See Iliffe J. "Tanzania Under German and British Rule", in *Zamani.* edited by B. A. Ogot and J. A. Kieran (1968).

6

AFRICAN METHODS OF WARFARE DURING THE MAJI MAJI WAR 1905-1907*

G. C. K. Gwassa

Herr Eduard Haber, Chief Secretary in German East Africa in the early 1900s, found evidence of skilled and systematic military planning in the Maji Maji war of 1905–07. In a communication to the Governor he noted that:

> The development of the movement was undoubtedly controlled in a logical manner by good strategists. Many suspect that discharged askari were behind it while others point to an Arab as the leader.[1]

Three points could be made with regard to Haber's observation. First, that there was good organisation in Maji Maji. Second, that such an organisation could have been the work of aliens; and by innuendo, that Maji Maji societies were incapable of such a feat. Thirdly, however, Haber has not explained why and how discharged askaris or an individual Arab could have decided to fight against the Germans and how it was possible to mobilise a population comprising over twenty different ethnic groups spread out over 100,000 square miles—the area roughly covered by the Maji Maji War.

However, recent oral research on Maji Maji has exposed a number of weaknesses in the purely archival sources. Shortcomings of German resources arose largely out of too heavy dependence on information supplied by their agents, who wished to please their masters, and by frightened captives who hoped to be spared their lives. Oral sources are agreed that it was safer to say what the Germans or their agents, especially the latter,

---

*This chapter is based on four years of research undertaken by the author. The research was done mainly within what is called in this paper the Matumbi-Ngindo complex, i.e. the outbreak area. Hence this chapter is limited in scale, but its content is highly relevant to the dispersal area. The chapter dispenses with the more generally known account of Maji Maji and concentrates on an aspect in which the German and other written records are particularly deficient. The reader will follow much of this account if he already has a fair knowledge of the Maji Maji War.

expected to hear, or to deny connection with *aji* and Maji Maji. Indeed suspects continued to be hunted and punished, usually by hanging, until after 1912.[2] Thus the classical German record of Maji Maji, Graf von Gotsen's *Deutsch Ostafrika im Aufstand*, remains both unreliable and apologetic. Since German sources revealed little about Africans, it is not wise to rely on these sources alone, especially as regards African techniques of fighting. This chapter, then attempts to relate Maji Maji events to social environments in order to expose and possibly expound African methods of warfare in the movement.

In a sense a discussion of methods of fighting in a mass movement like Maji Maji requires two approaches: an examination of its organisation and more specifically of its military tactics. Additionally it is equally important to determine what binds individuals or groups together, and how they get committed to a common cause. Further, in studying a mass movement, it is necessary to examine leadership, which in turn requires an understanding of the social groups of which the leaders and the led are members. In other words, this chapter ought to deal with three types of methods of warfare, viz. ideological techniques, organisational techniques and fighting techniques and their respective leadership. It may thus be possible to determine the nature and limitations to African Maji Maji participation—an aspect about which historians have remained particularly silent.

In order to place the events that follow in a political and social context it is necessary to present a sketchy background history of southern Tanzania. Before and during the nineteenth century, intense cultural admixture had been brought about by wars, migrations and intermarriages, and especially by raids of the Yao and Ngoni and their imitators. Caravan trade with distant lands and also slave trade had contributed to this cultural complexity. The general result of these developments was percolation, assimilation, adaptation and accommodation of various cultural traits, spread out over a wide area. At the same time most areas had been desolated by wars and raids. Father Maurus, travelling in the Lindi hinterland, remarked in 1894 that:

> Everywhere we meet fugitives carrying all their belongings with them, who, driven by panic fright announced that the Mazitu and Wangoni were coming tomorrow.... They plunder everything and stab everybody or make them their slave.[3]

Lieutenant Ewan Charles Smith travelling beyond Kilwa and Lindi had similarly noted that:

> There were absolutely no inhabitants, though the ruins of more

than one village indicated that the districts had been fairly well populated at a recent date.[4]

But there were pockets of dense population, at least in 1905. Ngindoland was said by Bell to be very heavily populated. The Matumbi, however, had become overpopulated and suffered acute land shortages by 1905 because they had been by-passed by the slave trade and raids had always stopped at the periphery of their hills. But it was probably because of the fear that they inspired in coastal Arabs and others that the Matumbi were able to remain relatively undisturbed. The first missionary in the area testified to this:

From the earliest among Europeans as well as among natives of the coast the Wamatumbi had a reputation for exceptional brutality. Not once did the Arabs risk themselves in their midst ... Even today it is extremely hard to find porters for the Matumbi country from the coast, not only on account of the high mountains and steep climbs and descents, but even more on account of the inhospitable nature of the inhabitants.[5]

In areas of overpopulation like Matumbiland, it was necessary for each individual to put in maximum labour in the production of food on every available piece of land. This was an important factor, among others, in the Matumbi hatred of the German cotton plantation system which diverted their valuable labour.

Politically, most Maji Maji peoples, except for the Ngoni and a number of their imitators, were organised in clans which had clearly established laws of political succession, based on an existing political philosophy. For instance, in the Matumbi-Ngindo complex, political authority was passed on to one of the sons of a dying clan head, (*mpindo* or *mwenye* in Kimatumbi and Kigindo respectively), but only on the basis of merit which itself was determined by performance in a kind of informal examination put to those sons. Thereafter the successor was elected according to the number of people who called to pay homage to the candidates. Thus, if the eldest son failed to get the majority, his younger brother stood for such elections until a successor was found through majority vote. Among the essential qualifications were wisdom, eloquence, kindness and impartiality, as well as hospitality to strangers. Therefore in the Matumbi-Ngindo complex, one essential feature of their political philosophy was that clans were equal and it was inconceivable that there could be a ruler of rulers or an *mpindo* over *bapindo* (plural). Unless there were reasons for hostility, such as land disputes, clans usually had some recognised "diplomatic" relations, and in time of war they defended their country together, though never under one central leadership. A second feature of their political philosophy was that authority could be just only if based on merit. In this sense, therefore, the German rule was unjust because it was an alien system based on force. It was also wrong because it sought to create a rule of *mpindo* over *bapindo*. In Matumbiland, from which Arabs had been debarred, people became increasingly hostile to the presence of corrupt Arab *akidas* who were now intent on taking advantage of the opportunity offered by the German colonial rule.

The Ngoni, on the other hand, had a centralised political system based on raiding weaker neighbours. But even these were divided into subdivisions—the southern kingdom of the Ngoni Njelu (Zulu) and the northern kingdom of Ngoni Mshope (Mbonane). By 1905 these kingdoms were ruled by Nkosi Mputa Gama and Nkosi Chabruma respectively. With the Ngoni too, however, authority was based on merit, usually characterised by courage and an unflinching will to face physical danger, for theirs were states based on military conquests. In this way the Ngoni were nearly always on the offensive, rarely did they wage defensive wars.

But amongst many of the political systems based on clan organisation, the concept of war was defensive. Only when attacked by an enemy could one beat the *lilunga* or *kilingondo* (war drum) to summon neighbouring clans to remove a common danger. Neighbours answered *lilunga* by beating their own drums and then mobilising themselves to go to the source of the original *lilunga*, where they then decided how to stalk the enemy or the man-eater. Largely for this reason the Matumbi can provide no evidence of having undertaken an offensive war against their neighbours.[6]

Also connected with warfare was a universal belief in and use of various medicines in order to get the better of the enemy. These war medicines can be divided into two groups. There were those that were used for divination to predict success or failure in an impending war. Usually these were objects such as the *liteho* of the Bena,[7] or *lihomelo* (drum) of the Pogoro.[8] There were also powerful experienced diviners such as Chikusi Kapungu and Kang'anda of Ngoni Njelu and Mshope respectively.[9] The second group comprised those war medicines which made the partaker, in one way or another, immune to weapons. There were many varieties. The Matumbi-Ngindo complex for instance, used *ndyengu* and *kilughe* respectively to immunise people against weapons such as bullets, spears or arrows, and to deflect enemy missiles from their targets.[10] The Ngoni had medicines which turned them into anthills so that their enemies could not see them. Thus when *maji* (water) was introduced with a promise of being able to turn bullets into water, or to cause them to drop off the body like raindrops from an oily object, the idea was that it was a war medicine, but a more powerful one, as will be seen below.

Similar to the oracular powers of such objects were the prophetic or superhuman powers attributed especially by Matumbi-Ngindo peoples to a possessed person, one who has *lilungu*. To them a person possessed by spirits has extremely wide social license. He can walk naked without offending anybody; he can kill but he cannot be punished; he can sleep in the open overnight and no beasts can harm him; and he eats freely. Further he hates the company of witches, who stink before him and whom he pursues and kills if he meets them. He can prophesy in a manner in which an ordinary person cannot. Thus it is important to see that the *mganga* (expert) Kinjikitila Ngwala or Ngarambe, the man who brought *maji*, was believed to be possessed. But Kinjikitile Ngwale was also possessed by a special god at the sight of which a person or his next of kin would die. This god could also hide in forests and open up the skulls of lonely travellers and drink up all their blood, leaving the empty carcass for others to see. This god was Hongo, a huge snake which normally lived under deep waters in rivers or pools. For this reason then, Kinjikitile was extra powerful for his body provided an abode for the god, Hongo.

Against this background, the Germans guided by Carl Peters burst with haste and vast economic appetites into a land about which they knew hardly anything. The architect of German East Africa, Peters is commonly known as *mkono wa damu*—the man with blood-stained hands—and one author has described him as "a thruster, adventurer, dreamer, liar and imperialist".[11] In 1884 Peters formed his German Society for Colonisation, and after he and his fellow adventurers travelled to East Africa and grabbed "bogus treaties" from the hinterland of Bagamoyo. Early the following year Peters and his compatriots got from Bismarck, the German Chancellor, a charter of protection (Schutzbrief).

Peters soon organised his Society into the German East Africa Company, which had administrative authority and a monopoly of trade over what subsequently became German East Africa. The new company had a number of problems, but from our point of view the most important of them was the coastal resistance led chiefly by Abushiri bin Salim at Harthi and Bwana Kheri in the latter half of 1888. The resistance extended from Tanga to Mikindani. In Kilwa the resistance was under one *Mtoro*; two German representatives were killed and their heads cut off and hung on poles outside their *boma* for everybody to see. Everywhere the Germans suffered heavily. However, African successes were short-lived, for Germany, intent on saving face, officially used the argument of abolishing the Arab slave trade to send von Wissmann as Imperial Commissioner to suppress the movement. By 1891 von Wissmann was satisfied that there was no more trouble, and the Imperial government soon took over the administration.

The German rule with a Governor and District Officers (Bezirksamtmanner) had instituted a system of local government under *akidas* and *jumbes*, usually in areas without a strong centralised political system. Therefore many of the Maji Maji districts came under the *akida-system*. But in Ngindoland there were only *jumbes* and no *akidas*. Through this system of local government it was hoped that the gap between Europeans and Africans would be bridged, and that colonial administration would be effectively carried out. But *akida-jumbe* systems were doomed to failure for various reasons. Firstly, the *akidas* were invariably foreigners, usually Arabs or coastal Swahili with a *mwungana* (freeman) complex, or ex-mercenaries, especially the Nubians. Being ignorant of the customs of the people over whom they ruled, and being educated only in Islamic law, these people not only were unsuited for the job but were themselves hated. In Matumbiland where hatred of Arabs and Swahilis was an established fact, they were hated even more because of their high-handedness as well as their extortionate and corrupt practices. Furthermore, in a society that was organised on a clan system, in order for the *jumbes* to be effective, they had to be selected from the clan. This, when it was done, created its own problems. In places like Liwale where the *jumbes* were the same as the former clan heads, there arose conflicts in responsibilities and authority. One person was supposed to discharge two conflicting responsibilities. This led to a very unhappy situation which probably caused nearly all the *jumbes* in Ngindoland to become Maji Maji leaders automatically. But where the new *jumbe* was a different person from the former clan head, as in Matumbiland, the new man did not enjoy the same respect, and in cases of conflict the *mpindo* had the upper hand. Moreover, since the *jumbes* were chosen from their own clans, it meant that when the Germans ordered them to impose harsh punishment, to conscript labour etc., it was against their own relatives or brothers. So there developed a typical colonial situation in which a person was being ordered to exploit and oppress his own brothers.

In southern Tanzania there were several examples of resistance against the Germans apart from the initial coastal fighting. In

1894–95 Hassan Omari Makunganya, operating from the immediate hinterland of Kilwa, waged war against the Germans. Makunganya was one of the Yao warlords who had grown in importance and influence through his participation in caravan and slave trade. His ability and fame spread widely in the hinterland of Kilwa and Lindi. However, the Germans defeated and caught him at Mavuji and Kilwa-Lindi Road. He was hanged at Kilwa-Kivinje on a mango tree, which has ever since been called *mwembe-kinyonga*, hangman's mango tree. Local sources show that twenty-seven others were hanged on the same day. The Ngindo, hearing of the defeat of Makunganya, sought the powerful German alliance against the Ngoni raiders who threatened to decimate their society.

Another Yao operating in the hinterland of Lindi, Machemba, continually resisted the Germans until he was defeated in 1899 and fled into Mozambique. Later, Maji Maji leaders were to follow Machemba's example. The Matumbi also fought the Germans in 1898 over taxation. Elsewhere in Maji Maji districts there was little fighting. In Ngoniland, German occupation was carried out in such a ruthless way that the Ngoni were in no position to fight them. The Africans had a terrible lesson.

In general therefore, German rule in the south had remained weak. After the turn of the century the Germans began to assert their influence in many ways, particularly in their attempts to make their colony self-supporting by producing raw materials for German industries. Thus after other attempts had failed to meet German economic expectations, it was decided in 1902 to introduce a system already operating in Togoland, of using African communal labour in the production of cash crops. The system began in Dar es Salaam and spread to Kilwa by about 1903. In Samanga Mdumbo, for instance, there was a huge experimental cotton plantation owned by a German settler, Steinhagen. Each *jumbe* was required to send fifty men at a time to work on this plantation under very severe conditions. But conditions were even worse because, as mentioned earlier, Matumbi society was over-populated and labour was very valuable, so that any diversion of this labour to another occupation was necessarily injurious to Matumbi economy. What made the problem even more acute was the fact that the Matumbi were required to work on the cotton plantations just at the very time that they needed to devote maximum efforts to both cultivating and protecting their crops against vermin, especially birds and wild pigs. Hence their grievance against the cotton scheme was very severe. Gradually Africans began to feel the need for removing German colonial rule, which was the source and basis of all the grievances put together.

But any African action against Germans had to answer certain fundamental issues. First, the military superiority of the Germans, which had taught the Africans a harsh lesson in the nineteenth century, had to be faced if the sad story was not to be repeated. In other words, the Africans had to devise better techniques or methods of warfare before they could feel confident of fighting the Germans again. Secondly, it has already been seen that Africans were too divided to be capable of working together beyond the level of the clan and with more difficulty, beyond ethnic groups or political boundaries. Africans had to evolve an organisational machinery that would assure participation by each of them, so that the weight of numbers could become a factor. Thirdly, a new organisational technique as a requirement amongst peoples so disunited necessarily created a crisis which had to be solved. In other words, and fourthly, a new organisational technique had to have a new ideology as its basis; a new ideological technique was a prerequisite for any mass commitment. A crisis-solving device became necessary. However, as has been shown above, there was a potential for unity from cultural similarities especially religious beliefs, on which a new ideology and unifying could be based. The crisis was potentially soluble, there had to be leadership to utilise a mass technique by working within the framework of a known and therefore acceptable ideology. In other words society and war in this case were very closely related. That is why a full understanding of Maji Maji is impossible without understanding the participating societies.

It is now essential to make a closer examination of Maji Maji leadership: military and ideological. These two patterns can be distinguished as Maji Maji and *maji* leadership. Strictly speaking, military leadership was not unknown, since as each people or clan had its own military leaders in case of attack. Let us first examine ideological leadership and organisation. To appreciate fully the role of *maji* leadership it must be remembered that in a war like Maji Maji, individual leaders and their followers are brought together to plan in order to ensure victory. By 1903 there was a crisis amongst the Matumbi-Ngindo peoples. In the words of Matumbi informants the crisis was clear:

> How could one clan face the Germans alone and not be wiped out? There had to be many![12]

and again:

> The problem was how to beat him (Germans) really well. Who would start. Thus they waited for a long time because there was

no plan or knowledge. Truly his practices were bad. But while there were no superior weapons should the people not fear? Everywhere elders were busy thinking, "What should we do?"[13]

Then in 1904 a powerful new leader emerged. He was Kinjikitile Ngwale, who lived in Ngarambe in the north western part of Kilwa district and was believed to be possessed by Hongo. His fame and power spread quickly in Matumbi-Ngindo complex. Clients flocked to Ngarambe to collect *maji*, the new war medicine that would cause Europeans guns to spurt water when fired, or their bullets to drop off African bodies. Eventually Kinjikitile sent representatives to different parts of the country to act on his behalf.

A comparison with the traditional role of the *mganga* or diviner in African society illustrates the importance of Kinjikitile and *maji* in solving problems of unity, thereby making possible Maji Maji movement. Whenever there is a social crisis such as death or illness from unknown causes, or suspected witchcraft the victim or his family consult a *mganga* or diviner who explains the crisis and usually prescribes a cure and suggests an expert doctor. Whether these explanations or prescriptions may or may not bring a cure which is scientifically verifiable is irrelevant. What is important is that people have faith in it and whenever there is a crisis they believe it can be both solved and explained. Similarly most people consult doctors when they are ill, when they have a crisis. Doctors stress that patients must have confidence (or faith) in the drugs they take. Likewise the number of church-goers seems to rise during times of crisis.

In a similar manner, Kinjikitile and his *maji* was a crisis-solving device. He provided a unifying ideology. His *maji* was not to be a war medicine of or for a single group or clan, but of and for all people; his was a universal war medicine having a universal appeal. Thus his message through the *maji* became the basis of a revolutionary commitment to mass action against the Germans. Furthermore Kinjikitile, and later his ambassadors, provided a forum for inter-group communication between individual leaders from different localities. But in order to examine this hypothesis in depth let us consider in more detail what is believed by the people to be the immediate antecedents to Kinjikitile's meteoric rise to leadership.

Kinjikitile Ngwale was a man of exceptional qualities. A middle-aged man about six feet tall, he had an extremely imposing personality. He was an astute psychologist, an able politician, and a man of great eloquence, wisdom and imagination. Previously he had held no special position in society, being simply a peasant and a recent immigrant into Ngarambe—a land where the Ikemba, Ngindo, Kichi, Matumbi and Pogoro peoples lived all together. Like everybody else he had suffered under the harsh arm of German colonial rule. In Ngarambe village two incidents took place before Kinjikitile was possessed by a spirit. These were a visit by a huge snake and the miraculous disappearance of Kinjikitile into the same waters into which the snake had disappeared the previous day.

A man presently living on the site of Kinjikitile's former homestead, and who was fifteen years old in 1905, has given the following story. A very large snake entered the hut of a certain Mzee Machuya Nnundu in Lihenga near Ngarambe pool. It was too large for the hut and its coils flowed outside. It had the head of a monkey, large red eyes and was the colour of a rainbow. One afternoon it disappeared, supposedly into Ngarambe pool. On the same afternoon two ladies who had been harvesting sorgum beheld a tall man dressed in an extremely dazzling white *kanzu* or robe. As the two women ran in fear, the trail of the mysterious snake which lead eventually to Ngarambe pool was interrupted by footmarks between the points where the man in the white robe appeared and disappeared before the two women. The next morning while basking in the sun with his family, Kinjikitile was dragged into the same Ngarambe pool by an unknown and invisible spirit, his wives and children failing to prevent it. Kinjikitile spent the rest of the day and night beneath the waters from which he emerged the following morning. "After returning from there he began talking prophetic matters", teaching that Europeans were *utupi nkere* (red potter's clay); lion was sheep, dead ancestors would be returned by God to help their children, and that all Africans irrespective of any differences were one and they had to fight *utupi nkere*.[14]

These events were explained in the following terms. The huge snake had been Hongo and Kinjikitile had been possessed by Hongo. Thus the attributes of a man possessed and of Hongo, the snake God, were merged into one person. But Kinjikitile's power was even greater because he operated within societies which also placed a high premium on the office of the *mganga*, which he was now believed to be. In Kimatumbi and related languages the title was *pundi* or an expert. One informant explained the role of the *pundi* or *mganga* in this way:

> It is not as these days when we all believe the doctor or *Bwana Mganga*, but the D.C. or Area Commissioner still stands above us all. The D.C. or Area Commissioner orders or rules the people.

But the *Bwana Mganga* cures the peoples of illness, including
the Area Commissioner himself! So if a *Pundi* said something we
agreed. Today if *Bwana Mganga* says something we do not believe.[15]

In that sense Kinjikitile was an even greater *pundi* or *mganga*;
"witchdoctor" the common English translation, merely distorts
realities.

Since Kinjikitile had not been a *mganga* or an influential leader,
it would be well to examine the methods he used in making himself and his teachings known and accepted over a wide area.
First, from Ngarambe, Kinjikitile mounted a whispering campaign
variously called *Njwiywila*, *jujila*, or *mtemela* which quickly spread
far and wide. *Njwiywila* was communicated on an individual basis,
but only between relatives and close friends. The communication
cost one pice, but only after the recipient had sworn to keep it
secret.

Given the time and circumstances, a movement whose basis
for expansion was kinship or friendship and a payment of money
had a great potential for rapid development. There are three
reasons for such a view. First, the movement was bound to spread
quickly within individual clans and with those clans that were
related through marriage. Besides, friendship was not and could
not be confined to clan boundaries. Secondly, in 1905 much of the
area under review was still largely under barter economy (and
thus taxation was still an impossible burden), so that the economic
value of even a pice was very high. There, to pay for *njwiywila*
became a real commitment to the new message. But it is not unlikely that, since it was required that nobody should part with the
message gratis, some people recovered the money they had paid.
Thirdly, the most important, *njwiywila* was directed specifically
towards an existing crisis. A participant in njwiywila put the
message as follows:

> This year is a year of war, for there is a man at Ngarambe who
> has ... Lilunga. Why? Because we are suffering like this and
> because ... we are oppressed by the *akidas*. We work without
> payment. There is a *pundi* at Ngarambe to help us. How? There
> is *jumbe* Hongo.... It spread quickly throughout Matumbi county
> and beyond.[16]

Thus it seems reasonable that the urge to pass on such information
to a relative or friend must have been irresistible. But the njwiywila
phase did not last very long, for people became curious and began
to go to Ngarambe to see what Kinjikitile had to offer.

However, *njwiywila* seems to discredit two arguments of the

Germans and other scholars of the subject. First, it is possible that the conspiracy thesis advanced by Marker and then by Von Gotzen, though it has already been demolished elsewhere, arose from an imperfect understanding of *njwiywila* and was therefore a distortion.[17] Secondly, the popular and German view that *maji* was originally a mere panacea that was cleverly diverted by die-hard rebels against the Germans, has been severely discredited by *njwiywila*. However, the proponents of such views of *maji* have shown neither why a panacea movement was then possible or necessary, nor why it should have won such wide acceptance at the time.

For lack of a better term, the second phase can be referred to as "pilgrimages" when people began to go to Ngarambe to fetch *maji*. The German view was that these pilgrimages were not clearly understood by the participants, who at least in the beginning, were not against the Germans. A German officer who believed in the conspiracy thesis was of the view that:

> The business appeared completely harmless, and was understood in a rather hazy way by the money people who made pilgrimage to the medicine men. In no way secretly but publicly and without ceremony, great crowds of people—some of as many as 300 adults were observed—made their way to the medicine man under the eyes of the Arabs, Indians and Coastal people who were all later to suffer.[18]

The German view is not corroborated by on-the-scene information, which shows that the pilgrims knew clearly what they were doing. They drilled. A resident in Ngarambe at the time showed the joy and inspiration of the pilgrims:

> It was like a wedding procession, I tell you. People were singing, dancing and ululating throughout. When they arrived they slept there and performed *likinga* (drilling) every one in his own group. The following morning they received medicine and returned home.[19]

There can be no doubt that the whole business was a source of inspiration to Africans.

Early in 1905, when rains affected the flow of people to Ngarambe, Kinjikitile sent out his representatives or ambassadors to various areas of the Matumbi-Ngindo complex. In Ngarambe and Matumbiland these representatives were called *mpokosi*. At Nandette in Matumbi there was an *mpokosi* whose real name is unknown to the author. In Ngarame itself were Ling'ang'a, a Mpogoro, and Njugwemaina Ngwale, Kinjikitile's own brother who took over from him after the Germans hanged him. Into the

present Utete district was sent Makingiliya, a Mngingo. In Ngindoland, there were three influential representatives: Ngarumbamika,
Kindamba Mkui and a woman, Binti Ireka, recorded in German
sources as Bitereka. In Madaba, an area of Pogoro-Ngindo peoples
north of Liwele, was one of the most powerful *mpokosi*-Ngameya,
a brother-in-law to Kinjikitile.

It is tempting to put on record here the proceedings of *likinda*
in Nandette, as an example of how it was done. The *mpokosi*
gave the orders according to Bw. Sebastian Upunda of Nandette
as follows:

> Nyime witi (I stand at attention)
> Tunanyima puputa (we are at attention)
> Mtabite niki? (what are you carrying?)
> Tutabite ngunde (we are carrying peas)
> Ngunde, ngunde gani? (peas, peas, what peas?)
> Ngunde, ngunde ate (creeping peas)
> Ate?
> Ate!
> Ate?
> Ate!

and so on as they marched, until the *mpokosi* ordered again:

> Nyime witi
> Tunanyima puputa
> Mtendebuke mnoli ku Ndonde (turn towards Ndondeland)
> Mtendebuke mnoli ku-machi mapii (turn towards the black waters)
> Utupi nkere, mbyu? (destroy the red potter's earth)
> Mbyu! (destroy)
> Mbyu?
> Mbyu!
> Mbyu?
> Mbyu!

The instructions were full of symbolisms. For instance, to turn
towards Ndondeland and to the ocean meant that war would
extend from the coast inland; "peas" were bullets and "creeping"
meant stalking the enemy, while "mbyu" signified the sound of the
gun in destroying *utupi nkere*—the Europeans.

In Ngindoland, unlike in Matumbiland, the three leaders, commonly referred to as *hongos*, went around the country addressing
public rallies on the powers of *maji* and the impending war. Ngindo
sources compare the activities of these three people with the early
activities of the TANU secretaries and chairmen, who had to
travel around spreading the message of *uhuru*.

Having dealt with the two phases of the *maji* movement (not
Maji Maji) it is now necessary to examine more closely the pro-

ceedings at Ngarambe. At the pool Kinjikitile had a permanent assistant who may be called his A.D.C. He had built a very large *kijumba nungu* (house of God) at which all pilgrims were required to make offerings of either salt, rice or a pice each, to an ancestral spirit. Here Kinjikitile, needless to say, instituted a very revolutionary practice, for a single *kijumba nungu* had come to serve for all the clans; moreover, in the past it had been the usual practice to propitiate the gods before going to war. Kinjikitile himself was then living in extreme seclusion in his former homestead, which had been fenced. The A.D.C. passed back and forth between the pilgrims and Kinjikitile, telling him of new arrivals or departures. After being summoned, Kinjikitile emerged from behind his fence, and dived into the deep waters of the pool where he remained for not less than five minutes consulting *hongo*. Afterwards he sat on an outcrop of rock in the pool or on a mat that floated in the water. Then he called out to each group and required its leader to come forward, whereupon he asked the rest of the group whether that was really their leader. He addressed each group in a manner that resembled a political rally, and his imposing personality and eloquence proved very useful. One old lady who went to Ngarambe to fetch *maji* and saw Kinjikitile has described him as *"mpindo* of wisdom".[20] Then Kinjikitile would give them instructions about the war and about the *maji*. Leaders got many types of medicines to make them stronger. Each group turned and left without looking back, a new condition that was required of all men in the impending war.

Kinjikitile's instructions and taboos to his clients were many and varied. He prohibited witchcraft, looting of any type, taking women captives on the eve of war, and the eating of pigeon peas. When shooting they were to say, "Maji-maji, maji-maji", which gave the war its name. But more specifically he talked of the war, around which all the instructions revolved. He always said:

> The Germans will leave. War will start from up-country towards the coast and from the coast into the hinterland. There will definitely be war. But for the time being go and work for him. If he orders you to cultivate cotton or to dig his roads, or to carry his load, do as he requires. Go and remain quiet. When I am ready, I will declare the war.[21]

And he always finished his address with a challenge that:

> Whoever does not believe me let him go and enquire from Bokero in Rufiji Ruhingo (i.e. Upper reaches of Ruhingo)

Kinjikitile had hoped to galvanise the Africans into one dynamic force spread over a wide area. The fact that war broke out before he was "ready" showed a fundamental conflict or disequilibrium between ideology (*maji*) and practical military realities and the respective leadership. Thereafter Maji Maji could never expect to have centralised leadership.

It will already have been seen that *maji* movement as an ideology provided for and made possible mass involvement in Maji Maji, and that without it, it is unlikely that the war as a mass movement would have taken place. But this does not preclude the possibility that in the absence of *maji* there would probably have occurred a series of resistances similar to those of the nineteenth century. *Maji* assured all of a mass commitment by all. But this should not be overplayed, for since the basis of this committment was not only a desire to fight but also faith, not all were fully committed to the war—especially when faith or ideology conflicted too sharply with realities.

It will now be useful to examine military leadership. It has already been seen that at Ngarambe pilgrims went in groups under their own leaders. These groups tended to remain the same, give or take a few members, when war was being fought. In the area under discussion, leadership was based on merit, which was itself measured according to existing social standards. Thus for instance in Matumbiland, leaders were chosen for their courage, proven military skills and ability to lead others; and usually they were tall and healthy-looking. Another factor was possession of guns and gunpowder reserves and many "sons" or followers. In other words, since selection was based on merit and the people were organised in clans, there could never be centralised leadership, since no single man could meet all the standards of all the classes. In Ngindoland the situation was similar, although there gunpowder was never a real factor since usually they used poisoned arrows.

It is likely that in meeting at Ngarambe and at various other places, individual leaders gradually developed common strategies and with time felt more and more united in a common cause. Leaders then communicated and discussed various proposals with their own peoples in their respective localities. Perhaps it is important to mention the more influential leaders in various areas.

In Nandette, where Maji Maji started, more or less the most important leader was Sikwako Mbonde, assisted by Kibanga Mpiri. In Tawa (or Mtumbei-Kitambi) the leader was Ngomile Kilindo, joined later by Abdallah Kitambi. In Pungutini there was Ngogota who appears as Gogota in German sources and who is said by Gotzen to have had 2,000 men with guns as late as September 1905. In March 1906, he was imprisoned in Mohoro.[23] In Kitunda, in central Kichiland, Mkina Mkechekeche (German Kechekeche) was assisted in leadership by Kunjabandu. German sources indicate that Mkechekeche surrendered in January 1906. Many more leaders could be assisted by name but it should be pointed out that in the Matumbi-Kitchi area, leadership did not always co-incide with existing political authority. Contrary to what one authority has suggested, those *jumbes* who joined in Maji Maji and even became leaders did so for reasons other than the fact that they had participated in the cotton scheme.[24] Abdallah Kitambi joined the movement at the threat of death, after it was discovered that he wanted to aid the escape of Hopfer in order to acquire his property. The hated *jumbe* Mtemangani in Nandette also had to join Maji Maji or be killed.[25]

In Ngindoland, however, leadership was assumed by *jumbes*—existing agents of the German administration. The one person who nearly wielded centralised leadership was Abdallah Mapanda, a firebrand politician, brave and eloquent, wise and experienced in elephant hunting. He was a deeply disillusioned debtor to Aimer, a settler-trader resident at Liwale *boma*. Other prominent leaders were Lihambi, Nassoro Mpwanga, Mpule, and especially Mebmbetu Ntule of Kingwichiro, as well as Omari Kinjalla, who took the *maji* to Ungoni. Each leader was in charge of his own *litapo* or section and there was no central leader.

The fragmentary nature of Maji Maji military leadership necessarily created problems of inter-group communication, especially regarding the making of decisions. The Matumbi-Ngindo peoples attempted various solutions, but still on a clan basis, and their effectiveness depended largely on a gentleman's agreement, which in turn was influenced by considerations of group commit-ment to a mass action. Usually neighbouring leaders met to decide something, whereupon each of the leaders would send his own messenger to communicate the contents of the resolution to those leaders nearest to him. On receiving the information, each of these other leaders sent his own messenger further out, to pass on information to their respective *litapo* or sections. These messengers travelled only at night and slept indoors during the day to avoid detection by German loyalists. Thus, for instance, when the Matumbi decided to uproot cotton as a form of ultimatum to the Germans and when subsequently a *lilunga* or *kilingondo* (war drum) was beaten calling all Matumbi, Kichi, and Ikemba to Nan-dette to prepare for an attack on the headquarters of the Kibata Akidate, they had all received the news already. Or when the Ngindo leaders decided to meet at Naruleo the night before the attack on the Liwale *boma*, all the *jumbes* came with their men. In Matumbiland, where gunpowder was a necessity, the night

buyers went to Kilwa Kivinje to barter rice for it. It was a dangerous occupation, and those caught were persecuted by the
Germans. In 1968, there were two old Indians in Kivinje who were
locked up for two weeks in August 1905, on suspicion of having
sold gunpowder to Africans. It is important to note that nearly
all of these activities were carried out essentially on a clan basis.
That is also the way the war was fought.

It is now clear that Maji Maji techniques had been influenced
by and dependent upon society and the colonial situation. The
interaction of these two forces was the deciding factor in turning
the impending war into a mass movement. The ensuing unity was
a revolutionary phenomenon. But it was essentially revolutionary
in its spirit of commitment and in the physical meeting at a rendezvous for joint action in a common cause. In battlefields and
especially later in guerilla warfare, the Maji Maji peoples still
charged or retreated as clans, or according to practices in existence
before 1905. This phenomenon necessarily militated against centralised leadership—a fact which came to be the very undoing
of the war as a freedom movement. However there are two reasons
why the African clan formation need not be seen as futile or as
showing a lack of military acumen. First, since every fighter carried
his own food, it was important to remain in clan formation, for
in case of need one could replenish only from one's relatives.
Secondly, in the event of death or injury only members of the
victim's clan would take care of him. Hence fighting in the company of foreign clans was both unreasonable and impracticable.

Actually military operations during Maji Maji occurred in
two main phases: pitched battles and guerilla warfare. The two
phases coincided roughly with periods of African victories and
of German repression and suppression respectively. But African
successes were usually accompanied by German nightmares and
an attempt to contain the Maji Maji war. Suppression was attempted once Germans had recruited enough mercenaries from, for
example, the Sudan, Somaliland or Zululand. The Africans
incurred heavy losses during the systematic suppression. But as
long as Africans fought pitched battles the Germans did the same.
When they resorted to guerilla tactics, the Germans were tested to
the fullest, and so they introduced a combing policy of extermination of entire families and villages. But in Matumbiland the Germans were disappointed, for usually they found mysteriously
deserted villages. The German askaris were bitter about these
desertions. Since systematic suppression and the combing policy
alone could not bring about a quick victory the Germans sought
alliance with hunger by applying a scorched-earth policy. The

words of Captain Richter made clear the importance the Germans attached to the scorched-earth policy. Commenting on the imminent famine facing the Africans he declared:

> That's right, the fellows can just starve. We shall be sure to get food for ourselves. If I could I would prevent them from planting anything. This is the only way that we can make the fellows sick of war.[26]

As early as October 1905 Captain Wagenheim, who had been in charge of German operations in Morogoro region, had been outspoken about the German alliance with famine. He had explicitly recommended the use of scorched earth. "In my view only hunger and want can bring about a final submission. Military action alone will remain more or less a drop in the ocean", he insisted. The German fear of defeat was clear. The use of famine as a weapon led to great loss of life long after the war had ended, and the area has not recovered since.

During pitched battles Africans were on the offensive, attacking usually at night. Their target might be German district headquarters or the residence of a German representative usually an *akida*—or else a centre of German supporters such as Nubian ex-mercenaries. It is interesting to note that nearly all such attacks were mounted on three fronts.

War began in Matumbiland on 20 July 1905 and not on 31 July 1905 as German records suggest. As Kinjikitile had delayed in declaring war, the people of Nandette became impatient and decided to uproot some shoots of German cotton as an ultimatum. When the akida of Kibata, Seif bim Amri sent people to spy on the uprooting they were hotly pursued back until at Kitumbi (hill) Mwando, two miles from Kibata, where the first pitched battle took place and where the first victim, Manyana, fell. The *akida's* men subsequently retreated into Kibata stockade. However, Kitumbi Mwando soon became a very important rendezvous of Maji Maji men.

After the first engagement the people of Nandette returned to reorganise themselves. Hence a *lilunga* or war drum was beaten, and the following night all Matumbi Kichi and Ikemba people assembled at Kitumbi Mwando, where each leader agreed to attack Kibata from the direction of his home. Thus people from Pungutini under Ngogota attacked from the north east, while those from Nandette under Sikwako Mbondo attacked from the south-west, with Kitumbi Mwando as a base. Ngomile Kilindo and his people of Mtumbei and Tawa moved on Kibata from the south or Chumo direction, so that the attack was on three fronts. They took up their positions during the night, and at dawn they closed in on Kibata, besieging it for about a week until the *akida*, running out of ammunitions, managed to escape to Kilwa Kivinje via Kiteja. The other large engagement at Kibata took place after the Germans had reinforced their number in an attempt to hold it. This attack too was carried out on three fronts.

After the second Kibata engagement, those doing the fighting divided so that each group of clans would attack those areas nearest to them. For instance, the Pungutini and Kinjumbi groups were assigned to Samanga, while Mkechekeche of the Kichi and the Ikemba were first to attack *akida* Milika of Mji Mpya, west of the present Utete, they were then to join forces with the Pungutini group in attacking Mohoro.

One morning at Samanga Ndumbo, Maji Maji fighters came in and uprooted cotton. On hearing of this action, *Kinoo* or Steinhagen, together with the *akida* and some askaris, marched to and attacked the Africans. After a short fight the Africans retreated into the interior. Later in the afternoon they came back and took up three positions—the Kinjumbi road, Kilwa road and Mohoro road *litapos*. As the Germans were expecting an attack from Kinjumbi, this *litapo* charged first and Steinhagen hit back very ruthlessly. But that *litapo* retreated, pursued by most of the Germans; simultaneously the Mohoro road *litapo* moved in to the attack. A remnant of askaris and supporters had to fight the Mohoro *litapo* which in turn retreated and was hotly pursued by the Germans. This left Samanga Ndumbo undefended, so the Kilwa *litapo* moved in and burnt the settlement down.

There are several other examples of a three-pronged attack. Liwale was attacked from three fronts. Those from Madaba road were based at Naruleo, while Abdallah Mapanda and those from Kingwichiro were based at Kilimalyo, and those from the south were at Nangongo on the Masasi road. At dawn the three forces converged on Liwale *boma*, and the incendiary arrow came from the direction of Nangongo.[28] There is also evidence to show that Mahenge *boma* was attacked from three fronts. Isongo, Gambiro and Ifakara. But German and oral sources are still silent about how this was possible.

Such prevalence of three-pronged attacks, as cited above, makes it tempting to suggest a modest explanation. It may well be that amongst these people three is a ritual number: that is, in order for prayer or ritual to be effective, the doer must repeat each act three times. Thus the number three or anything representing it becomes a symbol of success for the doer and for others of his faith. This view is further strengthened by the fact that Maji Maji fighters wore pieces of millet stalks or seeds in threes, possibly with ritualistic symbolism. The Zaramo had in the past three, but they now have seven as their ritual number.[29].

Guerilla methods of warfare tended to reflect more clearly the ethnic differences of the fighters particularly as there were considerable geographic variations within the Maji Maji districts. In practice organisational focus tended to be on the clan or the family and neighbouring families, because in most cases guerilla bands were small in number. In Matumbi the decision to adopt guerilla tactics seemed to have been arrived at unanimously.

> As we turned from there (pitched battle). Thereafter we talked amongst ourselves and agreed with each other that a group of fifty men, Then if the askari came from a certain direction we waylaid them and fought them.[30]

Ambushing and surprise attack were the order of the day in the guerilla phase. While some were fighting, others were hiding food, children, women and the aged in caves, thickets or dense forests. From the standpoint of topography, some areas were better suited to guerilla warfare than others. Ngindoland, an undulating plateau with scattered homesteads outside Liwale and scattered thickets, was so ill-suited for guerilla fighting that most Ngindo, as did the Mwera, ran to Kilima Rondo to hide. On the other hand Matumbiland—with intensely folded conical hills, steep slopes, many "V" shaped valleys with fast-running streams (especially in the rainy season) and large and small caves scattered around the highlands—was particularly suited to guerilla tactics. Matumbi, in those days lived on the hilltops which provided much more effective defence and this was an important advantage in the sentry system they used during Maji Maji.

The Germans usually attacked a village on an appointed day in their attempt to wage the war systematically. Therefore the Africans had to keep a permanent sentry, for it was not known exactly when the German askaris would attack a particular village. Thus at each homestead a sentinel was posted in a tree on one of the hilltops. This provided a wide view as all Matumbi hills incline towards the east and are at about the same altitude except for Mbinga range which, in any case, is on the edge of the highlands. In this manner the advance of the German askaris could be detected from a distance. On seeing the advancing columns the sentry cried out "Kilulu-kilulu (danger, danger), whereupon all children, women, the old, and the disabled went with food into hiding in dense bush or in one of the nearby caves. In the Nandembo area of Matumbiland, Father Ambrosius Meyer, who visited one of the largest caves in 1910, found numerous hearth fires and estimated that during Maji Maji, five thousand people could have camped unseen in its enormous vestibule.³¹ The cave is called Nang'oma, and Crosse-Upcott erroneously thought it to be the source of *maji*. However, in the process of hiding large bush grain/food stores were established.

While others hid in the bush or in caves the sentry more accurately mapped out the route to be taken by the German mercenaries or askari. All the able-bodied men armed themselves and took up their positions along the path of the Germans. Usually they chose a narrow pass between hills, a steep slope or a river valley difficult to cross. In actual combat the Matumbi had specific methods.

When an advancing German party fell into the ambush, half the Matumbi could attack from one direction so that when they later retreated into the bush, the askaris tended to follow them. But at that point the second group would attack them from behind, whereupon the askaris would have to turn back. After a while the first group would return and hit at the Germans from behind; and this technique would continue until the Matumbi would disappear into dense bush. A slightly more sophisticated method was one which can be called *kalinguli*. Technically *kalinguli* was a military spy. However, in the *kalinguli* method of fighting, after the enemy had been located the Matumbi laid an ambush arranged in a "V" formation with the apex away from the enemy. The *kalinguli* then went out, and when he was a reasonable distance from the enemy, he fired at them and ran back as quickly as possible towards the apex of the "V". On seeing the *kalinguli* the Germans nearly always pursued him mistaking him for a lone attacker. In this way the askaris gradually became engulfed in the "V" formation, and as they reached the apex they were attacked by fighters at that end along the sides of the "V". As fighting developed, those along the "V" closed in behind the askaris (that is, if the askari had entered right into the trap) and attacked from behind. It was in this manner that Sergeant Josef Schober was killed at Mbombwe on 2 October 1905 by one Abdallah Tosa.³² The Germans sources seem to indicate that Schober was killed on 8 October, but the slab on his grave at Mbombwe called by the Matumbi *iziko lya njunga* has 2 October inscribed on it.³³

By their guerilla tactics, the Matumbi reduced the German askaris to a state of famine, for the Germans had always depended on looting food from African reserves. On reaching a village they would take enough for themselves, and the remainder they would burn so as to deprive the Africans of food. In Matumbiland the askaris or mercenaries who were charged with much of the "combing" of the hills were filled with rage, for not only could they not kill or torture, but they could not get food from the deserted homes. The Germans themselves admitted that the Matumbi excelled in guerilla warfare.

> Rebels here (Matumbiland) had excelled all others in tenacity (and dexterity)[34]

The way the Germans responded to the skilled guerilla tactics of the Matumbiland was to intensify their reign of terror. Henceforth all bush was set on fire, and if they discovered a cave in which they suspected people were hiding, they built a big fire at the entrance to choke the occupants within. All villages and food crops were burnt down.

Elsewhere in the area of Maji Maji it was difficult to utilise Matumbi guerilla methods with the same results. The Ngindo, living in typical savannah vegetation in the *miondo* woodland, had neither dense bush, forests, hills nor steep-sided valleys. Consequently, in their hiding most Ngindo went south into Kilimarondo forest. In less hilly areas the Maji Maji fighters usually dug ditches or trenches called *handaki* (pl. *mahandaki*) on either side of the path and lay in ambush in them. When the German askaris passed between these, they were attacked first from one side and then the other. The Mwera seemed to have used this method.[35] Sometimes wide trenches were dug at a strategic point along a path and covered carefully with grass and small amounts of earth. The unsuspecting askaris came along and fell into the trenches; and as the others tried to rescue their friends, they were attacked by Maji Maji fighters hiding in nearby thickets. Another technique was to plant thorny bush or sharpened sticks along a route and attack the askaris as they removed these obstacles. But these guerilla skills proved of no avail as time went on, and the Maji Maji peoples were defeated very badly, suffering staggering losses.

Many other examples of guerilla techniques could be cited, but all lead to three conclusions. First, that for the Africans, these were not new techniques, as they had been in use long before the coming of Europeans. It will be remembered that in 1891 the Hehe attacked and defeated a German column under Zelewsky, with an ambush technique similar to that of the Matumbi: the Germans were attacked from both sides in a narrow gorge between two steep hills near Lugalo. The Matumbi themselves had used their techniques against invading Ngoni and Yao as well as in the 1898 War of Pumpkins. Probably the only new elements in their fighting was a repeated destruction of the telegraph line between Kilwa and Mohoro and Dar es Salaam. One was cut first on 28

July 1905 and again on 3 September, while the Lindi-Kilwa line
was in pieces on 27 August and many times thereafter.[36]

Secondly, guerilla tactics were themselves influenced by geographic conditions. It happened that 1905–06 was a time of exceptionally heavy rainfall.[37] German sources are full of reports of
flooding rivers that killed many of their numbers. Wangenheim,
for instance, failed to cross the Ruaha from Kidatu to Mahenge,
partly because of the floods and partly because the ferry had been
hidden by Maji Maji fighters. For the Matumbi, it is unlikely
that they could have continued with pitched battles even if other
circumstances had allowed it, because once it rains in Matumbiland, the swift-running streams are often dangerous to cross and
the ground becomes so sticky that it is impossible to walk long
distances with reasonable speed. Besides, in areas where the
vegetation was ill suited for guerilla fighting, methods of warfare
were also slightly different, as shown above.

Thirdly, from the nature of its organisational techniques, which
became increasingly incapable of mass military operation, guerilla
warfare was a reasonable if necessary alternative. Further, the
nature of guerilla tactics amongst these peoples was such that this
phase was characterised by defensive and not offensive operations.
But it should be stressed here that these divisions into pitched
battles and guerilla phases are only an academic exercise, and
in practice the two sometimes occurred simultaneously although
of course in different places. Thus when the Matumbi went into
guerilla fighting in September, Kibata continually suffered attacks
at night, although these were on a minor scale compared with
the July and August offensives.

In conclusion it is possible to advance several arguments out of
this discussion. First, that Maji Maji as a freedom and mass movement was too revolutionary and demanding for the methods that
the Africans employed. It seems that the unity of the movement
was more a matter of faith than practical military administration
and the fact that ideology or theory did not harmonise with practice
was the main source of weakness. Truly the ideology was very
revolutionary but the actual practice of war became revolutionary
essentially in organisational scale and not in the criterion and
rationale of organisation because traditional sectional loyalties
held sway. Secondly, that since such organisational techniques
failed to break through local attachments and loyalties, it became
more and more difficult to engage in pitched battles, which themselves had the colouring of guerilla elements from the very beginning. Hence guerilla techniques were a natural and reasonable
outcome of such weak organisation and leadership, which was

united only by ideology and hardly at all by centralised administration. In addition, however, Africans were at a disadvantage in pitched battles because of the superior weaponry of the Germans. Third, that whatever methods were used in any given area were influenced by traditional usages in existence before 1905 as well as by variations of climate and topography in the south. Fourth, that African methods of warfare almost forced the Germans to change their own methods. For instance, once Africans adapted guerilla tactics, to which Germans had no military answer, they resorted to the scorched-earth policy. It is likely that without the German alliance with hunger, the Maji Maji war would have taken much longer; and it is because of this policy that so many people died and so many epidemics attended the end of war in 1907. Nevertheless, weak organisation and famine apart, Africans were also defeated because of their inferior weapons. Although Gotsen records that there were 8,000 guns in Matumbi alone, this point should not be taken too seriously, for these were nearly all of a type inferior to ordinary flint guns.[38] Oral sources are agreed that arrows killed more.

Finally, it is significant that military organisation was never at any time transcended by ideological leadership. This phenomenon is generally true of other resistances such as that of the Ndebele and Mashona in 1896–97. But in both cases initial violence was inspired and turned into mass violence by ideological appeals. In Tanzania the people had not only to revise and improve on Maji Maji methods in their quest for independence in the twentieth century, but increasingly they rejected violence as a technique of liberation. This view suggests at least two arguments. First, that violence need not be the only technique of liberation. Secondly, that methods of violent protest are related to a people's historical, political and social experience—and depending on the outcome of violence, such methods may be discarded because of their inadequacy in changed circumstances. The implication here is that the context of historical facts must be understood and studied along with the economic, social, political and time factors impinging on a society as a unit.

NOTES

1. Eduard Haber to Graf Von Gotzen, 9 September 1905, Reichskolonialamt (R. Kol. A.) 726/81–90 in Deutsches Zentralarchiv, Potsdam, German Democratic Republic.
2. R. Kol. A. 701/112. In 1908 Mwichande Likapa, a Mgindo, was reported to Lindi authorities by Mohamed bin Issa in connection with Maji

Maji. He was hanged. Several similar incidents are reported in oral sources. Two people appearing before the D.O. Liwale in 1912 over a dispute between them were caught and hanged as Maji Maji suspects.

3. Fr. Elzear Ebner, "History of the Wangoni" (mimeograph, Peramiho n.d.), 134–5.
4. Quoted by J. M. Gray in *History of East Africa*, R. Oliver and G. Mathew (eds.) (O.U.P., 1963), p. 249.
5. P. Ambrosius Meyer, O.S.B. "Matumbiland in 1912", in *Missions Blatter von St. Ottilien Jahresbericht der Benediktinermission von St. Ottillen June 1912.* Also see a translation in Kilwa District Book.
6. A. R. W. Cross-Upcott, "The Social Structure of the Kingindo-Speaking Peoples". Ph. D. thesis, University of Capetown, 1955, 22 ff. unpublished.
7. J. M. Maketta, "Maji Maji in Ubona". Student research paper, typescript 1969, University of Dar es Salaam.
8. J. A. Kayera, "Report on Maji Maji in Mtimbira Area-Ulanga". Student research paper, typescript 1969, University of Dar es Salaam.
9. O. B. Mapunda and G. M. Mpangara, *The Maji Maji War in Ungoni* (E.A.P.H., Nairobi, 1969).
10. Mzee Ndundule Mangaya Kipatimu Kilwa, interviewed 8 August 1967.
11. G. L. Steere, "Judgement on German Africa" (London, 1939), p. 249.
12. G. C. K. Gwassa and John Iliffe (eds.) "Records of the Maji Maji Rising", Historical Association of Tanzania Paper No. 4 (E.A.P.H., 1968), p. 8. Also Mzee Elisei Simbanimoto Upunda, Nandette, September 1967.
13. Gwassa & Iliffe, pp. 8–9, also Bwana Sebastian Upunda, 4 September 1967.
14. Mzee Mohamed Nganoga Nimekwako, Ngarambe, interviewed 31 August 1967.
15. Mzee Ndungule Mangaya, September 1967.
16. Gwassa and Iliffe, p. 10.
17. Moritz Merker, "Ueber die Aufstandbewegung in Deutsch-Ostafrika", *Militar-Wochenblatt*, Vol. 91 (1906), Cols. 1022–3.
18. Gwassa & Iliffe, pp. 10–11, also Merker *loc. cit.*
19. Gwassa & Iliffe, p. 11.
20. Bibi Nambulyo Mwiru, Ngarambe. Interviewed 31 August 1967.
21. Gwassa & Iliffe, p. 12, also Mzee Ngapota Mkupali of Kipoto, Chumo and Matumbi-Ngarambe texts, *passim.*
22. Mzee Mohamed Nganoga Nimekwako, *loc. cit.*
23. Graf von Gozten, "Deutsch-Ostafrika im Aufstand 1905–06" (Berlin, 1909), pp. 133 and 156.
24. See John Iliffe, "The Organisation of the Maji Maji Rebellion", *Journal of African History VIII* (1967), pp. 495–512.
25. Mzee Ambrose Ngombale Mwiru, Kipatumu, 7 August 1967.
26. "Kingonsera Chronicle", Ferbuary 1906, quoted in Gwassa & Iliffe, p. 27.
27. Capt. Wangenheim to Gotzen from Kilwa, 22 October 1905, quoted in G. A. von Gotzen "Deutsch-Ostafrika", p. 149.
28. R. M. Bell, "The Maji Maji Rebellion in Liwale Districts", *Tanganyika Notes and Records XXVIII* (January 1955), pp. 338–57.
29. Information from Mrs. Marja-liisa Swantz.
30. Mzee Kibilange Upunda, Nandette, 4 September 1967, 19 October 1968.

31. A. R. W. Gross-Upcott, "The Origin of Maji Maji Revolt", *Man* (May 1960), Article 98, pp. 71–3.
32. Matumbi texts, *passim.*
33. Gotzen, *op. cit.,* p. 134.
34. *Ibid;* p. 159.
35. Mzee Bakari Ruvu, Ruvu texts, 19 January 1968.
36. Gotzen *op. cit.,* p. 58; see also "Deutsch-Ostafrikanisch Zeiting", Nr. 26 (30 June 1906).
37. Kilwa District Book., see also Gotzen, *op. cit.,* p. 140 & *passim.*

7

MUMBOISM—
AN ANTI-COLONIAL MOVEMENT

Bethwell A. Ogot and William R. Ochieng'

During the last five years, historians and political scientists have been engaged in a study of African "Primary" resistance movements. They have sought to know why certain individual African leaders or societies collaborated with the Colonial regimes while others resisted all approaches by the colonialists.[1] In such studies little attention has been given to the way traditional religious cults were adopted and used, usually after a military defeat, to organise a different kind of resistance to the intrusion of European rule. In this chapter, we have attempted to show how the Gusii, who had lost the military fight by 1908, adopted the Cult of Mumbo from the Luo and used it effectively to continue their struggle against the British up to about 1954.

I

By the Anglo-German Treaty of 1890 the respective spheres of influence of the two powers in East Africa were defined. In the scramble for territory that followed, both the Germans and the British worked feverishly to transform their spheres of influence into protectorates. In this way, two British protectorates were declared over Buganda and the territory between Uganda and the coast in June 1894 and July 1895 respectively. In the same way, most of the African peoples who now live in Kenya and Uganda gained admission into the British Empire without they themselves being aware of the fact.

How did the Gusii react to this free admission into the British Empire? Before we can answer that question, let us first of all say something about the people themselves. The Gusii, a small highland Bantu tribe, occupy the most southerly portion of the cool fertile western section of the Kenya Highlands. Their language places them within the family of the Bantu-speaking majority of

NYANZA PROVINCE

0 10 20 30 40 KILOMETRES

ALEGO

R. NZOIA

RAMOGI HILL

LUO

KISUMU

KANO

RUSINGA ISLAND

KARACHUONYO

R. SONDU

LAKE VICTORIA

LUO

KITUTU

KISII TOWN

NORTH MUGIRANGO

WANJARE

GUSII

KARUNGU

R. KUJA

NYARIBARI

KADEM

BASSI

MAJOGE

KURIA

R. MIGORI

R. MARA

NORTH MARA

sub-equatorial Africa, although their entry into the southern highlands, which is now surrounded by tribes of unrelated language
families, isolated them from other Kenya Bantu tribes. According
to their historical traditions, the Kuria (whose language is mutually
intelligible with Gusii), the Maragoli, the Kikuyu and the Gusii
were, in the distant past, the same people. They migrated from
their original home somewhere in north-western Uganda (some say
Egypt) and regrouped around Mt. Elgon, where there occurred a
major dispersal. The Kikuyu, according to Gusii traditions, moved
to central Kenya, while the Gusii themselves trekked southward
to Kisumu where they established a settlement which appears to
have extended up to Chemilil in the east and Kosele—Gendia in
Karachuonyo location in the south. It was at Kisumu that a section
of them which later became the Maragoli broke off. The Gusii
group entered their present homeland some two centuries ago,
having semi-circled the highlands by way of Gososia in north
Mugirango, the Masai district of Trans-Mara, and the Kabwoch
location in the Homa-Bay district.[2]

THE ESTABLISHMENT OF BRITISH ADMINISTRATION IN GUSII

The Protectorate which the British declared over Buganda in
1894 was soon extended to include the Kisumu and Naivasha
districts, which in 1900 became the Eastern Province of Uganda.
Until 1902, this province was merely regarded as a supply zone
for the route to Uganda. To bring the Eastern Province under firm
control, an administrative headquarters was set up at Mumias in
1894 under F. Spire, and in 1895 C. W. Hobely was instructed to
relieve Spire, build a permanent station at Mumias and gradually
establish an administration over the various sections of the turbu-
lent collection of peoples who were collectively known as the
"Kavirondo". And between 1895 and 1900 Hobely organised
several punitive expeditions aimed at bringing under control warlike
groups such as the Kager, Uyoma, Kitosh, Nandi, Kakalelwa,
Kakamega and Tiriki. He believed that the use of force in Africa
was inevitable and natural. As he was to write later:

> The reaction of a native race to control by a civilised Govern-
> ment varies according to their nature, and to their form of Govern-
> ment, but in every case a conflict of some kind is inevitable, be-
> fore the lower race fully accepts the dictum of the ruling power.[3]

The Luo, Gusii, Suba and Kuria inhabitants of South Nyanza
were still a law unto themselves and were to remain so until 1904

without realising, or being told, that they were already in the British sphere of influence.

In 1902 they were transferred, together with the rest of the other peoples in the Eastern Province of Uganda, to the East African Protectorate (Kenya). Two years later the British decided to set up a small administrative outpost at Karungu, where some representatives of the East African syndicate were already prospecting for gold. Karungu was to act as a base from which to bring the entire South Nyanza (which included Gusii) under British control.

Another reason why Karungu was chosen was that the Germans were known to be active in the border area between the German and the British sphere of influence. Indeed, in Kadem and Suna the Germans had already appointed puppet chiefs, and according to G. A. S. Northcote, one of the earliest British administrators in the area, there was scarcely a community within fifty miles of the border which had not suffered from a German punitive expedition.

Unlike Central and North Nyanza, South Nyanza was, up to 1904, practically unknown to the British officials in the Province. H. M. Stanley had visited the area during his famous circumnavigation of the Victoria in 1877 and named it Ugaya (the name by which the Luo were known to the Kuria).[4] Colonel George had tried, unsuccessfully, to explore the region in 1901, but African hostility had compelled him to abandon the expedition. In view of the German threat from the south, however, the British decided against any plans for preliminary exploration.

Early in 1903 a parcel of Union Jacks was sent to Karungu area with instructions that they be flown from all villages in the vicinity. A few months later, in August, Boughton-Knight, after camping on Rusinga Island, landed at Karungu with the designation of Acting District Commissioner. Because of the German threat it was essential that the Anglo-German paper boundary of 1890 be confirmed on the ground. In 1904, H. H. Horne, who had become the District Commissioner on the death of Boughton-Knight, surveyed the Anglo-German Border and established a recognisable boundary, which unfortunately created another problem which remains unsolved to this day. An artificial line was drawn right across the Kuria tribe, one-third finding itself in the British, and the remainder on the German side.

It has been suggested by one of the authors that one of the major reasons why the Luo of the Central Nyanza District of Kenya offered no serious armed resistance to the British intruders was because their diviners (*jobilo*), who in pre-European days wielded considerable influence in society, had advised against showing any hostilities to the intruders lest they incur the wrath of the ancestors.[5]

Like the Luo of Central Nyanza, the Gusii also had their diviners. Names of Gusii prophets like Sakawa of Nyakoe; Muraa, wife of Ngiti; and Bonairiri, wife of Owura, rank high in their traditions. Sakawa, for example, had foretold the advent of the "white strangers" and had advised against fighting them. The greatest and the most beloved of all the Gusii medicine men of the late nineteenth century, he is credited with all kinds of prophesies. He is supposed, for example, to have prophesied where the white man's hospital, police lines and houses would be. He had also prophesied that the young men would be disarmed by the newcomers if they showed resistance. All these prophesies are believed to have come true. Respected and trusted by his people as Sawaka was at that time, there is no reason to believe that the Gusii could not have received the British in the same way as the Luo of Central Nyanza had done. It was unfortunate, however, that a violent entry by the British was destined to destroy the ground unwittingly prepared for them by Sawaka.

But not all the Gusii subtribes reacted in the same way to the British landing at Karungu. The weaker subtribes, for example, were eager to win British support against their enemies. Ombati of the "buffer state" of Muksero lost no time in appealing to the British for assistance against their powerful neighbour, the Kitutu. Nyamusi of Majoge, whose territory had been torn by civil strife since 1902, is also reported to have visited Karungu in 1904 with offers of friendship. These collaborators, as we shall see later, greatly aided the British administrators in their task of establishing colonial rule in Gusii, and they, in turn, used the colonialists to continue wars that antedated the colonial period.

On the other hand, the reaction of the larger subtribes to the British presence in South Nyanza was indifferent. In fact, between 1904 and 1906, they continued to organise daring raids deep into the Luo and Kipsigis countries. As P. M. Gordon said, "If the British claim to protection of the Luo was not to be a mockery these predations had to be stopped."[6]

It should be realised that by this time the British had abandoned their so-called peaceful policy of gradually bringing the "natives" under their control "without using absolute force at once" and had come to rely increasingly on punitive measures as the quickest and surest method of bringing peace. As Hardinge once advised the Foreign Office, "In Africa, to have peace you must first teach obedience, and the only tutor who impressed the lesson properly is the Sword."[7] This was the method S. S. Bagge, the Sub-Commissioner for Kisumu Province, adopted when he dispatched a punitive expedition to Gusii in 1904 "on the receipt of the news that some Kavirondo tribesmen had been murdered by the Kisii". This expedition, characterised by wanton burning of huts and senseless human massacre, was to poison the relationship between the Gusii and the British administration throughout the colonial era.

It all started with a civil disturbance in the Kitutu. A Gusii clan called Abagusero who lived on the border between the Luo subtribes of Kasipul and Kabondo and the Gusii subtribes of Wanjare and Kitutu had, over the years, formed a nasty habit of ambushing Kitutu women who went to trade in Luo country. Muksero robbers would lie in ambush and suddenly pounce on the defenceless women, robbing them of pots, grain, milk and other items of merchandise. This kind of "highway robbery" disrupted the normal flow of trade between the two tribes.

In 1904, the Kitutu subtribe decided to put an end to this practice. In a devastating war, they trounced the Muksero. The slaughter was so great that the majority of the Muksero folk fled in terror: a large number ran to Luoland; an equally large number dispersed amongst the Nyaribari, Wanjare and Majoge sections of the Gusii; while a sizeable proportion fled as far south as Isbania in Butende, a few settling temporarily in the Luo area of Kadem, from where they were later dislodged by the Luo clan of Kakoth. It was at this time that Ombati, the self-styled chief at Muksero, took a small band of followers via Gekero to Kano near Kisumu where he hoped to obtain some medicine to use against the Kitutu. On hearing of the presence of the British at Kisumu, he appealed to them for assistance. It was partly as a result of this appeal that late in 1904 an expedition was dispatched "to investigate the activities of the Kisii".[8]

Ombati's interview with S. S. Bagge, the Sub-Commissioner in Kisumu, provided the British with the kind of pretext they needed. For some time, the administration had cast a covetous eye on the land of the Sotik and the related Gusii as "a large area of excellent land—which should be opened up to settlers . . .". In fact Governor Stewart had addressed a letter to the Foreign Office in which he stated that it was most important that the Gusii territory should be opened up since it was "well adapted to European settlement".[9] He noted with regret, however, that while some of the Gusii were friendly and wanted the administration to establish "a Government post in their country" a large portion of this tribe was "inimical" and would most likely give trouble.

However, on receipt of the news that some "Kavirondo tribesmen" had been murdered by the Gusii, a police detachment, under Sergeant Instructor J. H. Milton, was hastily ordered in September 1904 to join a company of the K.A.R. which at the time was based at Kericho under the command of Captain E. V. Jenkins, D.S.O., with G. S. A. Northcote, an Assistant Collector at Karungu, as a political officer. The platoon, comprising a hundred troops of the 5th K.A.R. and fifty policemen, was dispatched via Kisumu and was away for most of the month. They assembled at Karungu, and from there entered the Gusii country by way of South Mugirango, where they stayed from 20 September to 7 October 1904. The aims of the expedition were firstly to teach the Gusii a lesson for attacking the Luo, who were already under the protection of the British; and secondly and more importantly, to survey the area for a suitable site for an administrative station in Gusiiland.

The attempt by the Abagirango to enquire about the intentions of the "red strangers" was met with indiscriminate shooting, the burning of houses and the seizing of cattle. When one, Nyaruaba of South Mugirango, protested when a policeman led his fattest bull away, he was shot dead on the spot, and many like him suffered the same fate.

Shooting their way as they moved, the troops crossed from South Mugirango into Wanjare, where they erected a camp at Ngeri. This action was resented by the people, who were already angered by the brutal treatment meted out to the Abagirango by the British. When they advanced on the police camp, the platoon opened fire, killing hundreds. Oyugi, the chief elder of Wanjare, was then given a basket of Union Jacks which he was ordered to hoist on rooftops in the surrounding area. He was further ordered to confiscate cattle from all the ringleaders. And when Oyugi failed to obtain cattle in this way, as was inevitable, the invading troops raided the villages, impounding cattle and shooting everybody on sight.

The troops next attacked the Mariba clan in Wanjare. According to tradition, Ombati's sister was married to a man of this clan who had rudely refused to pay dowry. Since Ombati was acting as the local guide to the troops, he was determined to pay off old scores. The attempt by the Mariba warriors to put up a show was hopeless in the face of superior weapons. Having destroyed the Mariba village, they crossed into West Kitutu, where those who had murdered the Abagusero lived. Indiscriminate shooting forced the Kitutu who lived in the neighbourhood of Nyabururu to surrender. When Nyakina, an elder from the area, approached the troops to make peace with them, he was shot dead through the head, an act which was never forgotten by the Kitutu people. In the evening of 6 October, the troops retired to their base at Ngeri, and on the following morning, they collected all the cattle they had seized and left. The official estimate, which is conservative, put the number of Gusii killed in Kitutu at one hundred, and three thousand head of cattle captured.

For the operation, all members of the platoon under Captain E. V. Jenkins were issued with the East African General Service Medal with a bar (Kisii, 1904) in recognition of the fact that they had "dealt successfully with a revolt of the Kisii in Kisumu Province".[10]

The 1904 punitive expedition to Kisii had two major results. First, it enabled the British administration to reconnoitre the country, thus allowing Northcote to select a suitable site for an additional administrative *boma*. Secondly, and more important for our purpose, it demoralised the Gusii and poisoned their future relations with the British. True, warfare had occurred almost continuously among the seven Gusii subtribal units: the Kitutu, North Mugirango, Bassi, Nyaribari, South Mugirango, Majoge and Wanjare. It is also a fact that the Gusii fought regular intertribal wars against the Luo, the Maasai and the Kipsigis, especially during the nineteenth century. But in few of these wars were more than five people killed on any given fighting day; and wars in which more than ten people died, like the Battle of Muksero or the Battle of Saosao (the only battle in which the Gusii fought as a united people against the Kipsigis in 1892), were always remembered as the exceptions. That the British had killed over a hundred people and "for no good reason" was unforgettable and unforgivable.

For another one and a half years the district headquarters remained at Karungu. This was largely because the British force was recalled to deal with another resistance to their intrusion amongst the Nandi. But in 1907, it was decided that the district headquarters should be moved from Karungu to Kisii. The reasons given were (a) that the Gusii had demonstrated their belligerence and it was therefore necessary to keep a closer watch on them; (b) that Karungu was not centrally situated and this made it difficult to govern the district effectively; and (c) it was also situated in a famine-stricken and malarial area. For example, Boughton-Knight and two other European gold prospectors had died there of malaria. For these reasons, Northcote, the Assistant D.C., was instructed to move the administration centre to Kisii, which he did on 1 April 1907.

For the remainder of that year, he was busy building the new government station which came to be known as Kisii, and attempting to impose an alien rule over the Gusii. For the latter task, he relied heavily on the services of Ombati, who was made chief of the Abagusero, in recognition of his great assistance to the British. With the aid of forty African *askaris* (soldiers), Northcote was determined to introduce British rule in an area where, as he saw it, "Every small hill was at deadly enmity with the (sic) neighbours even in the same clan".[11]

Although he was conscious of the disputes amongst the Gusii, which he rightly believed militated against any kind of unity, North-cote seems to have been unaware of the bitterness which the Gusii, especially the Kitutu people, harboured against foreigners. On several occasions in Kitutu, he resorted to the use of force in order to obtain food for the soldiers and porters who were engaged in building the station.

To the Gusii, Northcote personified the new enemy, and as Muraa the prophetess declared, only his elimination could bring peace and freedom to her people.

On Saturday 11 January 1908, Northcote, accompanied by a few *askaris*, went to investigate a case of theft in Kitutu. The people refused to meet him, and he therefore decided to confiscate two cows belonging to a certain Otenyo. According to Kitutu accounts recorded by Robert Maxon,

> When Muraa saw the Assistant District Commissioner taking the cattle away, she became infuriated. She began to insult the young men nearby in very abusive terms. She told them that they were just like women; didn't they care that their cattle were being taken? On hearing this abuse, Otenyo, whose cattle they were, picked up his spear and went off along the route Northcote was following. He got ahead of the Assistant District Commissioner and lay waiting for him in the tall grass beside the path. As North-cote was passing on his horse, somewhat behind the police accompanying him, Otenyo threw his spear at the Assistant District Commissioner and struck him in the back.[12]

The Gusii assumed he was dead. They shouted with joy that there would be no more white men in their country and they would once more be free. Having imbibed prophetess Muraa's medicine, which they believed would turn bullets into water, several clans, particularly in Kitutu, Nyaribari and Wanjare, broke into open revolt in which two Indians and one Jaluo in the *boma* were murdered.

In a personal diary he kept, Northcote himself has left us a record of how the situation appeared to him on the following day. He wrote in a letter to his father:

> The worst time that I had was on Sunday 12th January, the day after they struck me; I had sent out two parties of police, one to escort letters, as I had heard that all my messengers had been killed,

which was all rot, and another to rescue any scattered *askaris* [police] who were out in the district—about noon when I had only 24 police in hand, the natives who were massed on the surrounding hills moved down to attack; they all believed that I was dead. I hastily armed four prisoners, one Indian and three Waganda, who knew a rifle from a mincing machine, and collected all the women and porters, boys, traders round my house, in all about 300 but quite unarmed. This, however, frightened off the Kisii, who disappeared at 3 p.m. About the same time 15 police got back, and I felt more happy.[13]

Six days later Downing Street had received a cable from Governor Sadler informing them of the incident. In Kenya, the news of the "revolt" had reached John Ainsworth, the Nyanza Provincial Commissioner at Kisumu, on 12 January. He immediately dispatched Dr. H. S. Beederker under escort to Kisii to attend to Northcote. On 14 January Ainsworth received further information on the events of the 12th and 13th, which he interpreted as a general revolt of the Kitutu people against the government. It was after he received this report that he decided to contact the Governor. A company of the 5th K.A.R. based at Lumbwa was to be sent with speed to Kisii. Ainsworth also ordered W. R. Foran, head of the police detachment of Kisumu, to hurry to Kisii with all the available police. In total a column of 54 African police and 150 porters—all under W. R. Foran's command—left Kisumu for Kisii.

On 15 January 1908 they were in Kisii, where several attacks of the Gusii "were repulsed and casualties inflicted". They found that Northcote's wound was not serious. The Gusii warriors, armed with traditional weapons, were massed on nearby hills, although they made no attempt to attack the *boma*. On the following morning Captain J. Bois arrived with 75 men of the 5th K.A.R. from Lumbwa. He reported that Lieutenant Colonel J. D. Mackay, commanding a punitive expedition comprising 14 British Officers, 327 N.C.O.s and men, a doctor, and 500 porters, was due to arrive in the district two days later; and that the punitive expedition had been approved by Sadler. The British appeared determined to teach the Gusii a lesson.

The K.A.R. column, according to Foran, entered Gusiiland in a violent manner. They burnt huts, destroyed crops and captured any cattle they came across. The punitive operations lasted from 15 January to 13 February 1908, when the K.A.R. and the Kenya Police were withdrawn. The Police wing was entrusted with the task of escorting to Kibos the captured stock—some 5,636 head of cattle, and 3,281 sheep and goats. It was estimated that about

250 Gusii had been killed during these operations, and that many more were wounded,[14] despite the fact that they never encountered the invaders in any serious fighting.

Major Kirkpatrick, Chief Staff Officer of the Kisii expeditionary force, confirmed this when he explained his tactics:

I have found from years' experience in this country that the native will never fight or be brought into action until his flocks or herds are laid hands on; and after my first day's experience of the Kisii tribe I found he was in no way different from any other of the Protectorate natives and could not be brought to attack us. I therefore decided to make every effort to capture his stock with a view of bringing him to action...but I never could induce him to close quarters.[15]

Even to men who desired a quick and effective control of the outlying districts of the Empire, the massacre of defenceless Gusii men and women was outrageous. Small wonder that when he received the news of this expedition, Winston Churchill's outburst was:

I do not like the tone of these reports. No doubt the clans should be punished: but 160 have now been killed outright "without any further casualties" and the main body has not yet been encountered. ...It looks like a butchery, and if the House of Commons gets hold of it, all our plans in E.A.P. will be under a cloud. Surely it cannot be necessary to go on killing these defenceless people on such an enormous scale.

As far as the Gusii were concerned, this definitely was a butchery! The views of the man on the spot, Northcote, were ignored by the soldiers who regarded the Gusii as their military enemy. The former recorded his disapproval of the manner in which the so-called war was fought in these words:

It [war] had been most shockingly mismanaged; they [the British Officers] refused my advice and were very sorry afterwards—all but 6,000 of the cattle got away with the young Kisii men and were not touched, they should all have been rounded up; instead of this they have killed about 250 of the wretched natives and I am very sick about it; it would take too long to describe the absolute idiocy, obstinacy and want of knowledge of military operations in this country, which they showed.[16]

It is perhaps more pertinent to ask why, after the senseless massacres of 1904, the Gusii had again decided to take up arms against the British. The answer would appear to be that the Gusii still believed that the white man was a sojourner in their area, and that his departure could be hastened by subjecting him to a few

unpleasant experiences. They also deplored the white man's sense
of justice, which involved random shooting even of innocent men.
A prophetess in Kitutu, the aforementioned Muraa wife of Ngiti,
had gone round telling her people that if they permitted even a
single white man to stay in the district, he would be joined by
others, and eventually the Gusii themselves would be enslaved. She
offered to give the warriors medicine "so that the bullets would
turn into water". She apparently had gained her reputation in the
old wars between the Gusii and the Kipsigis, where her medicine
was believed to have earned the former several victories. This time
she advocated the murder of Northcote.

Although there was general agreement among the Gusii that
Northcote should be killed, nobody seemed brave enough to do it.
Muraa therefore decided to use her foster son, Otenyo. She gave
him beer and medicine to protect him against the bullets. When
Northcote appeared in the neighbourhood, Otenyo, as we have
seen, ambushed and speared him. He was arrested by Chief
Angwenyi, one of the few loyal Kitutu chiefs, tried at the *boma*
and then taken to Nairobi, where it is believed he was shot. Muraa
was arrested on the eve of the 1908 punitive expedition and brought
to the *boma* for interrogation.

"The woman laibon was old, ugly and wizened," writes Robert
Foran, who was in charge of the Police Wing of the British expedition, "and looked an evil witch. At first she was inclined to be
truculent but Hemstead managed to convince her of the folly of
defying the government. The upshot of their interview was that she
promised to return to her village, assemble the chiefs and elders of
the tribe, and persuade them to offer their complete submission.
She further agreed to return to the *boma* at the conclusion of this
tribal conference and offer herself as a voluntary hostage for the
good conduct of the Kisii. . . . I felt confident that a guarantee would
not be honoured; nor was it . . . [A few days later after Kisii villages
had been completely demolished, their crops burnt to the ground,
and their livestock captured, the chiefs surrendered]. Two days
later Chief Angwenyi and another chief came into the *boma* and
offered to surrender with all their followers. Hemstead made the
acceptance of this surrender conditional upon them producing the
man that had speared Northcote. Rather to our surprise they returned in the afternoon with several other chiefs anxious to make
peace, also they brought in Northcote's assailant. The latter admitted the crime saying the *laibon ordered him to kill the Bwana
at the boma*. . . . We learned that the laibon had come in, surrendered unconditionally and would be deported to the coast."[17]

The "old, ugly and wizened" woman laibon was, however, no⟨

deported to the coast, probably because of her advanced age. She
was severely reprimanded and then set free. But the Gusii interpreted this release as a betrayal of her foster son Otenyo. The
leader of the anti-British movement, they felt, had become a collaborator and a traitor. Accordingly, they composed a song in
which they condemned Muraa's disloyalty to their cause:

Muraa you are a deceiver, oo yaye X 2
You deceived your son Otenyo, oo yaye X
To kill Nyarigoti,[18] oo yaye X 2
What is he looking for, oo yaye X 2
Striding across our land, oo yaye X2
What is it he is up to, oo yaye X 2
Oo yaye, oo yaye X 2.

The Gusii had thus been defeated a second time. They began
to realise the futility of an armed resistance against superior
weapons. Having won the military war, Northcote, who soon recovered from his wound, proceeded to establish British administration in the district. With the exception of the Kitutu subtribe, the
largest political unit in Gusii was the clan, normally headed by an
elder who performed certain ritual functions and therefore wielded
some political power. There were no traditional chiefs in the usual
sense of the term; and political power was, in the final analysis,
vested in a Council of elders. These councils, however, had little
authority over the young men, who led an independent life in the
cattle villages. In these fortified villages all clan cattle were kept
and guarded by the warriors, and no women were allowed in
except for the purpose of bringing food.

At the same time it is important to emphasise that despite clan
loyalties and interclan rivalries, the Gusii were also very conscious
of their subtribal groupings.

Northcote decided to convert the seven sub-tribal units into administrative locations, each headed by an appointed chief. Oyugi
was appointed chief in Wanjare, Angwenyi in Kitutu, Ombati in
Muksero, Nyamwamu in Nyaribari, Okech in South Bogirango,
Chore in Bassi, Nyamosi in Majoge and Ndubi in North Bogirango
and Sotik. Whereas in the past the chiefs wielded no tangible
political and juridical powers, now the chiefs were not only powerful and answerable to the British administration, but they also
ruled clans other than their own. Furthermore, the chiefs' powers
were further strengthened by the establishment of locational courts.
The Gusii territory was thus rapidly transformed from its fragmented stateless condition to a system of chiefdoms with specialised
political roles operating within a system of colonial administration.

In 1912, the only remaining foci of resistance, the cattle villages, were burnt down and the institution abolished because, as the administration put it, they were "potential centres of treason".

THE INTRODUCTION OF A CASH ECONOMY

With the new administrative machinery established, the colonial government next turned its attention to development. This largely involved the issuing of seeds for food crops such as maize, potatoes and beans and the construction of a network of roads. As in the rest of rural Kenya, little was done to promote agricultural development in Gusiiland prior to the 1930s because of the Kenya Government policy of concentrating on the "white highlands".

Compulsory labour for road construction, hut tax and the conscription of labour for European plantations were introduced at this time. Tax defaulters and absentees from official communal work were dealt with severely. Small wonder many Gusii people fled to Luo and Kuria areas.

While the administration was concerned with the material needs of the Gusii, the missionaries soon followed, armed with the Bible. First to arrive in the district were the Mill Hill Fathers who in 1911 founded a mission station at Nyabururu in Wanjare. Two years later, the S.D.A. arrived to set up their mission at Nyanchwa. Besides evangelising, the missionaries also built schools where reading, writing and some crafts were taught. But we also learn from the memoirs of Richard Gethin, the first permanent white settler and trader in Kisii, that these missionaries did not always leave the things that are Caesar's to Caesar. He recollects that when he first met Pastor Sparks and Carscallen of the Seventh Day Adventist Mission at Nyanchwa in 1914, he could not see anything religious about the two missionaries, who were "more interested in trading in buffalo hides", and their mission houses were more like stores for hides and other trade goods than the holy sanctuaries they were supposed to be. Gethin records:

> Preaching of the Gospel was conspicuous by its absence. Carscallan [sic] would see an old Jaluo native asleep in the shade of a tree. He would approach him, put his hands on his head and if he still slept, give him a kick on the backside saying. "Son, you are saved and you can thank the Lord it is me who has saved you; if it were one of the others you would be condemned to terrible torture when you died." With this, the convert would be roped into carrying a load on the next safari.[19]

There was also the contemptuous attitude of many of these missionaries towards Gusii customs and traditions, and the paternalistic "village government" established at the mission stations which soon alienated some of their converts.

There was thus a restlessness and resentfulness in Gusiiland caused partly by the punitive expeditions of 1904 and 1908, partly by the autocratic behaviour of the British administrators and their agents the chiefs, and partly by the holier-than-thou approach of the foreign missions. It is against this background of hatred and deep resentment of things European and foreign that the spread of Mumbo movement to Gusiiland should be examined.

II

MUMBOISM

In her paper on the "Cult of Mumbo",[20] Dr. Audrey Wipper criticises one of the authors for presenting Mumboism in "a way that stereotypes and obscures much of its real content". She continues:

> Even the historian, B. A. Ogot, overlooks any of its aspects that do not fit into his categorisation of Mumboism as "fanatical and non-programmatic" [whose] leaders preached complete rejection of everything European and a return to the African way of life!

Her own conclusion is that from one perspective Mumboism "was nativistic, in that it rejected European customs and advocated a return to the old prophets and old ways, while from another, and more revealing, perspective it was Utopian and innovative, rejecting the colonial regime, tribal authority, and introducing new norms and leadership roles".[21]

In this section of the paper, we wish to emphasise the point that Mumboism in Gusiiland was largely an attempt by the Gusii to use a traditional Luo cult for *political* purposes, following the defeat of the "primary resistances" in 1904 and 1908. We also hope to show that Dr. Wipper's second, and more revealing, perspective of Mumboism only succeeds in obscuring the nature of the cult, based as it is on a misconception of the traditional Luo cult and on an uncritical reliance on official reports.

THE ORIGIN OF MUMBOISM

Although the Mumbo movement only became active and political in 1913, the cult itself was as old as the Luo settlement in the lake region of Kenya.[22] And like another type of *juogi* (spirits) known as *Wagande*, Mumbo probably reached its most developed form as a religious cult in the nineteenth century.[23] Mumbo is believed to be a large sea snake which inhabits Lake Victoria. It is believed that it has in its possession goats, cattle, sheep and fowl, all of which are white and visible only to the possessed, being things of the spirit. In ordinary terms the lake shore folk refer to Mumbo as the fish mother (*min rech*) because it is believed that it is always followed by fish wherever it travels. The fish mother occasionally manifests itself as a giant snake which resembles a rainbow.[24]

Spiritually speaking, the Mumbo spirit appeared only to the selected and privileged few. Symptomatically, those called by Mumbo were first hit by a serious illness in the course of which they saw a rainbow. When the illness began to subside, the sick became possessed of the spirit, spoke in strange tongues and trembled. Having thus been spiritually prepared, the god Mumbo next revealed his message to the victims. This is how one, Ayuka Achieng' of Karachuonyo, South Nyanza, received his call about 1914.[25] This is how the famous Obondo Adenyo of Ajigo village in Sakwa, Central Nyanza, got his call about 1919. Obondo (popularly known to the Luo as Obondo Mumbo) had been ill for some time, when he became possessed and started to talk in strange tongues. One day he broke into a wild run towards Lake Victoria, where he threw himself into water. It is said and believed that he did not get drowned, "for the Mumbo spirits kept him afloat.[26] He stayed on the lake for some time "in the company of hippos, crocodiles and other mythical white sea creatures",[27] protected by the Mumbo spirits. The God Mumbo then gave him the powers of prophecy and healing.[28]

Sacrifices were made regularly to Mumbo. These consisted of slaughtering animals by the lake, and then throwing certain parts of the animal into water, for the spirits. A possessed Mumboite was adorned with heavy, white goat skins, with *ndede* or *bombwe* (certain aquatic soft plants) tied round the hands, legs and neck. Also, he never shaved his hair. This was the Mumbo cult as practised around Lake Victoria.

THE MOVEMENT BECOMES MILITANT

The militancy, racism and incipient nationalism of the Mumbo cult are normally attributed to a special call which a certain Onyango Dunde of the Seje clan in Alego, Central Nyanza, received from the God Mumbo. This call gave the traditional Mumbo beliefs political and racial interpretations which for the next forty years rocked the foundations of peace in the South Nyanza district of Kenya.

The change occurred in 1913. In that year, according to the holy chronicle of the cult, Onyango was sitting in his hut one evening when a gigantic snake appeared. It swallowed Onyango and almost immediately vomited him back, unscathed but shaken. Onyango may thus be regarded as a Luo Jonah.[29] The snake then spoke to Onyango:

"I am the God Mumbo, whose two homes are in the sun and in the lake. I have chosen you to be my mouthpiece. Go out and tell all Africans—and more especially the people of Alego—that from henceforth I am their God. Those whom I choose personally and also who acknowledge me will be forever in plenty. Their crops will grow of themselves, and there will be no more need to work. I will cause cattle, sheep and goats to come up out of the lake in great numbers to those who believe in me, but all unbelievers and their families and cattle will die out.

"The Christian religion is rotten (mbovu) and so is its practice of making its believers wear clothes. My followers must let their hair grow and never wash. All Europeans are your enemies but the time is shortly coming when they will disappear from our country.

"Daily sacrifice—preferably the male of cattle, sheep and fowl —shall be made to me. More especially I do prefer bulls. Have no fear of sacrificing these, as I will cause unlimited black cattle to come to you from the Lango (the Masai, Kipsigis and Nandi). Lastly, my followers must immediately slaughter all their cattle, sheep and goats. When this is done I will provide them with as many more as they want from the lake."[30]

Having said this the snake disappeared into the lake.

It must be emphasised that a proper understanding of the new Mumbo movement must depend to a large extent on a correct interpretation of this message, which henceforth became the new testament of the believers. Audrey Wipper, for example, in her paper already mentioned, attempts to explain the message in terms of the "millennial dream". She also misinterprets the role of bhang smoking in the movement and cites it as an illustration of the Mumbo "Utopia". Finally, she mistakenly assumes that the appeal of Mumboism was similar in all respects in both the Luo and the Gusii situations.

To the Luo among whom Onyango immediately set out to spread his gospel, the spiritual aspect of the God Mumbo's message was not new, as we have already seen. To them the new gospel was the denunciation of the European, his government, his religion and his way of life. This was definitely an anti-European resistance move-moment couched in the always appealing medium of religion. Indeed, one might go a step further and state that the cult, in its new garb, represented a beginning of cultural nationalism in the area. It was not a bankrupt philosophy which preached a return to a vacuum. It definitely drew its inspiration from the rich African traditions which were already threatened by the "civilising influence" of the European.

For example, did the Africans need the Christian God? Onyango, the self-styled prophet of Mumbo, drew the attention of "all Africans" to the fact that they needed no new God, since they already had their traditional god Mumbo. Instead of wearing the white man's clothes, Onyango reminded his fellow Africans of the traditional soft and beautiful goatskins which their forefathers had won.

The missionaries had been condemning their African pupils as dirty and smelly and they had laid great stress on the cutting of the hair. Mumboism, as an anti-European movement, enjoined the adherents to "let their hair grow—never cutting it . . . and they must never wash". This was not a traditional practice: it was a way of antagonising the European missionaries.

More importantly, the Christian religion had offered its followers an attractive millennium in the Kingdom of Heaven, where there would be no work or suffering and where the faithful would be singing joyful hallelujah songs to God. The missionaries stressed that this millennium was "at hand", and warned that those who held to their traditional religious practices would go to hell, where there would be never-ending suffering. On the contrary, to challenge the Christian Utopia, Onyango offered the imminent Mumbo Kingdom and the happiness and riches that would abound in it.

In short, this was a race in which both the African traditionalists and the Christian missionaries competed for the souls of Africans. The promises which the god Mumbo made to his followers were no more extravagant than those which the missionaries had made to their converts.

To moralise therefore, as Audrey Wipper does, that "unlike the Marxian Utopia, only the barest outlines [of Mumbo Utopia] were specified and unlike that Utopia, work did not play a significant role" is to express a prejudice. The Christian Utopia which the Mumboites were challenging has no specified outlines, and work does not play a significant role in it. Again for Wipper to conclude that the Mumbo Utopia would be "a relaxed happy life, free from worry, where Mumboites would smoke *bhang* (Indian hemp) to their heart's content" is to distort the facts. *Bhang* smoking was not part of the God Mumbo's message. When therefore the Mumboites decided to smoke *bhang*, they did this as a part of their anti-government activities, for the colonial government after the North-cote affair had declared *bhang* smoking dangerous to peace and orderly government.

From the above discussion, it is evident that the Mumbo movement was a bold and intelligent attempt by the African tradition-alists to resist the European, his religion and his culture; and one of the authors was therefore justified in describing Mumboism as "clearly anti-European and anti-missionary" and in saying that it preached "complete rejection of everything European and a return to the African way of life".[31] The Europeans, Mumbo had declared, were "enemies" and had to be forced to "disappear from our country". But since it was difficult militarily to dislodge them, a way had to be found to unite the hearts of Africans before final victory could be achieved. This was how the Mumbo message was understood, and this was the purpose for which it was applied.

THE CULT'S SPREAD AND DEVELOPMENT

From Alego, Mumboism extended to South Nyanza, where it spread like bushfire. The D.C. of South Nyanza spoke of a new religion, "Mumbo", making its appearance in his district in 1914, and of a prophet from Kabondo "promising cures of all evils" and predicting "the early departure from Kisii of all the white men after which the natives would possess their land in peace". Mosi Auma, the prophet, was arrested, tried by the D.C. under witchcraft Ordinance and sentenced to three years' imprisonment, later com-muted to one.[32]

Schools for the propagation of the gospel were built on the top of hills, and the movement quickly spread to Karachuonyo, Kochia and Gem (South Nyanza). As Mr. N. A. Kenyon, the D.C. for South Nyanza, 1920, later wrote:

> They attract the people to these schools by killing large numbers of cattle and sheep, providing food for them. The priests claim to be able to cure illness by vaccinating patients with ashes and cover-ing them with a grass called "Mumbo" and receive considerable fees in livestock for their services.[33]

THE SPREAD OF MUMBOISM TO GUSII

Initially the Gusii appeared indifferent to the new religion. But when in September 1914, the British actually evacuated Kisii *boma*, on the approach of German forces at the outbreak of the First

World War, the Gusii became convinced that Mosi Auma, the chief priest of Mumbo in Kabondo, "was a true prophet and that the European regime was over".[34]

Convinced that the prophecy had been fulfilled, they saw their duty as consisting in the obliteration of all the relics of European imperialism. It was in this spirit of frenzy that the deserted missions of Nyabururu, Nyanchwa and Asumbi, the trading centres of Riana, Rangwe and Homa Bay, and the Government offices at Kisii *boma*, were plundered, sacked and burnt.

The sight of the K.A.R. marching back to the *boma* in good form the following morning, to confront the Germans who had occupied the town, must have greatly embarrassed the enthusiasts. The Battle of Kisii was fought and the Germans pushed out, losing forty-five *askaris* against twenty-one British dead. It was then decided to take strong action against the Gusii and Luo for looting the missions and trading centres.

A punitive expedition was mounted under Richard Gethin, an Anglo-Irish entrepreneur and the first European trader in the district. The expedition, consisting of two companies of the K.A.R. and the police, "went out with the order to shoot all male Bagusii except children and to bring in all their cattle".[35] The operations were not successful, as the chiefs had leaked out the news of the planned expedition to their people, who either fled with their cattle in good time, or put up Union Jacks on their rooftops as a sign of loyalty and complete surrender to the British. Besides, it is reported that the African troops (a battalion of the K.A.R.) who carried out operations were more interested in "burning the huts and chasing the girls than they were in collecting cattle".[36] All told, the expedition's haul from both Gusii and Luo homes amounted to about three thousand head of cattle. About 150 Gusii were reported shot, and over a thousand huts burned.

To ensure security in the district during the war years, a policy of dispatching many young Gusii men to work outside the district either on European plantations or in the Carrier Corps was adopted. As one Government report revealed:

All labour sent out of the district has been for military requirements. In 1914–15 a very large proportion (50% was the amount ordered) of the able bodied men were sent out of the district for work as a punishment for rebellious conduct. It will be thus seen that in the two years 1914–1916, 21,864 men were sent out to work and of this period the bulk of men were not sent out until September 1914. ... It should be pointed out here that many of the men sent for work as a punishment for one year were kept considerably 25% over their time.[37]

One would have thought that with the return of the British to re-occupy the *boma*, the severe punitive expedition that followed the looting, and the new vindictive labour policies, Mumboism would be discredited in the eyes of the Gusii. Instead, in 1916 the chiefs reported an increasing number of adherents. And the year 1917 is traditionally remembered by the Gusii as "the year of the prophets". A great many Mumbo prophets, both false and true, rose to tell their credulous compatriots to keep their hoes and their pots indoors since *wimbi* would come by itself and fill their pots. The days of the European were said to be numbered, and taxes and other "burdensome jobs" would disappear with them.

The first Gusii subtribe to be affected by Mumboism was Wanjare, its leaders being Twara and Omwega. From here it was taken to Kitutu by Nayakundi and Ogwora, and thus to North Mugirango and Nyaribari, where the leaders were Muchoronge and Ondieki respectively. In Majoge, which was the last area to be affected, Ndigiti walked up and down the area recruiting converts. The Gusii, resentful of the presence of the Europeans in their country, received the message with enthusiasm.

In 1918 the D.C., alarmed by the Gusii response to Mumboism, described it to the P.C. as "exactly the sort of thing that might lead to the murder of an officer and another Kitutu war".[38] He therefore believed that firm and quick action was necessary. He arrested thirty Mumbo teachers whom he temporarily detained before handing them over to the P.C. and recommending their imprisonment at Magadi for six months each. The P.C. ordered the immediate release of the men. He reproached Campbell (the D.C.) on the ground that "no officer would deport men from their district without the sanction of His Excellency", a stand which was supported by the Chief Native Commissioner, John Ainsworth, who described Campbell's action as "undoubtedly *ultra vires*". Ainsworth felt that no repressive measures were necessary until the Government was satisfied that the cult had become "such as to lead to disloyalty".

When the prisoners were released, there was jubilation in the whole district with the Mumboites shouting "victory". The freed leaders, assuming that the Government had now accepted their religion, resumed their preaching with even greater fervour. This time, Ogwora, his wife and Ndigiti—the three leading personalities of the movement—were arrested and deported to Kismayu.

The year 1918 is traditionally called "the year of the famine of the false prophets" (*Enchara ya Oino*). There was a great famine which people blamed on the Mumbo prophets, who had advised them the previous year not to cultivate. Mumboites, nevertheless, did not lose heart, and in fact their activities intensified. But the famine continued on into the following year. Worse still, 1919 is remembered by the Gusii as the year when a strange disease "ate" the private parts of people (or the year of *Amaika Nse*). So alarming were both the famine and the disease that the D.C. in his annual report had the following to say:

> It was hoped that the end of the war might mean the end of most of our troubles, and that from then onwards more attention could be given to development and progress in the district. Unfortunately, as often happens, famine and pestilence followed hard on the heels of war. In the months of November and December, the influenza epidemic swept through the Reserve, discouraging everything and causing the deaths of some five thousand natives. There was a recrudescence of this disease, or something like it, at the end of the year, resulting on a considerable number of deaths in the Kisii locations immediately adjoining the station.[39]

Needless to say, famine and pestilence disrupted the normal flow of life in Gusiiland. One of the important practices affected, especially by the *Amaika Nse* disease, was the circumcision ceremonies, due to be held in the early months of 1920, but which had to be postponed until the following year. Circumcision ceremonies formed an important part of Gusii social and cultural life; hence they could not be suspended on some flimsy ground. During these ceremonies, which always followed harvesting, the youth would sing and dance; friendships would be made in ceremony camps; while goats and bulls would be slaughtered for the deserving youths to initiate them into adult life.

Unfortunately the year 1919, as we have seen, was marked by famine and pestilence. Also, the advent of a virus which attacked the private organs of people made circumcision virtually impossible. Hence, the locations which adjoined the station, especially Kitutu, which had been badly hit by the *Amaika Nse* and famine, were forced to put off circumcision ceremonies to 1921.

Audrey Wipper, obviously influenced by Robert A. Levine,[40] mistakenly attributes the postponement of circumcision in 1920 to Mumbo teachings. She cites this influence as evidence in support of her theory that Mumbo did not simply advocate a back-to-the-old-ways policy. She writes:

> Even more significant in establishing that the cult did not simply advocate back-to-the-old-ways was its several attempts to *abolish CIRCUMCISION*. In 1920, the cult ordered circumcision to be suspended for several years, some say nine. Apparently it was suspended at least in Kitutu and North Mugirango locations for the year 1921. People were dissatisfied with this situation and resumed

initiation in 1922 when many children were said to have died in seclusion. Their deaths were attributed to the violation of Gusii custom which took place in 1921.[41]

She explains this apparent paradox whereby *Mumboism*, which rejected Westernism, was at the same time seeking to *abolish* Africans customs, by saying that "when the political aspirations of Mumboism failed to materialise its protest then turned to attempts to abolish this traditional practice".[42] But why? Dr. Wipper does not explain. In fact, we found no evidence in the field to support Wipper's interpretation.

The important point to emphasise is that the famine and pestilence of 1919 was blamed on Mumboism by most of the Gusii, and consequently there was a sharp decline in the membership of the cult. Many of the rituals and practices of the Mumboites were of Luo origin and were therefore little understood by the Gusii. Even the Mumbo songs such as,

> Ramogi, Ramogi
> Wang' chieng'. Wang' chieng'.
> Wang'polo, wang'polo,
> Sabaye, Laesi, Sabaye,

were largely sung in Dholuo. Many Gusii people therefore joined a new cult, Sakawaism, which was of local origin, and which, fortunately for Mumboism, shared with it many elements in common.

As already mentioned Sakawa was a great Gusii prophet who lived at the turn of the century. It was he who had prophesied the advent of the white men, but he had also predicted their departure. Besides, he had warned the Gusii against fighting the Europeans. When the Gusii twice tried to expel the Europeans (in 1904 and 1908) and were defeated on each occasion, a myth began to develop that it was Sakawa who had brought the Europeans, and it is he who would get rid of them on his return, which was expected to be sometime in the middle of 1921.

By 1920 belief in Sakawa's second coming was rife in Kitutu and was spreading at an alarming speed to other areas. In the same year Bonairiri of Kitutu approached Chief Nsungu and asked for permission to set up a school for the teaching of Sakawaism. She was declared insane by the D.C. and thrown into a lunatic asylum. She was later released and was quiet for some time, but by November she had again gathered a large following whom she began to prepare for the return of Sakawa.

Throughout 1921, her movement continued to gather momentum. Two days before the predicted day for the return of Sakawa, the D.C. got alarmed and immediately rounded up the ringleaders and broke up the school. The junior members of the cult were dealt with under the Abuse of Opiate Ordinance the ringleaders like Kiburi, Owura, Marita and Ongeri (son of Muraa the laibon) were deported to Kismayu, while Bonairiri (the prophetess), Nyakundi, Kimuti, Uriogi and Nyamchara (the last two were sons of Sakawa) were sternly warned and given one final chance to reform. These "bastard religions", as the administration called them, can only be understood if one regards them as manifestations of social instability, disaffection with the new regime and a serious search for a more meaningful and purposeful existence.

The rise of Sakawaism did not end Mumboism in Gusiiland. The movement continued intermittently until 1954 when it was proscribed by the Government. For instance in 1922, Mumboites were active in North Mugirango where the Kipsigis ex-laibon was actively preaching both Mumboism and Sakawaism. In 1927, Mumboism was being preached in Majoge, Wanjare, Nyaribari, Kitutu and Basi. The leaders were promptly arrested and detained at Kisii town "where a closer watch could be kept on them". In 1931, the Mumboites, led by Ochodo daughter of Obeto—the first Luo prophetess of Mumbo—were actively preaching in Kadem. Major Bond, the Assistant D.C., ruthlessly suppressed it, sending the "incorrigible" ringleaders to the D.C. to be imprisoned. In the same year Mosi Auma of Kabondo, who had been appointed a foreman by the Government, apparently to wean him from Mumboism, informed the D.C. that he wished to resign. The D.C. refused, as he believed that Mosi "wished to resign to be free to restart Mumbo activities".[43]

Among the Gusii, the movement was even more alarming. The Mumbo leaders who had been exiled to Kismayu in 1921 returned. They immediately started to spread the gospel of Mumbo again. The Government became so frightened that it convened a special meeting of members of the Local Native Council, chiefs and headmen, who passed unanimous resolutions forbidding, once and for all, Mumboism in the district. But in spite of this, the Mumboites continued to preach, and on a District Sports Day, they organised a big demonstration in defiance of government orders banning their religion. The ringleaders were arrested and sent to Kipini. Finally in 1954, the Kenya Government officially declared Mumbo worship dangerous to peace and good government, and therefore illegal.

THE PRACTICES OF THE CULT

From the evidence we have so far examined, it should be clear that Mumboism was more violent and more political among the

Gusii than among the Luo. Indeed, to the Gusii the movement had a predominantly political appeal. They had not forgotten the 1904 and 1908 punitive expeditions and they joined the movement in the hope of driving away the white man. This attitude is reflected in the Gusii Mumbo songs such as the following:

> Sabaye Laesi Sabaye,
> Wuriande you are going
> George you are going,
> Sabaye Laesi Sabaye.

This is a straightforward political song, telling the Europeans to leave. And as is the case with all these Gusii songs, there is no religious element in it.

It is also signficant to note that in Gusiiland, unlike the situation in Luoland, there were no churches built for Mumbo, no schools and no rituals, although the adherents wore goatskins. Their main practice consisted in running along paths with spears and shields, singing "Sabaye Laesi Sabaye". In Luoland, on the other hand, Mumboism was largely a religious movement, with its churches, schools and rituals. This can largely be accounted for by the fact that the establishment of administration in Luoland was, as a whole, a peaceful affair.[44]

THE MUMBOITES

Throughout history, people have joined movements and organisations for diverse motives, some personal and others public. The Mumbo movement was no exception. There were those, especially in Gusiiland, who joined it for political reasons; many other members saw it as a God-given opportunity for amassing wealth quickly: there were the credulous few who believed in the imminence of the "Kingdom of Mumbo"; and others joined it because everybody around them had done so. But significantly, there were those who sincerely believed in the spiritual reality of Mumbo. It is therefore difficult to come to any general conclusion as to what motivated the different members to join the movement. But on the whole, it is correct to say that the majority of the Gussi joined the cult because of their hatred for the white presence in the district. To this extent, it was an anti-colonial movement.

But what complicates the picture somewhat is that in many cases both the personal and the political motives applied. For instance, Nyakundi, son of Bogonko, harboured personal grudges against the British or their agents the chiefs, and expressed his hatred by joining Mumbo and preaching Sakawaism. When the British selected the first chiefs, they bypassed the Bogonko heirs in Kitutu and chose a chief from a rival clan. This act was resented not only by Nyakundi but also by the entire lineage. Bogonko, the founder of this lineage, was one of Kitutu's great warriors and political leaders. As Levine has recorded:

> Old men enjoyed relating tales of the awe in which people held Bogonka, a 19th century hero and leader of the Kitutu tribe. It is said that when he walked out of his home area people fled from their houses until reassured that he would do them no harm. Songs in praise of his wealth, power and accomplishments were composed. When he attended his grandson's wedding, woven mats were laid down so that he should not have to walk on cow dung.[45]

The above account is evidently one-sided and was probably narrated by a man of Bogonko's lineage. Those who are not immediately related to the lineage remember Bogonko as a relentless tyrant, an avaricious man who took delight in seizing his neighbours' cattle.

To understand the bitter rivalry which influenced much of politics in Kitutu, and therefore Gusii, in the twentieth century, it is necessary to go back to the death of Nyakundi, the greatest and most beloved of Kitutu leaders. When he died, he was succeeded by a weak son, Barare, who failed to rally the Kitutu people around him: and allowed old grievances to flare up. A disunited Kitutu was constantly raided by the Luo and Kipsigis, and in fact, Barare himself was killed during one of these raids by a Luo warrior. Bogonko his brother, then usurped power, but clans in west Kitutu rejected his leadership and instead appointed Gichana. Bogonko, they said, was a tyrant, warlike and greedy.

Since neither Bogonko nor Gichana was capable of eliminating the other, they both ruled their respective areas—to the old men's dismay. Bogonko was supported by the east Kitutu clans: Mwabogonko, Mwabundusi and Mwamanoa, while Gichana ruled over the clans adjacent to Kisii town: Bugusero, Bonyagatanyi, Mwamonari and Mwagichara. On the arrival of the British, Angwenyi, the successor of Gichana, was chosen as the chief of Kitutu; and this naturally antagonised east Kitutu. Nyakundi, the son of Bogonko, was disgruntled and he led an anti-government movement in Kitutu, which later found inspiration in both Mumboism and Sakawaism.

But it is incorrect to conclude, as Dr. Wipper does, that the greatest support for Mumboism amongst the Gusii came from the Bogonko clan. Indeed, Bogonko is an insignificant section of the

Abasweta clans, which are closely related and which remained behind in Kitutu when their relatives, the Nyaribari clans, moved away in the middle of the nineteenth century. From the evidence we have collected, it would appear that the greatest support for Mumboism in Gusii came from Wanjare. And although there was a substantial number of Mumboites in Kitutu, many of them became converted to Sakawaism in the 1920s.

CONCLUSION

We have tried in this chapter to discuss the spread and message of Mumboism in Gusiiland against the background of the establishment of British administration in the district, for it was evident to us that it is only against this background that a meaningful interpretation of the Gusii version of the cult can be given. We have done this in a simple, unsophisticated style, because we believe much confusion has arisen from attempts to fit such movements into a preconceived typology of cults. The Africans of the early years of this century acted the way they did not because they were conforming to some lofty philosophical principles, but because their concepts of peace, good government and life were rudely shattered by the colonial rule. The Gusii, for example, did not formulate the kind of system they would implement on the departure of the Europeans. What they wanted was to be left alone to lead the kind of life which made sense to them. It would therefore be extremely difficult for Dr. Wipper to support her conclusion that "while advocating in a few specific and highly symbolic ways a return to the past, the cult represents, in the main, a drastic break with the past". Another of her conclusions which is even more difficult to understand is this: "What the members really want is not to return to the old way of life but the life of the Europeans." In other words, Mumboism, she thinks, was nothing but an attempt by Africans to shout "sour grapes" when they felt they would not be able to attain the material civilisation of the European. We hope we have shown that Mumboism was, in the words of Audrey Wipper... "another attempt on the part of the Gusii (and the Luo) to rid themselves of the foreigners".

NOTES

1. See T. O. Ranger, "Connexions between 'Primary Resistance' Movements and Modern Mass Nationalism in East and Central Africa", *The Journal of African History*, Vol. IX (1968), Nos. 3 and 4.
2. Research on the traditional history of the Gusii which was initiated by

Professor Ogot was carried on and completed by Dr. Ochieng, for his Ph.D. degree from 1968–71, in the Department of History, University of Nairobi. See also Ochieng, W. R., "Bantu Origin", *Target*, No. 61 (May 1971).

3. C. W. Hobley, *Kenya: From Chartered Company to Crown Colony* (2nd ed., Frank Cass, 1970), London, pp. 217–18.

4. H. M. Stanley, *Through the Dark Continent* (New York, 1879), p. 259.

5. B. A. Ogot, "British Administration in the Central Nyanza district of Kenya", *Journal of African History*, IV, No. 2 (1963).

6. P. H. Gordon, *Annual Report* (1946), Kenya National Archives.

7. G. H. Mungeam, *British Rule in Kenya* (O.U.P., 1966), p. 30.

8. Mungeam, *ibid.*, p. 141.

9. *Ibid.*, p. 142.

10. W. Robert Foran, *The Kenya Police 1887–1960* (London, 1962), p. 26.

11. Kenya National Archives, DC/KSI/3/2, Report of G. S. A. Northcote, p. 11.

12. R. M. Maxon, "The Gusii Uprising of 1908 and Its Suppression", *Transafrican Journal of History*, Vol. 2, No. 1 (January, 1972).

13. Kenya National Archives, DC/KC1/4/2, January 11, 1908. The Diary of G. A. S. Northcote, Letter dated 12 February 1908, from Northcote to his father.

14. W. Robert Foran, *The Kenya Police 1887–1960* (London, 1962), pp. 26–7.

15. Quoted by C. A. Brooks, in "The Conquest of the Abagusii 1900–1914", M.A. Thesis, University of East Africa (Nairobi), 1970, p. 44.

16. Kenya National Archives, DC/KS1/4/2. Letter from G. A. S. Northcote to his father, 12 February 1908.

17. W. Robert Foran, *A Cuckoo in Kenya* (Hutchinson, London, 1936).

18. Gusii's name for Northcote.

19. Richard Gethin's private memoirs, pp. 35–6, quoted by C. A. Brooks, *op. cit.*, p. 75.

20. A. Wipper, "The Cult of Mumbo", East African Institute Conference Paper, January 1966.

21. *Ibid.*, p. 2.

22. See H. O. Anyumba, *Spirit Possession Among the Luo of Central Nyanza, Kenya,* Mimeo, 1955, Makerere Institute of Social Research Library, No. 19.6/9b. Anyumba suggests that the phenomenon of spirit possession amongst the Luo is of recent origin, and probably dates back to the period of settlement in the various parts of Nyanza (pp. 3–4).

23. *Ibid.*, p. 9.

24. Many educated people have dismissed this belief as superstition, explaining that what the simple people mistake for a snake is nothing but a water-spout. And although mysterious creatures of the sea have been the subject of legends ever since man first took to the water in boats, Prof. J. L. E. Smith, writing in *Spear*, Vol. V, No. 1 (February 1961), explained why he believed that such creatures actually exist. In this important article, he reminds us that the first reports of the giraffe were discredited, so were those of the okapi. Regarding sea-serpeants, he explains that the existence of the terrible Kraken, for a long time dismissed as a fanciful tale of sea-faring folk, is now accepted. In 1939, his view that Coelacanth probably lived along East Africa had been greeted with universal disbelief. "It just shows how a large animal can live in one place in the sea, even close to the shore, and not be known to intelligent people there,

as was the case with the French at the Comores," p. 15. He concludes his article:

"There is so much evidence for their (sea-serpents) existence that it is surely only a matter of time until proper research reveals them. If the Coelacanth survived unknown, without any trace for seventy million years, why should there not be other unknown creatures in the sea, other living fossils? There almost certainly are." (p. 18.)

25. DC/KSI/27, *Kenya National Archives,* Nairobi.
26. Anyumba, *op. cit.,* p. 5.
27. *Ibid.*
28. A. W. Mayor, *Thuond Luo* (Luo Heroes), (The Kenya Highway Press, Nairobi, n.d.), pp. 26–9.
29. *The Book of Jonah* in the Old Testament. Jonah was in the belly of the fish for three days and three nights. He was then sent to Nineveh to preach the word of God.
30. "Nyangweso"—"The Cult of Mumbo in Central and South Kavirondo", *The Journal of East Africa and Uganda Natural Society* (May–August 1930), No. 38–39, p. 15.
31. B. A. Ogot, *op. cit.*
32. Letter written 21 July 1915—DC/KSI/27, KNA.
33. DC/KSI/28, KNA.
34. District of South Kavirondo Administrative Records, KNA. KSI/27.
35. *The Nyabururu Diary,* 17 September 1914, p. 35.
36. KNA/DC/KSI/3/4.
37. KNA/DC/KSI/1/2 Annual Report for the year ending 31 March 1916.
38. Letter written on 28 November 1918, DC/KSI/27, KNA.
39. South Kavirondo Annual Report 1913–23, DC/KSI/1/2, KNA.
40. Robert A. Levine, "An Attempt to Change the Gusii Initiation Cycle", *Man* (July 1959).
41. A. Wipper, *op. cit.,* pp. 17–18.
42. A. Wipper, *op. cit,* p. 18.
43. Letter written on 14 July 1931, DC/KSI/27, KNA.
44. B. A. Ogot, "British Administratioin in the Central Nyanza District of Kenya", *op. cit.*
45. Robert A. Levine, "The Internationalization of Political Values in Stateless Societies", *Human Organisation* (1960).

8

THE KYANYANGIRE, 1907: PASSIVE REVOLT AGAINST BRITISH OVERRULE*

G. N. Uzoigwe

Old men in Bunyoro vividly remember the *Kyanyangire*.[1] To some the manner of its suppression marks the final and emphatic humiliation of themselves as a people and the end of the glory that was Kitara.[2] To others it was a resurgence of national consciousness which brings back nostalgic memories of the valiant and revolutionary years of the Kabalegan era. And yet compared to the Shona and Ndebele revolts in Southern Rhodesia (1896–97)[3] or the *Maji Maji* uprising in Tanzania (1905–07)[4]—to take two well known examples from Central and East Africa—the *Nyangire* revolt was a mild and tame affair. There was no physical confrontation between Banyoro and the British authorities, and consequently there was no bloodshed. In fact the only outward manifestations that a revolt was in progress were the excited mood of the population, the ejection of Ganda agents of British imperialism[5] from their chieftainships in Bunyoro, and their retreat into Hoima for refuge.[6] In the physical sense therefore it was a revolt *manque*. For those who judge the importance of resistance movements against alien rule by the magnitude of their ferocity and bloodshed, the *Nyangire* revolt would prove a disappointment. Nevertheless, a young Kinyoro clerk, Mr. Isaya Bikundi,[7] considered the event of such national importance and significance that he used to go to Hoima "with a pencil and papers to record whatever was said at any important meeting."[8]

But the *Kyanyangire* must merit our attention for a number of reasons. First, it demonstrates a clear connection between "primary" and "secondary" resistances against alien rule. This is important because for some historians such a connection hardly exists.[9] The defeat and exile of Kabalega did not reconcile Banyoro to British overrule. On the contrary they felt themselves

* This chapter is reprinted from G. N. Uzoigwe's *Revolution and Revolt in Bunyoro-Kitara*, by permission of the publisher, Longman.

humiliated and this feeling was to create a psychological problem which made the establishment of colonial administration particularly difficult. Second, it merits a study because of the manner of its organisation and the baffling method of its execution. Herein lies the dilemma of "secondary" revolts: how to revolt again having been crushed the first time. Third, its consequences are important. It shows that, given certain situations, non-violent resistance against an overwhelmingly superior foe may be a better way of achieving politico-economic ends than a heady and thoughtless confrontation. And fourth, it destroys Professor Ranger's general thesis of the importance of religious leadership in resistance movements in East and Central Africa.[10] The *Nyangire* revolt had no religious overtones. It was purely a political and economic movement.

We still know very little about the ideology, the organisation, and the nature of many resistance movements in Africa. This is not to suggest, as Professor Davidson does, that "historians have not really raised yet the problems of African resistance to colonialism"; but he is certainly right to suggest that many such resistances existed, the significance of which historians have not yet discovered.[11] The *Nyangire* revolt is one such example. Its study has been neglected and its significance overlooked, presumably because like the Kalantan rising in Malaya (1915)[12] it was not characterised by its bloodiness.

In the work mentioned above, Davidson provides a useful periodisation of African resistance movements. The first phase starts with the earliest European contacts and ends in the 1870s. The second coincides with the period of European scramble and partition of Africa (1870–1900). The third covers the early years of European colonialism (*c.* 1900–14). The fourth deals with the interwar years "when the crisis of the colonial system and imperialism started". And the final phase concerns the epoch after World War II when the colonial edifice was gradually levelled to the ground, at any rate in its political superstructure.[13] In all these he sees, as does Ranger,[14] a basic and fundamental connection.

The central thesis of this study therefore is that the *Nyangire* revolt was much more than a revolt against Ganda "sub-imperialism"—as British officials believed it was—and rather drew its ideology and inspiration, if not its organisation and mode of execution, from the "primary resistance" of the Kabalegan epoch.

When in 1891 Captain Lugard made short work of Kabalega's reputed *abarusura*[15] guarding the valuable salt mines at Katwe as well as the important route leading to the East African coast through which Kabalega got his guns, and imposed Kasagama on the throne of Kaboyo's Tooro, Kabalega's hope of refounding the ancient empire of Kitara[16] received an unexpected and rude shock. Lugard, without knowing it, had achieved more than a mere victory. The ease with which it was accomplished marked the beginning of the end, the impending collapse of a dream. Baffled by the strength of the new foe, Kabalega decided to sue for peace. But he desired peace with honour and had no wish to compromise the independence of his kingdom. Lugard had other ideas and offered him humiliating terms for peace. And against the advice of his generals who had apparently made a correct assessment of the combined strength of the Anglo-Ganda forces, he elected to meet force with force.[17] The recall of Lugard to England and the withdrawal of the Tooro garrisons gave Kabalega a new ray of hope. Promptly he invaded Tooro, reconquered it, and drove Kasagama to the mountains.[18] But the victory was to be short-lived. In 1893 the British Government decided on the subjugation of Kitara[19] and the writing was on the wall. By 1895 all Kabalega's generals with the exception of Kikukuule had lost hope and the king himself had fled to Lango.[20] The bulk of the *abarusura*, however, scattered all over the country. Those who were captured had their guns confiscated and had no alternative but to become cultivators—for them a detestable occupation—to eke out a living. Some, wearied of war, did not cause any social upheavals in their respective villages. They swallowed their pride and acquiesced in their reduced social status. Some even became chiefs under the British.[21] But there were yet others who either evaded capture or refused to be reconciled to their conquerors. It was those of this persuasion who regrouped in their various hideouts from where they continued their resistance under the distant leadership of Kabalega. Indeed, according to Sir Tito Winyi, they were such an implacable enemy of the Europeans that they preferred to fight to the last than succumb to the new domination. In this struggle many of them lost their lives and among them were some of Kabalega's sons.[22]

Of the leaders of the *abarusura*, only Paulo Byabachwezi proved to be loyal, for some time at any rate, to the British administration,[23] probably because he wanted to emulate Ganda chiefs[24] and manipulate the British to get what he wanted. It has in fact been suggested that he even nursed ambitions of becoming *Omukama* himself,[25] a suggestion roundly dismissed by his surviving son.[26] But British administrators also speculated that his loyalty may have been determined by the fact that he was "believed to have stolen a considerable amount of Kabalega's property" and consequently feared reprisals should Kabalega succeed in stemming the tide of British advance.[27] At the other extreme was Ireeta who only surrendered after Kabalega had been captured in 1899.[28] The attitude of the rest, Rwabudongo and Kikukuule particularly, was characterised by convenient submissions and defections.[29]

Curiously enough, the chiefs whose authority had been deliberately undermined by Kabalega[30] appeared to have given him more sincere support in his hour of need than some of the *abarusura* generals.[31] But because they were no longer the source of military power,[32] they were easily forced to accept the new domination.[33] Nevertheless Kabalega retained sufficient influence and authority among his subjects while a fugitive (1895–99) to be able, as Jackson put it, to keep "together a sufficiently large force to put up several stiff fights, and to the very last was a nasty thorn in our side".[34]

The capture of Kabalega in 1899 and his subsequent banishment marked the end of Banyoro "primary resistance" against the imposition of British rule. But they offered no loyalty to their new overlords. The keenness shown by the Banyoro to be appointed chiefs in 1900 may have surprised officials[35] but this was the only way to salvage something out of the wreck. But their loyalty lay somewhere else. The courage with which Kabalega had defended himself to the very last had increased his reputation among his people and had in fact won the grudging respect of his enemies. And until his death in 1923 many Banyoro still regarded him as their legitimate *Omukama*.[36]

Worried by this attitude of the people the British authorities had, in 1898, engineered the coronation of his son, Kitahimbwa, who was a minor, as *Omukama* with elaborate pomp and ceremony. The whole idea was to induce Banyoro to forget Kabalega. But this plan misfired. Nor were they taken in by the mysterious rumour which had preceded the coronation that their fugitive *Omukama* was dead.[37] They continued "to apotheosise him as the national 'Ultra Munyoro' hero".[38] And those who had brought about his downfall and disgrace were a national enemy.

It is true that even before the capture of Kabalega certain of his chiefs and *abarusura* had collaborated with the British and had even accepted chieftainships.[39] It is equally true, as we have seen, that they changed sides with baffling frequency. With the exception of Byabachwezi, only Bikamba remained outwardly friendly with the British after his defeat, but it soon became obvious that his subordinate chiefs in the Masindi area remained hostile.[40] Collaboration in Bunyoro was half-hearted and in many cases basically dishonest. Nor were the British unaware of this. Indeed in June

1897 Captain Thruston was to confess that British administration of Bunyoro was not attended "with a satisfactory measure of success".[41]

There were many reasons for this state of affairs, as Thruston proceeded to show with his usual candour. First, he admitted that Bunyoro was "a country of which the whole population, though kept down by show of force, is at heart hostile to the administration and sympathising, in many cases actively, with the late dynasty". Second, he pointed out that "Kabarega, the native king", though driven out of the country, had with him "a large following consisting of the most important personages of the country" and was "maintaining a force on the frontier" and had "agents throughout the country stirring the people to sedition.". Third, he discovered that of the five chiefs collaborating with them "one only is of the number of the original chiefs", the others having "little or no influence in their provinces and one of them is probably in active league with Kabarega". And fourth, because the country had no king and because it was governed "with extremely limited and vague judicial powers", the result has been "the collapse of the original primitive but strong feudal form of administration, and the absence of any system of administration that can provide for law and order and civil and criminal jurisdiction". He concluded this analysis by admitting that:

> The country at present can hardly be said to be under a government at all: it is rather under military occupation or at most a weak military government—a weak government is always a bad one and a weak military one is the worst of all.[42]

By 1900 the situation, instead of improving, was perhaps getting worse.[43]

Why was this? Banyoro tended to blame the British for all the tragedies that had befallen them: the horrors of the long war of attrition, the depopulation, the famine, the diseases, and the loss of territories to their neighbours. They accused the British of hatred of themselves as a people and of being easily misled by Baganda who saw the opportunity as ripe for the extension of their influence into Kitara. Had the British not intervened in their affairs, they argued, Kabalega would have lived to carry out his grand plan of conquering Buganda and transporting its population *en masse* to the Congo! But the British had changed the course of their history and their praise and elevation of Baganda were highly resented.[44]

In dealing with a people of such persuasions, whether justified or not, the British authorities displayed a remarkable lack of

foresight. Instead of attempting to win the loyalty of the aristocracy with kindness and understanding, their attitude towards them
was harsh, punitive and contemptible. In 1896 the alienation of
Kinyoro territory by Colvile in 1894 was confirmed[45] and Baganda
moved in to establish effective occupation.[46] The government
recklessly made it clear to Banyoro that they were a conquered
people, that their land now belonged to the Crown, and that whatever concession was given to them was done at Her Majesty's
pleasure. They were made to understand that they were not in the
same category as Baganda who had collaborated and were now
reaping the rewards of their loyalty.[47]

Already in 1899 Baganda chiefs, having surveyed the situation,
decided to press home their advantage. They put forward the claim
that Kitara was a tributary kingdom to Buganda. And, without
hesitation, Col. Ternan considered their application favourably.[48]
The attitude of British officials toward Kabalega was such that
they appeared prepared to accept any stories Ganda chiefs cared
to tell them. And nobody would blame Baganda for making the
best of a favourable opportunity. The hoes they claimed had been
sent as tribute to them represent, as it had been pointed out, "not
tribute but an insult since women dug with hoes".[49] Surprised and
enraged by Ternan's decision, the principal chiefs of Bunyoro
made it clear that their country "has never been tributary to
(B)uganda". They admitted, however, that "the reigning rulers of
both kingdoms had from time to time exchanged presents". They
requested permission to send a deputation to Kampala to plead
their case. Evatt, the captor of Kabalega, begged his superiors to
deal fairly with Banyoro "as jealousy of the Waganda, and a dislike
of their being placed in authority over them, is a feeling which
appears to be strongly imbued in almost all Wanyoro".[50] The plan
was never heard of again and was apparently dropped.

This was not all. By 1900 it was being rumoured in British
circles that the annexation of Bunyoro to Buganda would not be a
bad idea. Banyoro were considered as inferior in intelligence to
Baganda. They were practically treated as children who were
incapable of managing their own affairs.[51] This belief was so strong
that already in 1899 the decision had been taken to send the young
Kitahimbwa to Mengo "where adequate arrangements will be made
for his care".[52] And when Mr. Spire was appointed Collector of
"(B)unyoro District" in 1900,[53] he was given a free hand to decide
"exactly how many or how few attendants the son of Kabalega
(i.e. Kitahimbwa) requires to look after him . . . say, not more than
ten". The young monarch was also required to build his palace near

the Collector's residence and consequently near the fort. The responsibility for feeding him and his officials was left, not to the government, but to "the surrounding chiefs". The instruction goes on:

> All but the followers who you permit to remain with him are to be told to go about their business and work for their living or they will be tied up and punished as vagrants. Upon their attempting the last nonsense do not hesitate to take very strong measures against them, as they are a curse to the country.

But if need be they could be arrested and deported to Kampala "from which place they could be sent to Port Alice (Entebbe) and sentenced to a term of hard labour". And as for Kitahimbwa:

> It would be better that you should tell the King of (B)unyoro that he is only king by courtesy. His father warred against the British Government until he compelled it to put forth in strength and depose him. (B)unyoro is a very different position to (B)uganda. We are well able to recognise Kabrega's son as *chief* (my italics) provided he behaves well. Otherwise we should send him away out of the Protectorate to live with his father at the coast, and their will be no native chief over (B)unyoro.[54]

This debasing of the ancient and sacred institution of Kitara kingship was hardly likely to appeal to a highly monarchical people. Kitahimbwa was practically treated as just another "native chief". But to Banyoro, though a minor, he was much more than that. He was an institution. But British officials, themselves with high monarchical predilections, somehow managed to ignore this emotional point. And even when Kitahimbwa was eventually deposed, they continued to treat his successor, Duhaga II, with contempt. One official dismissed him as "lately a domestic servant" in the service of a missionary[55] and another was censured for punishing the chiefs of Bunyoro from the king downwards

> in a manner for which he had not the slightest authority and which might easily have given rise to trouble throughout the country, and at the least is calculated to materially weaken the position of the chiefs over their people.[56]

To make matters worse the government hastily imposed a "Hut and Gun Tax" on the people.[57] Certainly it is the duty of any government to tax its subjects. But anyone with the slightest knowledge of Africa at this time would have realised that this was a difficult issue. To tax an African was to emphasise to him his subordinate position, and he invariably revolted against such an imposition. Examples of such revolts are too well known in

African history to require documentation here. Experienced officials usually approached the problem with tact and subtlety. In Bunyoro no official cared what Banyoro felt or thought.

And as if to drive home the point that Bunyoro was a conquered territory, no agreement similar to that of Buganda or even to those of Ankole and Tooro was signed with it until 1933. Nor were Kinyoro chiefs offered the same revolutionary land settlement that was offered to their counterparts in Buganda in 1900. This meant, in effect, that all Kinyoro land belonged to the Crown.

By 1900 Banyoro appeared to have lost hope and to have regarded themselves as Frantz Fanon's "Wretched of the Earth". the damned, but unlike Fanon they did not see the solution in naked, physical violence. They simply lost interest in the administration and had little enthusiasm for anything. It is little wonder then that the Bunyoro Annual Report for 1900–01 stated that "the Unyoro chiefs are almost absolutely under the influence of their old barbarism and are consequently very secretive as to matters of religion and fetishism".[58]

The administration so far had been run entirely through Banyoro chiefs, the most important of whom had been *abarusura*, and it was no wonder that no improvement was visible. With the exception of Byabachwezi, none of Kabalega's principal chiefs were still represented in this administration. Bikamba had been killed by the Nubians in Masindi in 1897. No definite guidelines seem to have been followed and it was apparent that the complicated administrative pattern which had been the feature of Kitara government was deliberately being ignored. The consequences were disastrous. The reliance on some erstwhile professional soldiers and some new upstarts, all basically disloyal and dishonest, and without previous experience of administration, instead of on the tried and tested traditional chiefs, was bound to lead to failure. When Kabalega had attempted to curtail the powers of his chiefs and centralise his kingdom, he had taken care not to interfere with the basic system of administration.[59] British officials did precisely what Kabalega had avoided and were amazed at the degree of failure that attended their efforts. The appointment of Rwabudongo, who never had a chieftainship under Kabalega, as *Katikiro* (Chief Minister) and of Byabachwezi as one of the three regents to to the young Kitahimbwa[60] was bound to cause friction. This friction would have led to some sort of civil strife had Rwabudongo not died in 1900.[61]

At the end of the nineteenth century therefore Bunyoro was in a pitiable and deplorable condition. British administration had proved a total failure. The country had been ravaged by wars and famine and the people themselves were confused and depressed. There was no national consciousness and no national spirit. British policy had been savagely punitive rather than conciliatory and it was rather naive of officials to expect loyal co-operation. And this naivety was such that when trouble broke out a few years later, they laid the blame squarely on the shoulders of Baganda and gloried in the fact that it was not directed against them. But it was clear to them that even before Baganda chiefs were introduced into Bunyoro, many Banyoro had degenerated into irredeemable fatalists who had refused to improve either themselves or their country. On the contrary, they sealed their lips and spent their time in utter idleness and "silent opposition".[62] When George Wilson, nicknamed "Tayali" by Banyoro, undertook a tour of the kingdom in 1900 he was appalled by the "entire absence of local enterprise among the Banyoro", a state of affairs which he attributed either

> to reaction from the immense energy they have put forth in sustained opposition to the introduction of order into the country, or it may be due to a feeling of insecurity in the present unsettled state of affairs or perhaps, but I hope not, and certainly the facility they showed formerly in designing mischievous schemes would not bear out this theory, to a lack of capacity for enterprise.[63]

Most officials who knew Banyoro less well than Wilson had not hesitated to attribute their behaviour to natural indolence and lack of intelligence. But neither these officials nor even Wilson— the so-called friend of Banyoro—ever imagined that Banyoro might be simply lodging a silent protest against their humiliation under British overrule.

In 1901 therefore the government had no choice but to look for outside help to reform the administration. It was not that Banyoro were incapable of governing themselves, as was generally claimed, but that they lacked enthusiasm to work for the new administration. The young Kitahimbwa was sent to the courts of Buganda, Tooro, and Ankole to learn at first hand how the kings of those kingdoms governed their subjects.[64] To some Banyoro and possibly to the king himself, this must have been a humiliating and embarrassing experience. It will be remembered that it is their claim that those three kingdoms were rebellious provinces which had established their independence of Kitara. In the same year it was decided to introduce an indirect system of administration on the Buganda model. The kingdom was to be ruled through a system of counties, subcounties and so forth with the corresponding hierarchy of chieftainships under the kings (and during his minority represented by regents) and assisted by a sort of local parliament, the *Rukurato*. In addition there were to be regular *barazas* (open air audiences) at which public business was discussed and grievances heard.[65]

As soon as this new-style *Rukurato* was established, George Wilson persuaded it to invite a Muganda, Jemusi Miti, who was a government Swahili interpreter, to come over to Bunyoro with the title of *saza* chief and teach Banyoro how to govern themselves.[66] According to Miti, he accepted this offer reluctantly after he had been threatened with losing his government job in Buganda should he decline it. He was instructed to organise the new administration after the Buganda fashion, and to respect and obey his superiors who had to be consulted before any administrative innovations were made. In addition, Mr. Lloyd of C.M.S., Namirembe, was appointed to help him out as secretary.[67]

Miti went about his new task with energy and purpose and by August 1901 had streamlined the administration. He divided Bunyoro into *sazas*, *gombororas* and *mirukas*. And of the ten *saza* chieftainships, two were held by Baganda, Miti himself who assumed the *saza* chieftainship of Bujenje with the official title of *Kaigo*, and Antoni Kirube who was made *saza* chief of Kibanda (Chope) with the official title of *Kangaho*. The new departure in this administrative set up was the subdivision of the kingdom into *gombororas* and *mirukas* which was alien to the Kinyoro pattern of government.[68] Almost immediately Banyoro protested vigorously and officially against the new system and accused Miti "of having made a mess of the whole kingdom". But the government was impressed with the Muganda's work and ignored their protests.[69] It is interesting that Banyoro who had for long sealed their lips were now to come to life once more over the issue of Baganda chiefs. The reason is obvious. As one informant put it, single imperialism is bad enough but "double imperialism" is intolerable. They were too scared to protest openly against British rule; to protest against Baganda "double imperialism" was not tantamount to an overt challenge of British authority, a challenge they could ill afford.[70]

But this was only the beginning of things to come. Already the young king of Bunyoro, as befitted the son of the redoubtable Kabalega, had begun to show an independence of mind which soon brought him into conflict with the British administrators. On several occasions he had complained that he did not receive a sufficient supply of food and had questioned the reduced number of his retinue. He demanded that all those who had served his father should be allowed to serve him, a demand which drove Spire, the Collector, to comment, "The young king does not realise

the position of the King of Unyoro to be a very different matter
nowadays."[71]

By 1902 the government had found it difficult to work amicably
with Kitahimbwa and took the drastic step of deposing him for
alleged incompetence.[72] But for Banyoro, Kitahimbwa abdicated
"in protest against what he regarded as the unjust treatment
accorded to Bunyoro".[73] Neither the king nor the principal regent,
Byabachwezi, had been happy with the new state of affairs and
both had been overruled over the decision to appoint Baganda
chiefs to Bunyoro.[74] In later years, Jemusi Miti was to write of
Kitahimbwa:

> (He was) too young to control the state of affairs in his kingdom.
> Moreover, his relations with the British Government were none
> of the best. His attitude towards the British Government and his
> own chiefs was such that it clearly bespoke a mind as yet unruly
> and incapable to handle state affairs. Owing to his queer and un-
> satisfactory conduct, therefore Kitayimbwa (sic) was, on the 17th of
> September 1902, expelled from the throne.[75].

It is clear from this statement of a man who was hardly his friend
that the submission made to Molson and his colleagues was basically correct. Kitahimbwa was not sacked for incompetence (for
the government was run by regents and not by him), but for
insubordination.

Prince Andereya Bisereko, his elder brother, was appointed to
succeed him. He took the title of *Omukama* Duhaga II. Byabachwezi and Miti were also to be regents to the new young monarch
for Bisereko too was a minor.[76] The prince's elevation was hardly
surprising. He was a great friend and admirer of Miti as well as
of Miti's assistant, Mr. Lloyd.[77] He proved to be a reasonable
and tactful, but to the authorities a cunning king.[78] He was reputed
to be a king who thought twice before he spoke out and was
nicknamed *omutuma gw'ibale* (literally "stony-hearted").[79] Nevertheless, many of his subjects detested his friendship with Miti and
may have unjustly accused him of inviting Baganda into Bunyoro.[80]
But even if this accusation was untrue, the fact remained that he
was known to have been very much influenced by Miti.[81] The result
was that many Kinyoro chiefs did not give him the respect due to
a king.[82] Some in fact went to the extent of plotting his overthrow.[83] The peasantry tolerated him simply because he was
"Kabalega's son".[84] Indeed to a majority of Banyoro Kabalega
remained their legitimate *Omukama* as long as he lived.[85]

Without this background it would be easy to fail to grasp the
real motives that animated the *Nyangire* revolt. It was characterised
by a strong appeal to history and to the past. To the British

authorities, the *Nyangire* revolt was a move to get not them but Baganda out of the country. But as we hope to show, the issues involved were much deeper than this simple conviction. Certainly the immediate cause of the revolt was the refusal by the colonial government to rid Bunyoro of Buganda "sub-imperialism". The appointment of Baganda chiefs to Bunyoro acted as a catalyst to already existing Banyoro discontent.

The policy to introduce Baganda chiefs in Bunyoro was as short-sighted—even if necessary—as it was ill-advised. As Banyoro saw it, since the eighteenth century the kings of Buganda and Kitara (Bunyoro) had been struggling for leadership and supremacy in the lacustrine region. For nearly a century Buganda had gained the upper hand in this struggle. Under Kabalega, however, Kitara had shown a remarkable revival and was a positive threat to the power of Buganda. Kabalega, they alleged, was in such a strong position that he had worked out the fantastic scheme of con-quering Buganda and transporting its inhabitants to the Congo. Already his *abarusura* had beaten Buganda disastrously in 1886 ("Battle of the Gangaho"); and by 1890 Kabalega was able to interfere in the civil war in Buganda. Indeed his *abarusura* was in occupation of Buganda for some months with Rwabudongo as a sort of Kalema's *Katikro*, before they were driven out by the Christian forces. By 1891 the British had intervened in the affairs of Kitara, and by 1895 Kabalega was a fugitive in Lango. And between 1894 and 1900 the British had annexed over two-thirds of Kitara (Bunyoro) to Buganda, Ankole and Tooro. And now the protectorate government had come to the conclusion that a kingdom which had been governing itself for about six centuries and had, for most of that period, acquired a large empire was now incapable of self-government.[86]

Banyoro saw the issue of Baganda chiefs as the last straw. It was like forcing a father to accept the authority of his son. Or as they put it: "How can people whom we surpass be placed over us?"[87] And the attitude of Baganda in this role made this situation unbearable.

The advent of Jemusi Miti and Batelamayo was followed by the influx of Baganda into Bunyoro. Almost immediately some of these newcomers got themselves

> installed into pleasant places, others coming in making and selling soap, trading in skins, or as boys, and gradually getting in as sub-chiefs, chiefs receiving *shambas* and getting their friends in as their *msigeres* (*musigire* is a Runyoro word meaning someone left in another's place as a caretaker or some sort of an assistant) to the gradual turning out of the rightful landholders, placing their

friends into the minor and subordinate positions of village headmen getting for them the benefits that accrue therefrom.[80]

Banyoro also complained that the Baganda had brought nothing
into their kingdom and accused them of ploughing back their
profits to Buganda, "thus impoverishing Unyoro and enriching
(B)uganda'.[89]

The case of Bunyoro in this context has been brilliantly sum-
marised for the author by John Nyakatura, the traditional historian
of Kitara. He says:

> The act of the British Government in giving away six counties to
> the Ganda had serious and profound repercussions in the minds
> of all the people of Bunyoro. And whatever evils (killing Nyoro
> in cold blood) Ganda did to Nyoro in those counties after they
> had occupied them became known to all the people in the remain-
> ing part of Bunyoro. Moreover only four months had elapsed
> after Ganda had been understood to have been responsible for the
> loss of Bulega to the Belgians.
>
> And because of its apparent dislike of Nyoro and scornful atti-
> tude towards them, the British government brought Jemusi Miti to
> become *saza* chief, *Kaigo,* of Bujenje which was in the remaining
> portion of Bunyoro; Jemusi Mito also took it upon himself to
> introduce a considerable number of fellow Ganda whom he made
> chiefs, and caused Antoni Kirube to assume the *saza* chieftainship
> of Kibanda (Chope) as *Kangaho.*
>
> And as it is their general nature of greediness (*okuswansuma
> kwabu*), they introduced other fellow Ganda into the palace of
> *Omukama* Andereya Duhaga II. One of these Semu Bulela, be-
> came the *Omujweki* (someone responsible for the clothes of the
> *Omukama*); and another Kahuta, was head of all the *Omukama's*
> cooks (*Omwokya*).
>
> And with the air of self-praise and self-adulation, the Ganda had
> accustomed themselves to adding abusive and debasing words when-
> ever they talked about a Nyoro person. It is clear that where this
> kind of situation persists, no co-operation can be forged. This kind
> of situation did not exist among Nyoro themselves except among
> the Hima (pastoralist class) only and that's why it was easy for us
> to co-operate readily with the peoples of the Northern and Eastern
> Regions.
>
> For these reasons, therefore, Nyoro chiefs and all the ordinary
> Nyoro were forced to develop hatred for all the Ganda in Bunyoro,
> and instituted secret councils to consider the situation. Many people
> in fact were demanding a fixed date on which all the Ganda would
> be clubbed to death...

The important point about these views of alleged Baganda mis-
deeds is not their veracity but the fact that they were generally held.
It is also important to note that present day oral evidence and the

official archival material are almost in complete agreement. These allegations coupled with the natural jealousy of Baganda[91] by Banyoro sparked off the *Nyangire* revolt.

But Banyoro were animated by other more fundamental motives. One of these concerned the issue of land settlement. It will be remembered that in 1900 Sir Harry Johnston had regarded the whole of Bunyoro as crown land and had refused to extend to them the same revolutionary land settlement he had introduced in Buganda. Now, in September 1906, the *Omukama* and his chiefs—probably on the advice of Miti—petitioned the Commissioner for the Uganda Protectorate, Sir H. H. Bell, to grant them *mailo* (estates).[92] He promised to consider their request but preferred "before coming to a decision, to consult Mr. George Wilson, who is well acquainted with the country". Personally, however, he did not appear disposed to meet their request in full.[93]

Somehow the Commissioner's reaction came to be misinterpreted by Banyoro. A rumour apparently began to circulate that their petition would be favourably considered. It was at this point that it dawned on them "that a lot of their land will be handed over to the Waganda".[94] This point was emphasised by a later official who was convinced that

> the base of the whole trouble is (B)unyoro before was the fear of the Banyoro that the Baganda whom we have placed in (B)unyoro would bring in their followers and take possession of so much land that practically the whole of (B)unyoro would eventually become alienated to their heirs and successors.[95]

It therefore became vital for them to get rid of Baganda first before pressing for the land settlement. It was not until 1909, when Banyoro saw which way the wind was blowing, that they reopened the matter.[96]

Another point to bear in mind is the attitude of the peasantry. Admittedly they did not initiate the revolt but once it was started they certainly took great interest in it and gave their chiefs unswerving support.[97] There is no doubt that during the early years of British administration, Kinyoro peasants did not hide their lack of enthusiasm for the new domination. They were therefore a ready-made tool for revolutionary activities if the proper leadership was available. Despite the fact that the government had begun to bend over backwards to alleviate their sufferings,[98] they appeared sourly unimpressed. They refused to work and preferred to eat wild fruits and roots than to cultivate their own crops. As Grant put it, the peasantry were "entirely oblivious to the benefits to be derived by the acquisition of money" and were so irresponsible as to fail "to provide for their own sustenance, being at times reduced like the beasts of the field to grub for roots". And consequently "aliens have to be introduced to supply the labour essential for the mere maintenance of the very system which has so earnestly fostered them".[99] The few willing to work refused to accept any rate of pay "less than 50 per cent per day increase on the Entebbe and Kampala current labour rates". And from Masindi it was reported that "not one Munyoro native can be got to run to Hoima for 1 rupee and rations, pay for 10 days in (B)uganda".[100]

The question then is: why should a once virile people be reduced to the pitiful situation of grubbing "for roots" like animals especially when it has been admitted that some of these peasants were "far more intelligent than the chiefs"?[101] George Wilson saw the answer in the nostalgia they felt for the rule of Kabalega. He wrote:

Kabelega had been a king whose despotism had appealed strongly to the natives. His barbarities had not approached the gross character of those of the (B)uganda kings, the executions and mutilations by his orders havng generally been punishments for crimes.

Every peasant, he continued, had the right to appeal directly to the king for justice, a practice which Kabalega had encouraged because it gave him the opportunity of dealing with the unduly ambitious chiefs who could be easily put out of the way when their pretensions became manifest and obstructive. He also noted that the peasantry were well disposed towards Duhaga II and were heard to exclaim: "Why should we not be loyal to Kabalega's son!"[102] But it did not occur to Wilson that this attitude of the peasantry might be their way of showing disapproval of the new domination.

If the peasantry dealt with the Europeans in sullen silence, they were certainly not going to deal with their immediate chiefs, many of whom were Baganda, in the same manner. In 1904 they rebelled against them.[103] The Commissioner appointed Wilson to investigate their grievances. In a lengthy report he showed that the peasantry disliked the new system of administration which gave them less freedom than during the days of Kabalega. The further division of the kingdom into gombororas and murukas was alien to the peasantry. They complained that they were being maltreated and down-trodden by the chiefs. Naturally, Wilson laid the blame not on the system but on the way the chiefs carried out their duties.[104]

The other, and perhaps most important, motive behind the

revolt was the indirect attack on the British administrative structure. Banyoro used the question of Baganda chiefs to undermine
this structure. This dimension of the affair began to emerge, in
the view of officials, as the revolt progressed to a climax. Mr.
Watson, Acting Collector at Mbarara, wrote afterwards:

> I had reason some months ago to believe that some correspondence
> had passed between Ankole and Toro on the subject of the Baganda,
> and that Kasagama, *Kabaka* (sic) of Tooro, had advised Kahaya,
> *Kabaka* (sic) of Ankole, to discourage as far as he could the in-
> clusion of Baganda in the list of chiefs eligible for membership of
> the Ankole *Lukiiko* (sic).
>
> I am confident that the action which has been taken in Unyoro
> will strengthen Kahaya and his chiefs in resisting any attempts
> which may have been, or which may be, made to induce them to
> go beyond the proper and satisfactory atitude they have up till the
> present manifested in regard to this matter.[105]

There is evidence to suggest that collaboration between Tooro and
Ankole was the result of some diplomatic initiative on the
part of Kinyoro chiefs.

In January 1907 two Banyoro, Petero and Zabuloni, were
reported to have been sent as emissaries to the other kingdoms by
their chiefs. Petero's mission was to win over the principality of
Budiope (in Busoga) to their cause "as the people of there are very
friendly with Banyoro". Zabuloni undertook the same mission in
Ankole and Tooro. They were instructed to examine first the
feelings of their hosts towards Baganda and to ascertain whether
or not they would press for their removal. They were also required to find two witnesses among the *saza* chiefs in each kingdom "who would back up the Banyoro in a *Lukiiko* (sic) composed
of representatives of the various countries in the Protectorate and
to arrange that their selected witnesses should be the ones chosen
to represent their countries". The government was to be pressurised
into arranging such a *Lukiiko* to sit in a neutral place such as
Kampala. The plan of Kinyoro chiefs was to demand at this
Lukiiko, when summoned, the removal of Baganda chiefs from
their kingdom. The issue would be left open to their neighbours to
decide and thus place the government with a *fait accompli*. If the
Lukiiko decided in favour of Banyoro, "then the representatives of
the other districts would get up and ask whether the question of
the Baganda remaining in their respective countries could not
likewise be considered and adjudged and that it could be a favourable time to discuss the matter as all countries were present".[106]

The aim of this diplomacy is therefore clear. Before the proposal for this *Lukiiko* was put before the government, Banyoro

must have secured the support of what amounts to an anti-Ganda
League and be assured of getting their proposal passed since without such prior support they had nothing to gain from such a
meeting. So having got their way, the next move was to "help
Tooro, Ankole, and Busoga to oust the Baganda".[107] Then if this
move too succeeded, they would finally play their trump card—
a demand through the same platform of the *Lukiiko* for a return
to them of the "lost counties". Having helped the other members
of the anti-Ganda League to secure the expulsion of Baganda they
had hoped to be supported on this point. It is interesting that a
separate delegation was sent to the "lost counties" to explain the
purpose of this diplomatic initiative and presumably to secure their
representation and support in what amounted to a national conference.[108] It was not until May, however, that Banyoro put their
proposal before the government, which rejected it and ordered the
immediate restoration of Baganda to the positions from which
they had been ejected. Banyora refused to obey this order and made
threats "against the lives of the Baganda".[109]

Certain intriguing questions, however, remain to be answered.
Why, for instance, was this proposal not put before the government during the important meeting at Butiaba where Banyoro
aired their grievances at length? Granted that the emissaries had
just returned at that time, and the chiefs needed time to consider
their reports, why then did they keep their plan secret until the
revolt had broken out?

Mr. Haddon, Assistant Collector at Masindi, has provided an
interesting explanation:

> One solution is that they wished this scheme of an interracial
> *Lukiiko* to appear like a spontaneous idea which they had just con-
> ceived as a way out of the difficulty. No one at the time would have
> suspected that this was a carefully thought out plan—thought five
> months earlier.

And as to why "they chose the most favourable time to put it
forward", he explains:

> It may be chance, but it is also a clever move.
> I would put forward another theory which without further evidence
> (which I am unable to obtain) cannot be fully substantiated. The ob-
> stinate refusal of the *sazas* to conform with His Excellency's orders
> may possibly be explained in this way.
> If what Mika Kagao says is true that (B)unyoro was pledged to
> Tooro, Ankole and Busoga to try to oust Baganda, then by an ob-
> stinate refusal to obey orders (B)unyoro might force the govern-
> ment's hand and obtain the desired interacial *Lukiiko* (sic). The
> pledge was probably mutual and (B)unyoro could help Toro and

Ankole after her own affairs were settled—(B)unyoro was leading the way and could not show weakness at the very first opposition to her plans. This is substantiated by the fact that from Toro came the message: "It is better to die than to give away...."[110]

This theory was confirmed by another official who noted that at the beginning of 1907 the chiefs' "claims for self-government" had been put forward strongly but in the proper manner. But by May:

> The tones of their meetings had entirely changed. There was a decidedly rebellious attitude on the part of the Banyoro chiefs and their immediate followers. This attitude was so unlike anything I had ever seen from any natives that it made certain that there was some strong motive for their intense desire to oust the Baganda.[111]

And Mr. Grant, too, who had left Bunyoro in 1905 without noticing "the slightest indication of a desire to get rid of the Baganda" was also led to believe "that outside influences were at work".[112]

A lot of space has been devoted to this point because the discovery of these documents must certainly change the prevailing view with regard to the *Nyangire* revolt. It is clear that it was no mere comic gesture against Baganda chiefs. Its animations were deep and fundamental and had a lot of appeal to history. Had Banyoro got their way, not only would British authority have been seriously undermined but also the subsequent history of Uganda would perhaps have been different.

The essential point, however, is not that there was ever a chance of such a scheme succeeding, but the fact that Banyoro were animated by such motives and were driven to adopt the rather clever tactic of an anti-Ganda League to achieve their goals. There was therefore much more to the *Nyangire* revolt than Thomas and Rubie discovered. They wrote:

> The whole movement was reactionary, though not anti-European; a gesture by the governing classes against the discipline represented by the Baganda, which progress was rendering inevitable.[113]

But Jemusi Miti, who was the key figure in the revolt, knew better. When British officials asked him why Banyoro hated Baganda so much, he was reported to have replied:

> These chiefs are remembering their former *Mukama*, Kabalega. Most of them were *abarusura*, and therefore they do not hate Ganda only but also you, the Europeans. After getting rid of the Ganda, they will attempt to drive you out too.[114]

The organisation of the Nyangire revolt is no less intriguing than the motives which had precipitated it. The first problem that confronted Kinyoro chiefs was precisely the problem we have posed at the beginning of this essay: How to revolt again having been smashed the first time. As we shall see they managed to to find a way out of this dilemma.

By 1906 the British administration was at last showing some sort of improvement and officials were forecasting better times ahead and patting themselves on the back.[115] By this time too only one Muganda—Miti himself—held a *saza* chieftainship in Bunyoro although there were many Baganda among the lower chiefs.[116] Nevertheless the authorities saw no indication that trouble was coming within a few months.

It is difficult to account why the revolt occurred in 1907. It is also not clear precisely when Banyoro started planning it. What is certain is that its organisation was done in strict secrecy.[117] All we know is that it was started by a few chiefs in Bugungu probably at a local bar.[118] They met on several occasions in secret and decided to use the question of Baganda chiefs to open their assault on the government. This was a convenient move, for the Baganda issue was an emotional one and was likely to attract a lot of sympathy without necessarily being interpreted as a challenge to imperial authority. But in reality they were continuing Kabalega's struggle only in a different way. The times had changed, so also did the methods. Gradually the news of the decision that Baganda chiefs must be driven out of Bunyoro spread in traditional fashion throughout the country and within a short time the plotters gained many adherents.

Soon the base of operations was shifted from Bugungu to Hoima and they "used to meet in Paulo Byabachwezi's house".[119] Byabachwezi does not appear to have been one of the original plotters. The official view was that he was a late convert although Jemusi Miti tended to see him as the ringleader.[120]

During these secret meetings the crucial question was whether or not force should be used. Eventually the pacifists led by Byabachwezi got the upper hand.[121]

That such a decision was arrived at is no surprise. The use of force would have been the surest way of failing in their objectives. The country was in effective military occupation, and more importantly. "the fifth battalion (sic) was stationed at Hioma—plus a number of policemen".[122] Moreover, Banyoro had no guns. The *abarusura* had been beaten, disarmed, and scattered. Kabalega was in exile. Rwabudongo was dead, Kikukuule and Ireeta in exile, and Byabachwezi a collaborator, even if now a discontented one. And Duhaga II was a puppet of Miti and the Europeans. There was therefore no national hero to command the loyalty of the entire people. Banyoro also believed that the British administration had installed Ganda chiefs in Bunyoro and "were certain to fight in their defence" and were likely to seize the occasion of any "exhibition of violence to remove *en masse* Kinyoro chiefs and replace them with Baganda ones". They therefore "opted for a non-violent approach; they all agreed to fight verbally". Their supporters were advised, in their best interests, to be "passive onlookers" in the physical sense but must at the same time resolutely "refuse to take orders until their demands were granted".[123]

Another crucial problem that they dealt with would appear to be the question of external support. We saw how emissaries were sent to Ankole, Tooro, Busoga and to the "lost counties".[124] Part of the task of the emissaries to the "lost counties" was to cause discontent among the people. Throughout these moves Kinyoro chiefs were particularly careful not to be seen to be challenging the power of the imperial overlord, but rather emphasised that their aim was simply to secure the peaceful removal of Baganda chiefs.

So far the government had been unaware that a revolt was being organised. Apparently Duhaga was not informed about it until some time in January 1907. His chiefs had little confidence in him because of his alleged Baganda sympathies. Apparently, too, he secretly backed the revolt but, afraid of losing his throne, refused to come out in the open.[125] He refused to forward the matter to the District Commissioner, Mr. Cubitt, on the ground that he was ill and advised his chiefs to take up the matter directly with him. But Mr. Cubitt refused to listen to them until they had passed through the proper channel, that is, through the king himself.[126]

It had become a tradition in Bunyoro since the establishment of the British administration that on Wednesdays the District Commissioner (originally known as Collector) held *barazas* where grievances were heard and possibly settled. It was during one of these *barazas* that the issue of Baganda chiefs was first brought before the notice of the government. The spokesman at that time was a man called Nikodem Kakoko, "a former *murusura* who feared nothing". He was given enthusiastic support by everyone present. Mr. Cubitt, greatly shocked and amazed, was inclined to dismiss it as a matter of minor importance. But Banyoro left the meeting determined to press the matter to the end and were openly condemning the British for imposing Baganda chiefs on them.[127] The matter was reported to Entebbe but no action appears to have been taken.[128] In the meantime it had excited great interest throughout the country and by 5 February another delegation supported by thousands of followers was before Mr. Cubitt. Bikundi noted in his diary:

People came to Hoima from all corners of Bunyoro: Kibanda, Kihukya, Buruli, Bujenje, Bugahya, etc. It was terrible. There was a big multitude of people.

Byabachwezi demanded, in the name of all the people of Bunyoro, the removal of Baganda chiefs from their kingdom. Duhaga was not present at this meeting and Mr. Cubitt insisted that he must be present as well as every *saza* chief. Until then, he refused to do anything.[129]

During this period Jemusi Miti was home in Buganda. The situation was quickly deteriorating and urgent appeals were made to him to return at once.[130] Banyoro now appeared to be abandoning their pacific approach and gradually assuming a violent posture. But Cubitt and his staff still treated the matter with levity. Obviously they had not yet comprehended its seriousness. Jemusi Miti, on his part, refused to return to Bunyoro and responded to the occasion with cool professionalism. He telegraphed to one of his closest supporters:

I have seen your telegram. We have been placed by the Government among the Banyoro. He (sic) is able to drive us away. I am unable to return as you say.[131]

In essence Miti is saying that it was the duty of the government and not his to deal with the situation. He and his Baganda were merely civil servants.

At last Cubitt decided to act and summoned a big *baraza* for 21 February. Bikundi noted that "all the people of Bunyoro" were present and "those who did not turn up must have been seriously sick". Ibrahim Talyeba, the assistant to Miti at Bujenje, expounded the Kinyoro case. It is remarkable that at this *baraza* Kinyoro *saza* chiefs sealed their lips while the attack was spearheaded by *gomborora* and *muruka* chiefs, aided by a *mubiito* (prince), Zakaliya Omwangamwoyo. The theme was the removal of Baganda chiefs from their kingdom. Duhaga, at last forced to show his hand, decided to save himself by dissociating himself from the demand of his subjects. Cubitt advised the chiefs not to force the matter and promised to forward their grievances to the governor.[132] But the attitude of Duhaga "enraged the Banyoro chiefs so much that they openly and most rudely objected to their master's ruling, and expressed an intention of sending Jemusi Miti and his followers packing as soon as possible".[133]

Entebbe was informed of these developments.[134] But while the official machinery took its time to act the situation deteriorated further. Byabachwezi continued to preside over secret meetings of Kinyoro chiefs, closely watched by Miti's agents, while Duhaga cleverly retreated to Masindi and washed his hands of the whole affair.[135]

More and more Banyoro were becoming very aggressive. They began to make life miserable for Baganda. They began to arrest them on trumped-up charges and somehow managed to secure their conviction. They even made it impossible for them "to reap and eat their own food crops". And, according to Miti, Cubitt did nothing to alleviate the suffering of Baganda.[136] Perhaps encouraged by their success, Banyoro took the drastic step of turning Baganda out of their chieftainships and estates and forcing them to retreat to Hoima for safety.[137] And simultaneously a plot was in progress to depose Duhaga. This plot aimed at turning out Miti and his followers and Mika Fataki[138] first so as to be in a strong position to secure the deposition of Duhaga and his replacement with a Kinyoro prince of their choice.[139]

Now that events had got out of hand a telegram was received in Hoima which warned Banyoro not "to interfere with the scheme of chieftainships". Failure to comply with this order would "meet His Excellency's severe displeasure".[140] Finding their position intolerable, however, Baganda sought leave to return to Buganda but this request was refused.[141]

On 1 April, Mr. Tomkins, P.C. Buganda, was sent, as an official who knew Bunyoro well, to inquire into the disturbances at Hoima.[142] He arrived at Masindi on 12 April[143] and his first act was to convene a *baraza* at Butiaba. This was held on 14 April and all the *saza* chiefs including Miti and Duhaga were present. At this meeting Banyoro, led by Byabachwezi, spelled out their grievances in detail. They were careful, however, not to mention the anti-Ganda League and the multi-national *Lukiiko*. Nor did they raise the issue of the "*lost counties*". The tone of their speeches was fiercely anti-Baganda and their immediate goal the removal of Baganda chiefs and the assumption of Kinyoro self-government. They made it plain that the introduction of Baganda chiefs was entirely George Wilson's idea, a move they had opposed at the time but were overruled.[144]

Tomkins promised to consider their complaints and urged them to keep calm. And in his report provided the following solution:

> I strongly recommend that no more Baganda be allowed to hold chieftainships in (B)unyoro, unless under very special circumstances and that those there at present be replaced by Bunyoro (sic) as soon as opportunity offers—I should say as soon as possible for the peace of the country.

And as to the complaint that Miti had tremendous power over the *Rukurato*, he recommended that steps should be taken to keep him in check.[145]

Banyoro were not satisfied with the outcome of the Butiaba meeting. They continued to persecute Baganda.[146] Meanwhile the revolt had spread to Ssingo county where Kinyoro peasants refused to obey their chiefs[147]—a situation which got progressively worse further west.[148]

In May, Cubitt was recalled to Entebbe and was succeeded by Mr. N. G. Eden from Nimule. The government apparently did not consider Tomkins' recommendation favourably and Eden was instructed to reinstate Baganda chiefs forthwith and to make Banyoro "clearly understand that it is a conquered country and more than in any other the disposal of authority lies directly with His Majesty's Commissioners.[149] Eden convened a big *baraza* at which the governor's decision was read out. The Collector was amazed at the reception he got. Everyone was heard to exclaim *"Nyangire"* ("I have refused").[150] It was from this incident that the revolt took its name and later on Banyoro began to refer to that episode in their history as the *Kyanyangire*. Indeed Eden was warned by the chiefs that they would not be held responsible for the safety of Baganda should they return to their posts and estates.[151]

Eden made several unsuccessful attempts to get them to obey the governor's orders and on each occasion Banyoro expressed stronger defiance of the authorities.[152] The situation became very tense throughout the colony[153] and Banyoro chiefs decided to play their last card. They put forward the proposal of the multi-national conference to decide the matter.[154] But the governor refused to allow such a conference until his orders had been carried out. He went further to warn that until this was done "the presence of (B)unyoro chiefs here on Empire Day would be ill-timed."[155] In other words, they would be an embarrassment to the government in the presence of chiefs from the other districts.

What then should be done? Banyoro declined the use of physical force but were profuse in their verbal confrontation.[156] Their tactics baffled Entebbe as the following flurry of telegrams testifies:

(i) Your tel. today: do you mean situation requires force and if so reinforcements?

(ii) Is (B)unyoro contemplating armed resistance or insurrections?

(iii) Early insurrection or ultimate insurrection—that is if any chance of resistance or early insurrection reinforcements will be at once sent. If Byabachwezi has to be arrested I will take measures ready for whole country.

(iv) When do you expect *sazas* (*saza* chiefs) and what do you pro-
pose to say to them?

(v) I cannot understand position at all. You say no information of
armed resistance yet you have military ready. From your messages
I understand position critical so far politically and affecting *Lukiiko*
(sic).

(vi) Send away escort. A previous message not clear. I meant rather
than arrest Byabachwezi I prefer to take measures affecting whole
Lukiiko (sic). Do not now precipitate any disturbance until I am
ready.[157]

This was certainly the kind of situation in which colonial administrators hated to find themselves. In "primary resistances" the
enemies were well known. Their motives were clear and they were
in most cases armed. So it was easy to know what to do. But
here the situation was different. The authorities believed that Banyoro had no intention of getting rid of them; some even admitted
that they had a legitimate case; and others were convinced that
they could not stage any effective armed resistance.

What then should the government do? They had tried persuasion. When that failed they had tried bluff and bluster and
when that failed too they resorted to precautionary military
measures. It will be noted that such measures were not considered
necessary until Banyoro defied the governor's ruling. To people
like Cubitt the suffering of Baganda had registered little impression
and yet it was the administration which had imposed Baganda
on Banyoro. For five months these Baganda had suffered in Bunyoro and little had been done to obtain redress for them. But as
soon as the government's authority was challenged, the tone of
the despatches began to show an uncompromising bellicosity. "I
cannot realise", telegraphed Wilson, "that they (Banyoro) actually
understand that a decision has been given by the government
which they are refusing to accept."[158] And this was why Banyoro
concentrated their onslaught on Baganda rather than on government officials, thus creating the false impression that the whole
movement was a purely anti-Ganda affair.

The government's dilemma still remained. Up till now no effec-
tive measure had been taken to implement the governor's decision.
Even the threat to prevent Kinyoro representation at the Empire
Day celebration was abandoned[159] but the *Omukama* and his
chiefs politely declined to attend.[160] By now it had become clear
that the government was running the danger of losing its authority.
Military preparations were therefore intensified.[161] At this point
Bunyoro's principal chiefs decided to turn off the heat a little.

They accepted in principal to obey the government's order but pleaded inability to carry it out for fear of their subchiefs and out of consideration for the safety of Baganda. Eden dismissed this explanation as eyewash and not "altogether sincere", and consequently telegraphed Entebbe that he had reached the conclusion "that only arrest of neighbours (sic) should suffice to assert government authority and to prevent feeling running high".[162] Accordingly he ordered troops to be placed at strategic places including the premises of the Christian Missions and the *saza* chiefs became "absolutely mute".[163]

> Position is serious. This morning chiefs rather apt to go back on their word. I held small *baraza* this morning. Chief spokesman Byabachwezi with three to five hundred *batongole* and natives outside. Many detected with knives and have been cautioned to be on my guard.[164]

They "openly defied Mr. Eden in his order to reinstate Baganda". The fiercest of them was Kaboha, *saza* chief of Buruli. And the crowd was in such a "high state of excitement" that "Mr. Eden sent for the troops".[165]

At last Banyoro had played into Mr. Eden's hands. The complicated plot was too good to last without a hitch and the denouement was at hand. He took the decision to charge the chiefs with disobedience and order their arrest.[166]

These developments had gone slightly against Wilson's calculations. He had been confident that "(B)unyoro should (not) be plunged in war" and had warned Eden not to "precipitate disturbances", but to obtain Reverend "Fisher's frank opinion on matters".[167] This was accordingly done and Fisher advised Eden to "arrest the underlings who are the originators. I do not believe they will raise the country as the ill-feeling is not against government but against Baganda".[168]

Eden therefore convened another meeting during which the arrests would be made. This information leaked out to some chiefs who consequently went into hiding.[169] Nevertheless many people gathered in front of the General Post Office (Hoima) oblivious of what was going to happen. Eden ordered the army and police to parade "to show authority". But in spite of the presence of the military the chiefs "were in such a frenzied state that they were incapable of listening to reason, refusing absolutely to allow Baganda back in (B)unyoro chieftainships and shouting that they would die rather than see such a thing happen". Consequently, Eden arrested fifty-three chiefs "and then had to attend to the crowd of followers who were in an equally frenzied state beating the ground and even throwing themselves down saying they were equally to die in the cause".[170]

Another version of this story states that the *Omukama* denounced his subjects once more for flouting his own authority as well as that of the government and that the chiefs, cowed by the military exercises performed by the soldiers, decided to climb down.[171]

Whichever is the correct version of events, the arrest of the chiefs can be said to mark the end of the *Nyangire* revolt. But that was not the end of the affair, as the following song shows:

> Ekya Mubende Kirija
> Kirija mawe kirija
> Ekyatwaire abami boona
> O Kahwa na Rujumba
> Ekya Mubende Kirija
> Ebijunju bita embeba, kirija
> BaKabateza amabingo; karija
> Ekya Mubende Kirija . . .

This song may be roughly rendered into English as follows:

> There is more to come
> Resulting from this affair
> Which has led to the
> Arrest of the chiefs.
> Oh, Kahwa and Rujumba
> Have been taken away
> And sticks are used
> To beat and kill rats.
> And chiefs were beaten
> With pieces of reeds.
> (*Refrain*) More should be expected
> From this incident which
> Has culminated in the
> Imprisonment of chiefs in Mubende.[172]

As soon as this news reached Entebbe, Wilson decided to go to Hoima to clear up the mess left "owing to mismanagement of affairs in (B)unyoro by Eden" and "to make sure there should not be reason for alarm". He was convinced, however, that there was "no reason to fear disturbance".[173] Meanwhile, Eden had decided to send the political prisoners to Kampala. But anticipating that Wilson was unhappy with the way he had handled the affair, he begged him not to bring the prisoners back to Hoima with him because "the majority of (them) are of Kabalega's blood and those who are not have been fanatically contaminated with it.[174]

Meanwhile people in the "lost counties" and the other kingdoms were anxiously awaiting events. Southwards and westwards,
Mr. Leakey, P.C. Buganda, who had been instructed "to move
into counties south of the Kafu to inquire into affairs there",[175]
reported that "the Bakopi refuse to obey the chiefs and will not
see us. I have only been able to get but a few whom I may describe
as loyal Banyoro". Indeed many of them had already gone over
to Hoima to attend a secret meeting where they were to arrange
the division of the sazas of Buyaga and Bugangaiza between the
non-collaborating chiefs after the expulsion of Baganda. Those
who had remained behind had no wish also to resort to armed
resistance but were "quite ready to go further if the agitation
against Baganda in (B)unyoro should succeed".[176] With the suppression of the rising in Hoima, the revolt there also petered out.

Wilson arrived in Hoima on 22 May "riding on a horse".[177]
And having studied the situation, he meted out punishment to
the ringleaders. First, Byabachwezi suffered reduction in salary
and rank. He was made to hand over one-third of his estates to
the Omukama and was to pay a fine of Rs. 7,500 within a period
of three years. This amount was to be deducted from the percentage
due to him from the taxes collected in his county. Second, Kata-
likawe (Kitunzi), saza chief of Busindi, Daudi Katongole (Seki-
boobo), saza chief of Kihukya (Chope), and Leo Kaboha (Kim-
bugwe), saza chief of Buruli, were deposed. Third, forty-two chiefs
below the rank of saza chiefs were sentenced to six months' detention in Buganda. Fourth, twelve chiefs were deported to Kitui
in Kenya for three years. Fifth, Baganda were to be returned
to their chieftainships and estates under the escort of the D.C.
and the police. And sixth, the government cancelled all claims
on it because of loyalty and good services and threatened to be
even more severe on Banyoro if they attempted to rebel again.

The peasantry were exonerated because it was believed that
they had not precipitated the revolt. The Omukama himself went
unpunished apparently because he had openly dissociated himself from the malcontents and also because he had personally
been the object of their intrigues.[178]

Banyoro licked their wounds in private and attempted no further
disturbance. But in January 1908 there was an outbreak of incen-
diarism in Hoima. The victims were those chiefs who were
suspected of supporting the government in 1907. Among those
connected with this incident were two of Kabalega's sons, who
were also accused of sympathising with another plot to overthrow
Duhaga.[179]

The harshness with which the government treated Kinyoro chiefs was characteristic of the administration of Sir Henry Hesketh Bell.[180] But though the revolt was quelled simply by a show of force, Banyoro emerged out of it with considerable political and economic gains. Had there been an armed resistance and a protracted one as such, their defeat nevertheless would have been a certainty, and it is likely they would have lost everything they fought for. It is true that the government forced the reinstatement of Baganda chiefs but Banyoro claimed—a claim which had some substance[181]—it was privately made known to them that no more Baganda chiefs should be appointed to their kingdom, and that the existing Baganda chiefs remained in their posts subject to good behaviour. Proven evidence of insolence, disobedience, incompetence, or corruption against any of them would automatically lead to dismissal and replacement by a Munyoro. Indeed, as an informant put it, this was tantamount to making Banyoro "act as policemen over Ganda chiefs and they used all their ingenuity to have them eliminated as quickly as possible". Trumped up charges, and sometimes genuine ones, carefully arranged and cleverly executed were brought up against them and some were in this way sacked. Some were even blackmailed into confessing to some crimes which they had not committed or into doing certain things. "If you refuse to do this or that, *gulihwera Entebbe* (i.e. the matter will be submitted to Entebbe)."[182]

Official sources, however, are silent on such practices. All that is evident is that by 1914 only a handful of Baganda chiefs remained in Bunyoro.[183] And by 1930 Jemusi Miti was the only Muganda chief left in the country. He had clung on to his post precariously and primarily on account of his loyal service.[184]

The second political gain was the readiness with which British officials accepted the application of the *Omukama* and his chiefs to be granted control over the tombs of the *Abakama* of Kitara situated in provinces now under Baganda occupation. This question appears to have been first raised in 1909,[185] and after they had won this point,[186] Banyoro went on to request control over the sites containing the jawbones of their *Abakama*. It was their custom, they pleaded, as well as that of Baganda, to bury the jawbones of their kings separately, and that it was "the part they preserved most carefully and paid the greatest respect to", the assumption being that that part of the body contained the soul.[187] The Buganda *Lukiiko* was pressurised by the government into acquiescing in these demands.[188]

These gains were important, for although the struggle for the return of the "lost counties" continued until well after independence, the issue of the burial grounds of the *Abakama* of Kitara was to play a significant part in the return of Buyaga and Bugan-gaizi to Bunyoro and in the neutralisation of Mubende.[189]

Economically too Banyoro made some gains. We saw that the question of land settlement was one of the underlying motives of the *Nyangire* revolt. With the collapse of this revolt it became evident that Banyoro, still afraid that Baganda might be given estates in their kingdom, were reluctant to press the matter. Indeed it would appear that British officials had become more interested in the matter than Banyoro themselves. In 1909 Grant reported that "they do not appear to be very greatly concerned as to whether they have estates or not".[190] It was not until 1910, how-ever, that the *Rukurato* formally renewed the application of 1906.[191] By this time it must have become clear to them that the days of Baganda hegemony in their kingdom were numbered. In forwarding this application, Mr. Knowles, P.C. Northern Province, observed that "their petition is reasonable".[192] And when Eden became Acting P.C., Northern Province, he was instructed to submit a comprehensive scheme for land settlement which he duly did.[193] Before he submitted his report, however, he advised that Baganda chiefs "who have done good work for the government should be granted estates".[194] This advice was rejected by Knowles, now Acting Chief Secretary. He did not, he minuted, wish to have any more revolts on his hands and dismissed the contention that Baganda chiefs would resign if estates were not granted to them. "I don't think it at all likely, however, that any of the Baganda chiefs in (B)unyoro, from my personal knowledge of them," he concluded, "will be so foolish, as besides the position the chieftain-ship gives them, they earn a considerable income from the post, which I feel sure they would not voluntarily relinquish".[195]

It will be seen therefore why many Banyoro claimed victory after the *Nyangire* revolt. In their view they had lost the war but won the peace.[196] But it was still clearly evident that they had not yet genuinely accepted British overrule. Such an acceptance was unlikely so long as the "lost counties" remained lost. Nor were they concerned with driving the British out of their country by violent means. Such a view was seen by them to be impractic-able. Collaboration with, and manipulation of, officials became the policy of the chiefs as indeed it had always been. But there was little loyalty, or at least there was divided loyalty. A. R. Dunbar writes:

To add to the difficulties the chiefs who were the agents of the ruling power had two opposed loyalties, one to the British Administrators and the other to the *Omukama* and the people. Both sides judged them entirely by different standards so that it was virtually impossible for them to please both sides. As long as the British were in the ascendancy the problem of choice confronting a chief was not so acute, but once it was known that the British were leaving a dilemma existed.[197]

As for the majority of Banyoro—especially among the elderly and the educated—there still exists the belief that Europeans caused the decline of their once great kingdom. They are convinced that Europeans disliked them and had shown a lot of disregard for their interests. Consequently they distrust and fear the European. Even the educated find it difficult to get on intimately with them. John Beattie gained this impression in the early 1950s.[198] It is the present author's impression in the 1960s. Banyoro still have the feeling that the world has left them behind and they blame it all on nineteenth-century colonialism. With Banyoro the European can never win. And when nationalist politics became important in Uganda in the 1950s they contributed their share to remove the Europeans.[199]

In a certain sense this study is a sequel to the writer's earlier studies in the history of Kitara.[200] More importantly, however, as the reader may have noticed, it drew its inspiration from the ideas of Davidson and Ranger. These authors have provided a general theoretical pattern in relation to the various stages of African resistance to alien rule. This study is partly an attempt to justify their thesis and partly an attempt to expose the difficulties and dilemmas of collaboration after defeat and of "secondary resistance". Implicitly it is submitted that enforced collaboration is no collaboration at all but a tactical and diplomatic move to avoid sinking into obscurity. Basically there is continuous resistance.

Therefore to see the *Nyangire* revolt as a comic and tame protest against Baganda chiefs is an incorrect and simplistic view of the animations that lay beneath the African revolts or the so-called rebellions of the beginning of this century. Even granted that Banyoro of the *Kyanyangire* were only concerned with forcing Baganda out of their country, such action in itself is a revolt against British overrule; and its success or failure must be seen as victory or defeat respectively, not in relation to Baganda sub-imperialism, but rather in relation to those who had placed them in the position under attack.

NOTES

1. Banyoro refer to this episode in their history as the *Kyanyangire*. But the incident is popularly known as the *Nyangire* (I have refused) revolt.
2. Originally the district known as Bunyoro today was merely a province

of Kitara. With the decline of this empire, however, its kings retreated to the north of the lacustrine region and by the nineteenth century began to call what was left of Kitara, Bunyoro-Kitara. Gradually, and especially during the colonial period, it came to be known popularly as Bunyoro.

3. *Vide* T. O. Ranger, *Revolt in Southern Rhodesia 1896–97* (Lond., 1967); T. O. Ranger, "The Nineteenth Century in Southern Rhodesia", in Ranger (ed.), *Aspects of Central African History* (Lond., 1968).

4. *Vide* John Iliffe, "The Organisation of the Maji Maji Rebellion", *J.A.H.*, VIII (1967), pp. 495–512.

5. For the role of Baganda in British Administration of Uganda *Vide* A. D. Roberts, "The Sub-Imperialism of the Baganda", *J.A.H.*, III, 3 (1962), pp. 435–50.

6. Secretariat Minute Paper, Entebbe (henceforth S.M.P.) 267/1907, Mika Fataki to Wilson, 6 May 1907, No. 95; Tomkins to Entebbe, 18 April 1907, Minute No. 18.

7. He still lives near Masindi and is 102 years old.

8. K.H.T., No. 35, Isaya Bikundi (*Dairy of the Kyanyangire*).

9. *Vide* sources cited in T. O. Ranger, "Connections between 'Primary Resistance' Movements and Modern Mass Nationalism in East and Central Africa, Part I", *J.A.H.*, IX, 3 (1968), pp. 437–53.

10. *Vide* T. O. Ranger, "The Role of Ndebele and Shona Religious Authorities in the Rebellion of 1896 and 1897", in Eric Stokes and Richard Brown (eds.), *The Zambesian Past* (Manchester, 1966); *idem,* "African Reaction and Resistance to the Imposition of Colonial Rule in East and Central Africa" in L. H. Gann and P. Duignan (eds.), *History and Politics of Modern Imperialism in Africa*, cited by J Iliffe, *loc. cit.*

11. A. B. Davidson, "African Resistance and Rebellion against the Imposition of Colonial Rule", in T. O. Ranger (ed.), *Emerging Themes of African History* (E.A.P.H., 1965), p. 181.

12. For the study of this rising, *vide* J. De V. Allen, "The Kelantan Rising of 1915: Some Thoughts on the Concept of Resistance in British Malayan History", in *Journal of South East Asian History*, Vol. IX, No. 2, 1968.

13. A. B. Davidson, *loc. cit.*, p. 178.

14. *Vide* T. O. Ranger, "Connections Between Primary Resistance in East and Central Africa" (2 parts). *J.A.H.*, IX, 3 (1968), pp. 437–53; and *ibid.*, IX. 4 (1968), pp. 631–41.

15. For the *abarusura*, see Pt. I of the study from which this *chapter* comes.

16. *Vide* G. N. Uzoigwe, "Kabalega and the Making of a New Kitara", in *Tarikh*, Vol. 3, No. 2 (Longman, 1970). The author is also engaged in a full length study of the life and times of Kabalega entitled: *Kabalega of Kitara, 1850–1923: The Revolutionary Years* (East Africa Literature Bureau, forthcoming).

17. J. W. Nyakatura, *History of Bunyoro-Kitara*, edited with an introduction by G. N. Uzoigwe (Uganda Publishing House, 1970); K.H.T. No. 28, 12 May 1968; *Parl. Pap.*, Africa No. 7 (1895), *Papers re Uganda*, Colvile to Cracknell, 5 December 1895, No. 6.

18. *Ibid.*

19. *Parl. Pap.* No. 7 (1895), *Papers re Uganda*, Colvile to Kabalega, 5 December 1893.

20. Entebbe Secretariat Archives (henceforth E.S.A.), A4/2/1895, Cunningham to Entebbe, 17 July 1895; Ibid. Madocks to O. C. Troops, Bunyoro, 18 August 1895.

21. *Ibid.*, Madocks to O.C. Troops, Bunyoro, 18 August 1895; K.H.T., Nos. 21, 56 and 57.

22. K.H.T. No. 53, Interview with Sir Tito Winyi, 25 September 1969.

23. E.S.A. A4/10/1898, Fowler to Entebbe, 17 February 1898, No. 97.

24. For the way Baganda manipulated British Officials *vide* J. A. Rowe, *Lugard at Kampala* (Longman Uganda, 1969), Makerere History Paper No. 3; Michael Twaddle, "The Bakungu Chiefs of Buganda under British Colonial Rule, 1900–1930", *J.A.H.*, X, 2 (1969) pp. 309–22.

25. K.H.T., No. 55.

26. K.H.T., No. 17. Zakayo Jawe, Interview, 18 December 1968.

27. E.S.A. A4/8/1897, Thruston to Ternan, 21 June 1897, No. 320.

28. E.S.A. A4/17/1899, Evatt to Entebbe, 13 May 1899, No. 22.

29. E.S.A. A4/2/1895, Cunningham to Entebbe, 17 July 1895; *ibid.* Ternan to Entebbe, 26 October 1895; *ibid.* Madocks to O.C. Troops, Bunyoro, 18 August 1895, *ibid.* Same to Entebbe, 12 September 1895; E.S.A. A5/3/1897, Wilson to Dugmore, 13 December 1897; E.S.A. A5/6/1899, Ternan to Sub-Comm. Bunyoro, 6 September 1899; *vide* also E. C. Lanning, "Kikukuule: Guardian of Southeast Bunyoro". *Uganda Journal* 32, 2 (1968) pp. 119–47.

30. *Vide supra*, Part One.

31. K.H.T. No. 21.

32. *Vide supra*, Part One.

33. K.H.T., No. 21.

34. F. Jackson, *Early Days in East Africa* (Lond., 1930), p. 274.

35. Thomas and Rubie, *Enquiry into Land Tenure and the Kibanja System in Bunyoro, 1931* (Entebbe, 1932), p. 9.

36. K.H.T., No. 55; Uzoigwe, "Kabalega and the Making of a New Kitara", *loc. cit.*

37. E.S.A. A5/4/1898, Wilson to Fowler, 5 March 1898; E.S.A. A34/4/1898, Entebbe to Salisbury, 16 March 1898, No. 27.

38. Thomas and Rubie, *op. cit.*, p. 5.

39. E.S.A. A4/6/1896, Ternan to Berkeley, 27 November 1896, No. 224.

40. E.S.A. A4/2/1895, Ternan to Entebbe, 26 October 1895.

41. E.S.A. A4/8/1897, Thruston to Ternan, 30 June 1897, No. 312.

42. *Ibid.*

43. E.S.A. A12/1/1900–1901, "Report on Nyoro to Sir Henry Johnston", 1901.

44. K.H.T., Nos. 20(a), 20(b), 21, 22, 28, etc.; *vide* also, Nyakatura, *History of Bunyoro-Kitara, loc. cit.*

45. E.S.A. A33/2/1896, F.O. to Berkeley, 8 August 1896, No. 115 and Tel. No. 120. E.S.A. A4/7/1897, Forster to Ternan, 30 December 1896. E.S.A. A5/2/1896, Note by Berkeley, 19 November 1896.

46. E.S.A. A4/6/1896, Forster to Entebbe, 29 September 1896.

47. E.S.A. A5/5/1899, Trevor Ternan, "Outline of Method to be adopted in the Administration of Unyoro", 3 June 1899; E.S.A. A5/9/1900, Entebbe to Spire, 13 April 1900 (Draft); E.S.A. A4/27/1900, Spire to Entebbe, 28 November 1900, No. 5; S.M.P. 1019/1906, Entebbe to Hoima, 4 December 1906. *Vide* also Thomas and Rubie, *op. cit.* p. 9.

48. E.S.A. A5/8/1899, Ternan to Sub. Comm., Bunyoro, 13 October 1899, No. 42.

49. A. R. Dunbar, *A History of Bunyoro-Kitara* (O.U.P., 2nd ed., 1969), p. 106 citing Sir John Gray. *Vide* also Kenneth Ingham, *The Making of Modern Uganda* (Lond., 1958), pp. 68–9.

50. E.S.A. A4/22/1899, Evatt to Entebbe, 21 November 1899.
51. E.S.A. A12/5/1904, Fowler to Entebbe, 31 December 1904, No. 193; Banyoro informants are unanimous on this point. *Vide* also Thomas and Rubie, *op. cit.*, p. 9 and p. 11; James Miti, *History of Buganda* trans. by G. Rock (1938), MS. in Makerere Library, pp. 784–5.
52. E.S.A. A5/8/1899, Ternan to Sub. Comm., Bunyoro, 14 December 1899.
53. E.S.A. A5/9/1900, Entebbe to Owen, 8 March 1900.
54. *Ibid.* Entebbe to Spire, 13 April 1900 (Draft).
55. E.S.A. A12/5/1904, Fowler to Entebbe, 31 December 1904, No. 193.
56. E.S.A. A13/2/1904–06, Entebbe to Hoima, 22 February 1904.
57. E.S.A. A5/10/1900, George Wilson, Memo, 29 May 1900.
58. E.S.A. A12/1/1900–01, "Report on Unyoro", 1901.
59. See Uzoigwe, *Revolution and Revolt in Bunyoro-Kitara*, Pt. I.
60. E.S.A. A5/4/1898, Berkeley to Major Price, 4 September 1898; *vide* also E.S.A. A5/5/1899, Memo by Ternan, 3 June 1899, E.S.A. A5/6/1899, Memo by Ternan, 28 June 1899.
61. E.S.A. A4/17/1899, Evatt to Entebbe, 21 May 1899; E.S.A. A4/18/1899, same to same, Letter No. 43.
62. E.S.A. A4/8/1897, Thruston to Ternan, 30 June 1897, No. 312; *vide* also E.S.A. A12/2/1902, Tomkins to Entebbe, 16 June 1902.
63. E.S.A. A12/1/1900–01, "Report on Unyoro", 1901.
64. Princess Lucy Olive Katyanku and Semu Bulera, *Obwomezi Bw'Omukama Duhaga II* (Nairobi, 1950), p. 38.
65. Thomas and Rubie, *op. cit.*, p. 9.
66. *Ibid.*
67. Jemusi Miti, *op. cit.*, pp. 784–5.
68. *Ibid.*
69. *Ibid., vide* also E.S.A. A12/2/1902, S. Bagge, "Report on Unyoro District", 16 May 1902.
70. K.H.T., Nos. 21 and 58.
71. E.S.A. A4/27/1900, Spire to Entebbe, 28 March 1900, No. 5.
72. Katyanku and Bulera, *op. cit.*, pp. 37–9; Nyakatura, *op. cit.*
73. Molson, *Report of a Commission of Privy Counsellors on a Dispute between Buganda and Bunyoro* (H.M.S.O., Lond., 1962), Cmnd., 1717, p. 5.
74. S.M.P., 267/1907, Mika Fataki to Apolo Kagwa, 7 March 1907; *ibid.*, Tomkins to Entebbe, 15 April 1907; Bikundi, *"Diary"*, K.H.T. No. 35.
75. Miti, *op. cit.*, p. 787.
76. *Ibid. Vide* also Katyanku and Bulera, *op. cit.*, pp. 40–2.
77. Katyanku and Bulera, *loc. cit.*
78. E.S.A. A12/5/1904, Fowler to Entebbe, 31 December 1904, No. 193.
79. Dunbar, *op. cit.*, p. 108.
80. *Ibid.*
81. S.M.P., 267/1907, Cubitt to Entebbe, 21 February 1907, No. 1.
82. This was particularly true of the chiefs.
83. E.S.A. A12/3/1903. Memo by Tomkins, 26 May 1903; also *vide* S.M.P., 267/1907, Fataki to Kagwa, 7 March 1907.
84. E.S.A. A12/5/1904, George Wilson, Report, 10 March 1904.
85. K.H.T., No. 55.
86. The best account of the history of Kitara is J. Nyakatura, *op. cit.; vide* also Ruth Fisher, *Twilight Tales of the Black Baganda* (1911; 2nd ed., Frank Cass, London, 1970); J. Roscoe, *The Banyoro of Bakitara*

(C.U.P., 1923); A. R. Dunbar, *op cit.*; J. H. Beattie, *Bunyoro: An African Kingdom* (Lond., 1960); M. S. M. Kiwanuka, *Empire of Bunyoro-Kitara: Myth or Reality?* (Longman, 1968), Makerere History Paper No. 1; *idem,* "Bunyoro and the British: A Reappraisal of the Causes for the Decline and Fall of an African Kingdom", *J.A.H., loc. cit.; supra,* Part One.

87. S.M.P., 267/1907, Fataki to Kagwa, 7 March 1907.
88. *Ibid.*, Cubitt to Entebbe, 21 February 1907, No. 1.
89. *Ibid.*
90. K.H.T., No. 22, Interview, 22 May 1969.
91. S.M.P., 267/1907, F. M. Isemonger to Entebbe, 18 June 1907, No. 100; Miti, *op. cit.,* p. 795.
92. S.M.P., 1019/1906, Omukama and Chiefs to Entebbe, 14 September 1906, No. 1.
93. S.M.P., 1019/1906, Entebbe to Hoima, 1 November 1906, No. 6; *Ibid,* same to same, 4 December 1906, No. 7.
94. S.M.P., 207/1907, Cubitt to Entebbe, 21 February 1907, No. 1.
95. S.M.P., 2083, Eden to Entebbe, 9 August 1911, No. 1.
96. S.M.P., 1019/1906, Entebbe to Hoima, 1 March 1909.
97. K.H.T., Nos. 58, 73, 75, 35, etc.
98. E.S.A. A6/17/1904, Wilson to Entebbe, 28 May 1904; E.S.A. A12/5/1904, Pendergast to Entebbe, 2 January 1904, No. 4.
99. E.S.A. A6/17/1904, Wilson to Entebbe, 28 May 1904.
100. E.S.A. A12/5/1904, Wilson to Entebbe, 10 March 1904.
101. *Ibid.*
102. E.S.A. A6/17/1904, Wilson to Entebbe, 10 March 1904.
103. Katyanku and Bulera, *op. cit.,* p. 41.
104. E.S.A. A. A6/17/1904, Wilson to Entebbe, 10 March 1904.
105. S.M.P. 207/1907, Watson to Entebbe, 18 June 1907, No. 99.
106. *Ibid.*, Haddon, Report, 19 May 1907, No. 101.
107. *Idem.* Information supplied to Haddon by Mika Fataki, *saza* chief.
108. S.M.P., 267/1907, Isemonger to Entebbe, 18 June 1907, No. 100.
109. *Idem.*
110. S.M.P. 267/1907, Haddon, Report No. 101, 19 May 1907.
111. *Ibid.*, Isemonger to Entebbe, 8 June 1907, No. 100.
112. *Ibid.*, Grant to Entebbe, 27 May 1907, No. 1044.
113. Thomas and Rubie, *op. cit.,* p. 11.
114. K.H.T., No. 25.
115. E.S.A., A12/6/1905, Wilson to Entebbe, 22 August 1905; S.M.P. 1019/1906, same to same, 18 November 1905; *ibid.*, same to same, 21 October 1905, No. 38. S.M.P. 267/1907, Wilson to Tomkins, 1 April 1907.
116. E.S.A., A12/7/1905-06, List of Members of Bunyoro *Rukurato,* 8 February 1906; K.H.T., No. 25.
117. K.H.T., No. 21.
118. K.H.T., No. 25.
119. K.H.T., No. 20(a); Miti, *op. cit.,* p. 797.
120. Miti, *op. cit.,* pp. 795-800.
121. K.H.T., No. 22.
122. K.H.T., No. 21.
123. K.H.T., No. 21 and 22.
124. See Uzoigwe, *Revolution and Revolt in Bunyoro-Kitara,* pp. 43ff. for analysis of motives behind this diplomatic initiative.

125. S.M.P. 267/1907, Cubitt to Entebbe, 21 February 1907, No. 1; K.H.T., No. 21.
126. Miti, *op. cit.*, p. 795.
127. K.H.T., No. 22.
128. S.M.P. 267/1907, Cubitt to Entebbe, 21 February 1907, No. 1.
129. K.H.T., No. 35, Bikundi, "*Diary*".
130. S.M.P. 167/1907, Nakiwafu to Miti, 6 February 1907. Tel.; *ibid.*, Mudiru to same, 16 February 1907, Tel.; *ibid., Omukama* to same, 18 February 1907. Tel.
131. *Ibid.*, Miti to Mudiru, February (no date)
132. K.H.T., No. 35, Bikundi, "*Diary*".
133. Miti, *op. cit.*, p. 797.
134. S.M.P. 267/1907, Cubitt to Entebbe, 21 February 1907, No. 1.
135. K.H.T., No. 35, Bikundi, "*Diary*"; Miti, *op. cit.*
136. Miti, *op. cit.*, pp. 798–9.
137. S.M.P., 267/1907, Mika Fataki to Entebbe, 9 March 1907.
138. Mika Fataki was a Musoga who had come to Bunyoro as a boy, became naturalised, and rose to importance.
139. S.M.P., 267/1907, Fataki to Kagwa, 7 March 1907; *ibid.,* Leakey to Entebbe, 2 April 1907.
140. *Ibid.*, Entebbe to Hoima, 13 March 1907.
141. Miti, *op. cit.*, p. 799.
142. S.M.P. 267/1907, Wilson to Tomkins, 1 April 1907, No. 4.
143. K.H.T., No. 35.
144. S.M.P. 267/1907, Tomkins to Entebbe, 15 April 1907.
145. *Ibid.*
146. Miti, *op. cit.*, pp. 798–802.
147. S.M.P. 267/1907, P. Nsubuga Kadoma to Kagwa, 26 April 1907; *ibid.,* Leakey to Entebbe, 2 May 1907, No. 23.
148. *Ibid.,* Leakey to Wilson, 25 May 1907, No. 103.
149. *Ibid.* Entebbe to Hoima, 6 May 1907, No. 22.
150. Katyanku and Bulera, *op. cit.*, p. 42.
151. Miti, *op. cit.*
152. S.M.P. 267/1907, Eden to Entebbe, No. 26, Tel.; *ibid.,* same to same, No. 43, Tel.
153. Uganda became a Colony in 1906.
154. S.M.P., 267/1907, Eden to Entebbe, No. 37, February.
155. *Ibid.,* Entebbe to Hoima, 12 May 1907, No. 45, February; *ibid.,* same to same, No. 44.
156. *Ibid.,* Hoima to Entebbe, 17 May 1907, No. 85.
157. *Ibid.,* Entebbe to Hoima, 15 May 1907, No. 42.
158. *Ibid.,* same to same, 15 May 1907, No. 39.
159. *Ibid.,* Entebbe to *Omukama* and chiefs, 15 May 1907, No. 238, Tel.
160. *Ibid., Omukama* and chiefs to Entebbe, 15 May 1907, No. 37, Tel.
161. *Ibid.,* Hoima to Entebbe, 15 May 1907, No. 40, Tel.; *ibid.,* Entebbe to Jinja, 16 May 1907, No. 77; *ibid.,* Hoima to Entebbe, 16 May 1907. No. 40, Tel.
162. *Ibid.,* Hoima to Entebbe, 15 May 1907, No. 40, Tel.
163. *Ibid.,* same to same, 16 May 1907, No. 72 Tel.
164. *Ibid.,* same to same, 16 May 1907, No. 49.
165. *Ibid.,* Isemonger to Entebbe, 18 June 1907, No. 100.
166. *Ibid.,* Hoima to Entebbe, No. 45(a) Tel.
167. *Ibid.,* Entebbe to Hoima, 16 May 1907, No. 50, Tel.

168. *Ibid.*, Fisher to Eden, 16 May 1907, No. 69, Tel.

169. K.H.T., No. 25.

170. S.M.P. 267/1907, Isemonger to Entebbe, 18 June 1907, No. 100; K.H.T., No. 35.

171. Miti, *op. cit.*, p. 804.

172. K.H.T., No. 57. The chiefs were detained in Kampala and Kenya Mubende may have been chosen either out of ignorance as to where the chiefs were taken or for the purposes of rhyme.

173. S.M.P. 267/1907, Wilson to C.O., 18 May 1907, No. 94, Tel. No. 16; *ibid.*, Wilson to Bell c/o Chapelries (Lond.), 17 May 1907, No. 92; *ibid.*, same to same, No. 1.

174. *Ibid.*, Eden to Wilson, 20 May 1907, No. 102.

175. *Ibid.*, Entebbe to Hoima, 16 May 1907, No. 81.

176. *Ibid.*, Leakey to Wilson, 25 May 1907, No. 103.

177. K.H.T., No. 35.

178. Miti, *op. cit.*, pp. 806–7; K.H.T., No. 35.

179. Thomas and Rubie, *op. cit.*, p. 12.

180. *Vide*, for example, H. F. Morris, *A History of Ankole* (Kampala, 1962), pp. 39–45 for the way he handled the Galt affair.

181. *Vide* S.M.P., 2083, Eden to Entebbe, 9 August 1911, No. 1.

182. K.H.T., No. 58.

183. For changes in chieftainships and their personnel in Bunyoro *vide* S.M.P. 1251/09 Part I. It contains 234 minutes.

184. K.H.T., Nos. 58, 37 and 21. For Miti's own account of his stewardship in the period after 1907 *vide* Miti, *op. cit.; vide* also P. M. K. Lwanga.

185. S.M.P. 1313/1909, Knowles to Entebbe, 1 September 1909.

186. *Ibid.*, Entebbe to P.C. Buganda, 21 September 1909, No. 5; *ibid.*, Knowles to Entebbe, 10 October 1909, No. 6.

187. *Ibid.*, same to same, 10 October 1909, No. 6.

188. *Ibid.*, Regents, Buganda to P.C., Buganda, 29 October 1909; *ibid.*, *Katiikiro*, Buganda, to same, 12 February 1915.

189. For dispute over the "Lost Counties" *vide* Molson, *op. cit.;* A. D. Roberts, "The Lost Counties of Bunyoro", *Uganda Journal*, No. 26 (1962); and "The Petition of *Omukama* and his People to Queen", (Lond., n.d.).

190. S.M.P. 1019/1906, Grant to Entebbe, 9 March 1909.

191. *Ibid.*, *Omukama* and chiefs to Grant, 6 August 1910.

192. *Ibid.*, Knowles to Entebbe, 22 May 1911.

193. *Ibid.*, Eden to Entebbe, 26 September 1911.

194. S.M.P., 2083, Eden to Entebbe, 9 August 1911, No. 1.

195. *Ibid.*, Knowles to same, 19 August 1911, No. 3.

196. K.H.T., Nos. 21, 58, etc.

197. Dunbar, *op. cit.*, pp 111–12; *vide* also A. O. Richards (ed.), *East African Chiefs*, pp. 121–3; p. 365.

198. Beattie, *op. cit.*, p. 4.

199. For Nationalist politics in Uganda before Independence, *vide* F. B. Welbourn, *Religion and Politics in Uganda* 1952–62 (E.A.P.H., 1965).

200. See Uzoigwe, *Revolution and Revolt in Bunyoro-Kitara*, Pt. I; Uzoigwe, G. N., "Kabalega and the making of a new Kitara", *loc. cit.*

9

THE GIRIAMA WAR 1914–1915

A. J. Temu

The Giriama are the most populous of what have commonly come to be known as the Mijikenda people inhabiting the hinterland of the Kenya coast. According to the 1948 census, the total population of the Mijikenda amounted to 126,000 while the 1962 census recorded 400,000 out of a total population of 600,000 for the whole of the Kenya coast. In 1914, when the Giriama war broke out, the Giriama alone numbered 61,000 of whom 47,000 lived in Giriama district, 11,000 in Takaungu District, and 3,000 in the coast zone![1] Today most of them live in the Kilifi district and in Galana and the Sabaki river plains of the Malindi subdistrict. The other Mijikenda peoples are the Digo, the Chonyi, the Rabai, the Kauma, the Ribe, the Jibana, the Kambe and the Duruma.

The Giriama are believed to have migrated from Shungwaya, a place near what is now Fort Dumford in present day Somalia, as a result of Galla pressure early in the seventeenth century.[2] When they reached their present home, they built a fortress, *Kaya Giriama* (more commonly known as *Kaya Fungo*) on top of a hill in what is now Kilifi South; and here they lived cultivating grain and rearing sheep and goats. In the Kaya were buried the Giriama pots, the sacred political and religious symbols of authority.

The Giriama were divided into clans, each headed by a ruling council of elders known as the *kambi*. Senior elders of each clan formed the highest ruling *kambi* and resided in *Kaya Fungo* as the highest court of appeal for all social, political and civic matters. This *kambi* also dealt with criminal and civil matters which were referred to it either by the *kambi* of each clan or by individuals. Below the elders, who were known as *enyitsi*, were the prophets and prophetesses, the *wafisi*; they were the authority for all religious and ritual matters of the Giriama. As such, they were the only ones with power to administer oaths to individuals during criminal and civic trials and to the whole people during times of trouble. In addition, they officiated in

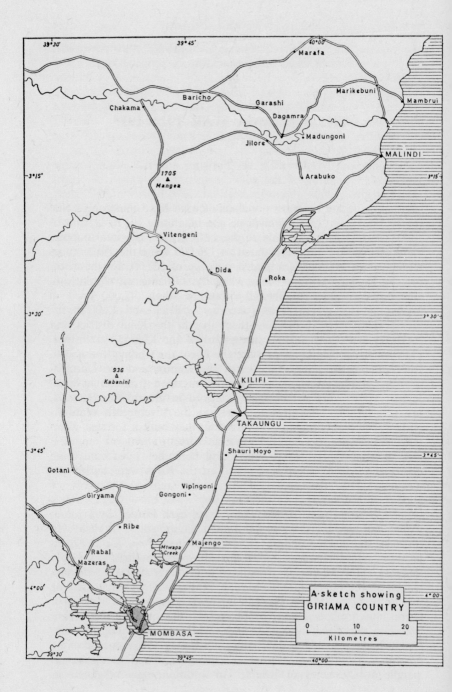

A·sketch showing
GIRIAMA COUNTRY

0   10   20
Kilometres

the practice of magic; and serving as *waganga*, they performed certain practices believed to be beneficial to the tribe. Such might include giving protection from personal danger, loss or illness; averting the envy, hatred and malignance of a rival and enemy; assuring good hunting, a bountiful crop or a journey without mishap; protecting house and gardens against robbers, etc.

The other grades can be distinguished in Giriama society: the *waya* whom William Hichens has called the ordinary fathers of the people and who formed the first ladder in the administrative and ritual structure of the tribe; and next to them the *nyeri*, the warriors. While the *nyeri* had already been initiated, their youth and lack of experience disqualified them from any of the grades above.

By the middle of the nineteenth century, the population of the Giriama had far outgrown the *kaya*; and in the latter half of the century they gradually expanded northwards and settled on both sides of the Sabaki river valley, bringing with them their political, social and religious structure. They continued to look upon *Kaya Fungo* as the centre of this structure, their capital and their ancestral home.

This paper attempts to analyse the background, rationale and reasons behind the Giriama War of 1914–15, its organisation and its effects on Giriama society. The main sources of information are, first, the colonial records of the war—mainly in the form of letters, reports and memoranda by the colonial administrators of the District and of the coast; there is a surprising abundance of such documents. Secondly, oral traditions, records of which were collected during the 1968–69 vacations, by two Giriama students —G. S. Ngombo and G. S. Mkangi. These students collected their information from different parts of the Giriama territory, thus covering a wide area.

According to Giriama tradition, war began on 4 August 1914 when the colonial administration dynamited *Kaya Fungo* and declared a state of emergency throughout Giriama country.[3] However, it was on 16 August that open hostilities broke out when a party of policemen in Northern Giriama was attacked with bows and arrows. And the following day saw the first casualty of the war, with the killing of a policeman, Kilunji wa Mutua, at Vitengeni. The Giriama followed this up with a heavy attack on the Government camp at Vitengeni, which they burnt; they then launched successive attacks on Mt. Mangea where the District Commissioner, Mr. Arthur Champion together with armed policemen had pitched camp to defend the government post and to launch expeditions against the Giriama. Another attack was made at Magarini Syndicate forcing the Manager to flee for refuge to Malindi. According to oral tradition, Champion and his party were besieged for several days and were saved from destruction only by the arrival of Charles Dundas on 24 August at the head of twenty-five armed policemen, and by a detachment of the King's African Rifles under the command of Major G. M. P. Hawthorn with Captains Reynolds and Carew. However, Major Hawthorn and a large column of the K.A.R. detachment were withdrawn immediately for service in German East Africa.[4] Continuing the offensive, the Giriama cut the Malindi-Lamu telegraph line at Fundi Issa and removed 600 yards of wire; they burnt shops, mission stations and the villages of all converts and of all headmen loyal to the British government. Mzee Tsumu, a loyal government headman, was attacked and barely managed to flee before his village was burnt down. At about the same time at Jilore Captain Carew with a motley of men faced a Giriama force about a thousand strong. The official record of this engagement lists thirty Giriama killed and two soldiers wounded.[5]

Hitherto fighting had been confined to the north but towards the end of the month, it spread to the south as well.[6] On 8 September, a government headman, Fundo wa Nyama, was killed; and immediately thereafter attacks were made on mission stations at Kaloleni and Baya Nyundo. As in northern Giriama, the houses and villages of missionaries, converts and government headmen were burnt, and European missionaries were driven out and forced to take refuge at Rabai or on the coast. It can therefore be said that by the beginning of the second week of September, fighting had broken out throughout northern and southern Giriama. Meanwhile the K.A.R., now reinforced, had returned to engage in what the District Commissioner of the District called "the little war".[7]

Fighting continued throughout the rest of the year. The Giriama adopted hit-and-run tactics—tactics that today have proved to be successful for the Vietnamese, although with modern weapons rather than bows and arrows. The thick bush into which they could vanish and reappear at will, gave them great advantage over their adversaries and lent itself perfectly to the guerilla style warfare which they adopted. The K.A.R. responded with horrible cruelty, much as the Americans are doing in Vietnam. All diaries of the operation which were available to the writer reveal an orgy of burning and destruction of Giriama houses and villages and capture of stock. To cite only a few examples, Lt. A. A. Hughes recorded:

(2) have been going on these lines, i.e. burning villages and trying to capture stock.

(3) 14th instant (September) I burnt villages close to the Mission.

(4) 15th instant (September) moved at 2.00 p.m. and burnt 5 villages. On the return journey we were followed by a number of natives—some of these were killed before they left us.[8]

And again Lt. P. F. Carew recorded:

September 26, 220 sheep and goats captured.

September 27, patrolled as far as North Mombasa, burnt all villages in the locality, captured 30 sheep and goats, 1 native killed.

September 29 all villages round Mugadini burnt, also villages at Shankadulu. 145 sheep and goats captured.

1st October. Finished burning villages at Bungale. Some natives had fled . . . 1 native killed, 200 sheep and goats near Gurashi and a large amount of property hidden in the bush found and destroyed.[9]

But the government frankly admitted that in such a situation, it at no time inflicted defeat on the Giriama, and its forces were reduced to resisting opposition and destroying villages. The Giriama therefore remained on the offensive throughout. "Thus the expeditions", wrote Charles Dundas, "by no means impressed upon the natives the ability of the government to force them to submission; they submitted rather by consent because they were tired of living in the bush than from fear of their lives and property."[10]

Nevertheless, the British had to negotiate for peace right in the middle of the war because the K.A.R. had to be withdrawn for service in German East Africa.[11] Anxious to prevent further destruction of their property and capture of their stock, the Giriama also agreed to come to peace terms. Official records, however, say that the Giriama elders had approached a certain Fathili Bin Omari, an Arab, to intercede between them and the British.[12]

On 4 October, terms for peace were arranged and the Giriama were forced to

(a)   pay a fine of 100,000 rupees or goats at 3 rupees each.

(b)   raise 100 labourers.

(c)   surrender all bows and arrows.

(d)   move from the northern bank of the Sabaki river.

(e)   surrender all heads of the tribe and leaders of the rebellion. (Report on the Giriama Rising Annual Reports, Nyika District 1914/1915).

All these conditions were to be fulfilled within ten days.[13]

Since they had not been defeated, the Giriama seemed to have bluffed the British when they came to the conference table. For they almost immediately resumed the offensive and refused to pay the reparations.[14] They had most probably believed that once they had agreed to peace, the British would withdraw their forces from their land and thus give them time to recoup for further engagements. Had the governor of Kenya not instructed the K.A.R. to remain in Giriama land to finish the war and to ensure that the reparations were paid, the war would most probably have taken a different turn.

Once the Giriama opened the offensive, they again adopted their hit-and-run tactics. The K.A.R. could do no more than burn a large number of villages and houses and capture some stock. Two expeditions were launched against the Giriama, and a heavy attack was made on the Mt. Mangea area; over 3,000 goats and 100 head of cattle were captured. By the end of the year active fighting had at last ended, and the government could now embark on the second stage of the war—that is, to collect the reparations and to ensure the evacuation of the northern side of the Sabaki river. This phase took the government about eleven months.[15] Commenting on the situation, F. Trail wrote:

> I regard the spirit of active opposition among the Giriama as completely crushed now.... They cannot be described as a loyal or amenable tribe now but remembering their characteristics and their past behaviour this can hardly be expected. A certain amount of passive resistance must always be looked for from them....[16]

At this stage it may be useful to analyse the background of the war, starting with the earliest contacts between the Giriama and the British in the 1840s. The C.M.S. established its first mission station at Rabai in 1843 though effective missionary work on the coast and particularly among the Giriama did not begin before 1873 when the slave trade was abolished and a settlement of freed slaves was established at Freretown. Between 1873 and 1904, it was mainly from the two stations. Freretown and Rabai that missionaries, particularly African catechists, made frequent tours of the Giriama country. In 1890 a mission station was established at Jilore in Northern Giriama. By 1904 a handful of mission stations were sprinkled throughout the Giriama country. The catechists and missionaries spoke about the kingdom of heaven with earnestness and attentiveness, but Giriama stuck stubbornly to their traditional religion, which they considered superior to Christianity. By 1914, therefore, there were hardly any Giriama Christians. In 1911, the Assistant District Officer of Rabai, Kenneth MacDougall, thus summed up the effect of the missionary contact with the Mijikenda people:

> The native Christian adherents number 700-800 but only a minority of these are Rabai and Wagiryama; the majority are resident aliens;

many of the Watoro have gathered round the mission and settled by William Jones, who was at one time in charge of Rabai, with what is admitted by the missionaries to have been great excess of zeal, since most of them were very far from having attained the knowledge of religious matters and the manner of life befitting Christians.[17]

It is no wonder then that the Missionary contact produced no results. Nor could it be argued that the British East African Company, 1888–95, had any effect on the Giriama, much less on their polity and customs. For one thing, the company was primarily interested in making profit, and therefore was not prepared to do anything that would interfere with this goal. Certainly the coast offered no opportunities for immediate profit and if in the coastal stations the Company's rule was only nominal, then it must have been nil in the interior where the Giriama and the rest of the Mijikenda peoples lived. Sir Arthur Hardinge, Commissioner of the newly created East African Protectorate in 1895, when he took over found that:

Neither at Gazi or Takaungu were the chiefs troubled by the presence of resident English officers. The District Superintendent at Vanga and Malindi paid short visits to Mbaruk of Gazi and Salim of Takaungu but they found it necessary to ignore or affect not to be aware of very many offences of both chiefs against the laws such as the slave dealings of the one and the imposition of taxes on British Indian subjects by the other.[18]

When Kenya became the East African Protectorate in July 1895, the officials of the Company formed the protectorate's new administration, and the Company's stations on the coast as elsewhere became centres of this new administration. Almost immediately the new administration was faced with the Mazrui rebellion, in which the Mazrui family tried in vain to re-assert its independence. This issue was finally settled on the battlefield, with the defeat of the Mazrui family in 1896. Up until the second decade of the 1900s the British were content to use the existing Arab/Swahili administrative and judicial structure and to pacify the coast through reconciliation as much as possible. As with their predecessor, the Company, the protectorate officials did little to bring the adjacent peoples within effective control outside the stations. Indeed, as part of the reconciliation policy, Hardinge had, in 1896, suggested the creation of a middle cadre of Arab/ Swahili civil servants as an intermediary stratum between the British and the African population; the Germans were successful with this policy in the then Tanganyika after the Abushiri rebellion of 1888–89. The British, however, became too concerned with expanding into the interior and with opening of the highlands to white settlement, to bother about either establishing effective control and implementing the new policy, or developing the economic resources of the coast and its immediate hinterland. Emphasis at once shifted from the coast to the highlands. By the turn of the century this emphasis on the highlands became permanent, when the colonial administration decided to open them to white settlement and to develop Kenya through the agency of white settlers. In 1901–02 the first settlers arrived, and in 1907 the capital was moved from Mombasa to Nairobi. Henceforth Mombasa and its hinterland were relegated to a secondary position.

Even the Arabs, whose long rule on the coast was replaced by that of the British in 1886, were neither able to conquer the Giriama nor to enslave them. The vast area in which the Giriama moved certainly contributed towards their independence. But perhaps more important was the fact that they were sufficiently independent in agriculture and in trade. For the most part they grew enough food and they had always surplus grain for sale. From the beginning they established trade with the Arabs and the Swahili to whom they sold grain, ivory and slaves. They raided the slaves far into the interior and at Kitui they were known as the manufacturers of arrow poison and as slave dealers.[19]

By the end of the nineteenth century this trade had assumed great importance and as a result a number of Giriama had become wealthy and influential men. One such man was Ngonyo wa Mwavuo of Marafa. When the British arrived on the Giriama scene and began to look for influential men to appoint as chiefs and headmen, they appointed him a headman of Marafa. Elsewhere in Kenya, the British did likewise, in their desperate search for men of influence to act as their agents.[20] Regarding Ngonyo, Kandenga wa Mwachinga says:

> Ngonyo was a very rich man. He was made a chief by the British because he was wealthy and influential. He earned his riches by selling slaves, ivory and cattle. He was connected with the Arabs in trade. Ngonyo was liked by people in our country. He went into hiding when we were fighting the British and people said they would not stop fighting before Ngonyo told them to.[21]

And again Mzee Hinzano says:

> My uncle (Ngonyo) was a very interesting man. Upon my grandfather's death he (Ngonyo) inherited all the wealth and became the most wealthy man in the whole of Marafa region. He became an elder and spokesman of all elders in the region. Whenever there was a *shauri* to be settled with the *serikali* (government) Ngonyo was

called. But he was so independent that he always quarrelled with Champion.[22]

Unlike the Rabai and the Digo, their kindred, who entered the cash economy of the coast and worked on the coastal estates and plantations as labourers, the Giriama were sufficiently independent economically to resist successfully integration into the coastal communities. So too did they remain culturally independent. Unlike the Rabai, the Ribe and the Digo, they became neither Muslims nor Christians, considering their own religion and ritual superior to Islam and Christianity. From the beginning the Digo and the Rabai became Muslims, while the Ribe became Christians.[23] C. W. Hobley, who was District Commissioner on the coast commented:

> They have, in the old days, been the despair of both Arabs and Portuguese, neither of whom appeared to be able to control them effectively and, considering the long period they have been in contact with the Arab civilisation, the comparatively slight extent to which they have been affected by it is remarkable. . . . The persistent manner in which they have generally clung to their ancient beliefs, although they have for several hundred years been in contact with Islam and, during the last fifty years, with Christianity, is a remarkable fact and evidence of either their tenacity of character or the unreceptive nature of their minds.[24]

Unlike the other peoples of Kenya, such as the Maasai, Gusii, Nandi, Kikuyu etc, who by around 1910 had been conquered and their land alienated the Giriama did not begin to feel the impact and pressure of the colonial administration until August 1912, when Arthur Champion was appointed Assistant District Commissioner over their country. The following year he established his headquarters at Mr. Mangea. Hitherto the country had felt little control from Malindi, Takaungu or Rabai, where administrative posts had been established in the 1890s. In 1914, Charles Dundas remarked that the "arrangement left a major part of the country unadministered, and the Giriama scarcely ever saw the same officer twice; they came to regard the government as a side-issue to the mission work, only less permanent than this."[25] And the Annual Report for the Giriama district in 1913 commented:

> Up to now, except for a superficial collection of taxes once a year or so the existence of the tribe has with one or two exceptions been ignored by the Malindi authorities and as this policy of inaction has gone for many years, it will naturally take some time for the people to realise that we have come to stay.[26]

Clearly the first task of the newly appointed officer was to bring the Giriama under effective control—which control, according to the British officials, was about ten years behind that of a well administered district up country. Such control was primarily intended to facilitate the systematic collection of taxes which, it was believed, would in turn force the Africans out of their homes and into the labour market. Such was certainly the rationale behind effective administration and particularly the institution of African taxation. In 1901 all Africans were required to pay a tax of two rupees per hut. On the coast labour was required for public works at Mombasa and elsewhere and for private plantations at Sokoke Rubber Plantations and Magarini Sydicate. Towards the end of the year these plantations were facing ruin due to shortage of labour. The Giriama, however, refused to enter the labour market and to pay tax. The bulk of the labour was provided by the Kikuyu and the Akamba. Even when, at about the same time, severe drought had resulted in crop failure, food shortages in Giriama, and government had followed this up with a vigorous collection of tax, the Giriama preferred raising loans from Indian and Arab moneylenders to offering their labour for sale. Some of the hard-pressed ones chose to work for short terms with their neighbours as this arrangement left them free to leave when rain fell or when they obtained relief somewhere, whereas working on European farms required them to stay for long stretches of time, often under cruel discipline.[27]

Taxation as a means of inducing the Giriama and indeed many of the African peoples in Kenya to enter the labour market proved a failure, even after hut tax had been increased from two to three rupees and an equivalent poll tax instituted. Save during times of famine, the Giriama produced enough grain and had enough stock to sell to get money for taxes. In 1890 W. W. A. Fitzgerald, travelling through Giriama country, found that the Giriama had large flocks of goats. Regarding grain he wrote:

> The produce grown by Wa-Giryama appeared to be maize—very extensively grown both for food and for sale. Castor oil grown in patches among the maize. Beans and pulse were also a great deal grown. Tobacco grew and were largely cultivated.[28]

In 1909–10 the district's total export of maize through Malindi alone amounted to 33,102 cwt and was valued at 84,174 rupees. The following year it rose to 49,472 cwt and realised 135,462 rupees.[29] Considering the fact that a substantial amount was exported through Takaungu and Mtanganyiko as well and that Indian middlemen extracted large sums of money which are not included in the above figures, one cannot overemphasise the strength of the Giriama as an agricultural people. They did not, therefore, have to labour on European farms to earn money to pay tax. Moreover, the sort of labour they were required to do, such as working for Europeans, carrying loads and digging roads, ran counter to their traditional norms of what kind of work was acceptable for females and what kind for males. Giriama porters were often derided as *Watumwa wa Serikali* (slaves of the government). Having no alternative therefore, the government invariably had to resort to collect tax and to recruit labour from the Giriama, even for public works. Regarding recruitment of labour, particularly for private plantations on the coast, the government ordered the District Officer and headmen to encourage the Giriama to come out to work. The enthusiastic Assistant District Commissioner and some headmen interpreted it as a licence to obtain forced labour from the Giriama. In 1913 the government answered the settlers' demands for the reduction of the African reserve as a method of forcing them to enter the labour market by ordering the Giriama to move from the fertile northern bank of the Sabaki river into one reserve in the arid southern part.[30]

The Giriama opposed the establishment of the colonial adminitration and the collection of taxation, and refused to enter the colonial labour market from the onset. Immediately upon taking up residence in Giriama, Arthur Champion began to mark out the boundaries of different headmen and to take a census of the tribe as a first step towards establishing control and facilitating the collection of tax. But the Giriama of various locations opposed him. They also refused to help with the construction of the road he had begun.[31]

Giriama opposition to these pressures took different forms: One of the commonest was for the adult male population to take to the bush upon the arrival of hut-counters and the administrative officer. Another was for various villages or groups of individuals, particularly the *nyeri*, (warriors), to attack tax collectors, hut-counters and loyal government headmen. Yet another form was refusal to pay tax or to turn up for labour on public works. When the government stepped up its measures and began to burn down houses they found deserted, to fine and imprison defaulters and to capture goats, the Giriama retaliated with collective attacks on the officials.[32] During the second half of 1913, the Giriama became violently opposed to the government.

On his visit to the Sabaki river valley to collect tax between August and October 1913, Champion faced persistent opposition from the Giriama. For example, all the inhabitants of Chakama location joined together and attacked him and his police when he visited their location; the rising was quelled only after a large contingent of police had been called in from Malindi. At Njalo location the elders refused to meet him; at Karwitu he found the villages empty; while at Mlango Baya in Merikani location he met a party of warriors armed with bows and arrows.[33] He reported:

> My orders and those of the government headmen have been totally disregarded.... The elders say they are helpless and are completely boycotted by the Wawiryama who have broken into little knots and hold their shauris in the bush. Acts of violence are more and more frequent and there is no law in the land.[34]

The following month the Provincial Commissioner paid a visit to the District with a large police force, to demonstrate to the recalcitrant Giriama the might of the colonial administration. He held a large meeting at Biria in the Sabaki river valley where opposition was more violent than elsewhere. Biria seems to have been the focal point for the Giriama of the north, and elders of the section certainly seem to have regarded it as their capital, albeit not a *kaya*. At the meeting the District Commissioner announced that the Giriama living on the north side of the river would move to the south, where together with those of the south, they would be concentrated into one reserve. Meanwhile he ordered them to move their *kaya* from *Kaya Fungo* and to build a new one at Vitengeni. He imposed a collective fine of 1,500 rupees on all of them and ordered them to take another oath which would undo the effects of the earlier one—that is, bind the Giriama into obeying and accepting the colonial administration instead of their own traditional government with its centre at *Kaya Fungo*.

Although the administration maintained that they wanted the *kaya* to be at a more central point, the move was certainly aimed at destroying it as a centre of authority to which all Giriama owed unquestioned loyalty. One administrator had called it a hot-bed of sedition, only to emphasise its hold on the Giriama and the hatred with which it was looked upon by the colonial administration.

The government certainly believed that once these measures were carried out, the Giriama would accept colonial control and its policies. The government felt that moving the Giriama from the northern bank of the Sabaki would serve as a severe punishment, particularly to those of the northern bank who had been most active in opposing the colonial administration. Champion maintained that the loss of the fertile plain would be long-lasting punishment to those who had been most unmanageable. Also the government hoped to open to European occupation the area so vacated. This was the most fertile area of all the Giriama country and it would, so the government argued, attract settlers. And since it was adjacent to what would be an overcrowded reserve, there would not be the problem of labour since Africans would flow out of it to work on the settlers plantations. In a way the government was responding to the demand which the settlers had put forward in 1907, for the reduction of the reserves as a means of solving the shortage of labour even though the Labour Commission of 1912–13 had refrained from recommending such a step.[35]

In March 1914 the Giriama took an oath at Vitengeni, as required by the administration. Two British officials took part in the ceremony. Obviously such an oath could neither undo the effects of the earlier one nor bind the Giriama to accept the colonial administration. In the first place it was not conducted with the sanction of the *kaya* elders and it was not even taken at the *Kaya*. Clearly the Giriama agreed to taking it in order to mislead the administration. The District Commissioner, F. Traill, painted a magnificent picture of the affair. He wrote: "Its performance must have been, at the time, a source of no small amusement and gratification to those who took part in it."[36]

By the beginning of August 1914 the Giriama had begun neither to move from the north nor to build the new *kaya*. The government had fixed the end of August as the deadline for the move to be completed, but the Giriama elders had taken an oath to fight to the death rather than to move. Regarding the transfer of the *Kaya*, the Giriama saw it as a serious affront to their traditions and, in general, as an attempt by the government to destroy the very basis and meaning of their existence as one people. They maintained that they could not move the *Kaya* and still remain one. Nor was it possible to move the medicines buried underneath the *Kaya*. Moreover, they maintained that if anyone did so he would die.[37] They therefore refused to move the *Kaya*. The administration dynamited it on 4 August 1914, and declared a state of emergency over the land.[38]

The dynamiting of the *Kaya*, the central shrine of the Giriama, brought things to a climax. So strained were the relations between the Giriama and their oppressors that war could not be averted. "The Giriama retaliated", says Edwin Mwinga, "by burning down government chiefs' homes beginning with Mzee Toya's home in Manyimbo. This was the beginning of the war."[39] In 1952, similar overt actions by the colonial administration in Kenya —the declaration of emergency and the indiscriminate arrest of Kikuyu leaders—precipitated the Mau Mau war.[40]

It is interesting to note that the Giriama war broke out at the same time as Britain declared war on Germany; their colonies were drawn into World War I, and Africans of Kenya fought against those of what was the then German East Africa. Soon after the declaration of war by Britain, the protectorate forces were haphazardly mobilised for engagement against German East Africa. By 16 August the German forces in East Africa had indeed occupied Taveta on the terminal head of the Voi-Taveta railroad and had also attempted to occupy a section of the Uganda-Mombasa railroad from the Taveta base. British officials resident in Giriama, Malindi and Takaungu widely believed that the Giriama war was precipitated by the activities of German agents—ivory traders and the families of the late Mazrui whom the Germans sent out to incite the people to rise against the British. Charles Dundas averred that the rising would not have taken place were it not for the fact that "they were told we were at war and that we were powerless to retaliate."[41]

To be sure there had been contact with the Giriama and the Germans through the ivory trade. When the British established themselves in Giriama country they prohibited the trade; nevertheless it continued. Bought from the Giriama by the Baluchi middlemen, ivory was smuggled into German East Africa and sold to Indian agents. There is no doubt that the abolition of the ivory trade adversely affected the wealth of influential people like Ngonyo wa Mwavuo and other middlemen, and gave them cause to hate the British. Indeed it is most probable that Ngonyo joined and led the people of Marafa region against the British in an attempt to recapture the wealth he had lost as a result of the abolition of the ivory trade. But perhaps an even more important reason he decided to fight the British was in order to prevent the loss of his land and the ruin which would have resulted from the government's announced decision to take over the land in northern Giriama. Thus he did not need any outside encouragement in order to rise against the British at this time.

During the Mbaruk rebellion of 1895–96, the families of the late Mazrui had sought and had been granted political asylum in German East Africa, having fled across the border rather than face capture and possible execution at the hands of the British after their defeat. They too would have tried to enlist the support of the Kenya coastal peoples on the side of the Germans against the British. However, according to available evidence including evidence from the Giriama themselves, they rose against the British in an attempt to maintain their independence. The Giriama would have taken up arms against the British even if World War I had not broken out. Both Ngombo and Mkangi have recently discovered that the Giriama had no prior knowledge of the outbreak of the World War I. Summarising the reports of the persons he interviewed, Mkangi says:

> They rose against the oppressive government; they could not have cared less whether that government was made up of British or of German people.[42]

And Mzee Hinzano of Mandunguni said:

> We did not rise in order to help the Germans, or because any of them would come to help us. We had nothing to do with them. (Our) leaders did not realise that our war would help the Germans indirectly. We rose because of intolerable conditions.[43]

Clearly so widespread an opposition, culminating in war from so decentralised a people as the Giriama, could not have come about without careful prior planning and organisation. Moreover it required a high degree of political and social commitment to the cause. Behind this opposition were the activities of a prophetess Me Katilili wa Menza, and her chief assistant and son-in-law, Wanje wa Mwadarikola.[44] About June/July 1913 the *Kaya* elders convened a large meeting of *Kaya Fungo*, which was attended by Me Katilili and Wanje. At this meeting an oath was taken binding the Giriama to the use of violence against the British and all Europeans. "The Giriama", writes Ngombo, "swore to fight the British and their mouthpieces—the chiefs and loyal government headmen—so that there would be no more taxation and no conscription into private farms."[45] And Arthur Champion excitedly wrote:

> the women swore the *kiraho cha* Mukush Kush (oath of Mukush Kush) which was to kill all government headmen who held councils or arrested anyone, all who attended their councils, all who became government police, karani (clerks) etc. all who went to read and write at the mission schools, all who assisted government in any capacity and even went so far as to include those who wore clothes of European make or any clothes other than the greased calico.[46]

At the same meeting traditional elders of each clan were reconfirmed undoubtedly by the priests, and set against those the government had appointed. Henceforth the Giriama would take orders from them rather than from those of the government.

When the meeting at *Kaya Fungo* broke up all the witchdoctors carried medicines in calabashes and sprinkled them in waterholes and rivers all over the Giriama territory to kill those who would dare break the oath. Me Katilili and Wanje toured the country and held meetings at which the same oath was taken. "At Bamba and Biria, about fifty miles from *Kaya Fungo*", writes Ngombo, "an oath-taking ceremony was held. The oath was taken against the British, their clerks, chiefs, headmen and askaris. All these were to die."[47] In his tour of inspection through Giriamaland, Arthur Champion found that Me Katilili and Wanje had preceded him at each place he stopped, and had preached the same gospel of violence and administered the oath. What shocked him the more was the large following they had attracted. When he reached Gurashi, at the northern end of the territory, he found them: he arrested them and held them until November, when they were sent off to detention at Kisii.[48] About the activities of Me Katilili he wrote:

> The curious soon came to see what was happening and in no time the witch Me Katilili got their attention and told them that the government had received each 1000/- to sell young men to the Europeans over the sea and never see their native land again. That now was the time to resist, for the European had no power. They had taken the power of judgement from the very headmen they had appointed and given it back to the Wagiryama at their old kambi. That now they must use their kambi and throw off the yoke of the government headmen and leave to rot the council houses they had built which stunk with the authority of the hated government. They would go into the bush and hold their little kambis as of yore without interference. They would bind themselves under sacred oath and spell to carry out this plan and all who dared thwart them or disobey them would fall under the spell and die.[49]

Colonial pressures apart, for these have been amply discussed, the *kiraho* and the activities of Me Katilili and her chief male assistant seem to have been central organisation and the mobilisation of the Giriama for the war. In southern Tanzania, it was through the maji ideology that the leaders of the Maji Maji war against the Germans (1905–07) were able to unite and to secure the highest degree of mass commitment from a greatly diversified people spread out over a vast region. Once unity and commitment had been achieved, fighting was conducted in clans as had been done in the past. Prophetic religious leaders were therefore crucial in the war, for they administered the *maji* and spread the war over the whole region.[50]

In the Nandi rebellion of 1893–1906, Arap Ngeny tells us that the Nandi were organised against the British around a central figure, the *orkoiyot* Koitlel Arab Samoei.[51] In 1890 the Nandi had clubbed to death the previous *orkoiyot*, Kimnyole Arab Turukat, for having failed to prevent the epidemics which struck the land and caused great loss of life both to stock and to humans. The

Nandi also held him responsible for the defeat of Nandi raiding units. Traditionally it was the role of the *orkoiyot* to avert disaster —a role more socio-religious than politico-military. Soon after the *orkoiyot* murder, they were struck by famine and threatened by European invasion both of which threatened to destroy them as the murdered *orkoiyot* had predicted. Hence, in order to prevent disaster and degeneration, the Nandi once more rallied around the *orkoiyot*, Samoei starting in the late 1890s, although for a time after they had murdered Kimnyole they lost faith in the efficacy of the *orkoiyot*. Thus united they resisted the British. The British were able to defeat them only after shooting down Samoei in 1905.

The Giriama seem to have used two organisational principles. Unlike the peoples of southern mainland Tanzania, the Giriama had one central place, *Kaya Fungo*, to which they owed unquestioned loyalty and from which all Giriama derived religious and political powers. The *kambi* at *Kaya Fungo*, it has already been shown, served as the highest court of appeal for all matters political, social and religious. When required the elders of the *Kaya*, the *wafisi*, administered *viraho* (sing-*kiraho*) (oaths of ordeal) which bound the Giriama to carry out whatever the elders required of them. In the nineteenth century, when the Giriama fought with the Kwavi and the Galla, the elders administered *kiraho* by which the *nyeri* and the rest committed themselves to fight. Likewise, when the British invaded Giriama and began to impose a variety of pressures on the whole society, the elders of the *kaya* in 1913 administered the *kiraho* through which the Giriama committed themselves to fight against the British. It seems clear that the Giriama used the *Kaya* as a symbol of unity and the oath as an ideology of mass commitment to the war. Most probably as the Giriama expanded into the north in the late 1890s and many clans were separated from the *Kaya* by long distances, the role of the *Kaya* as a centre of unity for all of the Giriama may have been diminished. Certainly all the day-to-day business of the clans was carried out in the clans. But more important perhaps was the fact that more and more power centred around them and they were more often called upon to deal with matters which would otherwise have been dealt with by the *Kaya* elders.

By the first decade of the twentieth century, Biria in northern Giriama seems to have developed as a semi-capital for the Giriama of the north. It is most likely therefore that at this time the elders of the *Kaya* certainly relied more and more on the oath to evoke obedience to them and their orders as well as to secure the highest form of commitment to whatever cause they espoused. From oral research it does not appear that there was any conflict or internal division between the elders and the rest of the Giriama, especially the young men, which would have required a more rigorous application of *viraho*. Certainly an alliance between the *enyitsi* and *wafisi* to reinforce their power over the rest of the society was not necessary, since the two grades were the same, and the *enyitsi* qualified for their particular function as well as that of the *wafisi*.

Oaths have been used in African societies at all times. During the Mau Mau war, oaths came to play an equally important role in that the Kikuyu used them as symbols of unity and ideological commitment to the Mau Mau war.[52] But oaths were used in African societies not only for this end; in Giriama society they were used as a last resort in settling disputes. For example, if one party to a dispute felt that the decision of the elders was not fair, often he would ask to take an oath as a last appeal. If the appellant was guilty he would die, so the Giriama believed.

As mentioned earlier, apart from the *kiraho* itself, the prophetess Me Katilili wa Menza and her son-in-law, Wanje wa Mwadorikola, served as powerful agents in spreading the gospel of violence between the British and in mobilising the Giriama for the war. There are very few studies of the role of prophetesses and women in general in African resistance against the colonial powers. Mr. Brazier tells us that Muhumusa, the widow of a Rwanda king who had died in 1895, fled to Ukinga in what came to be western Uganda and used the *nyabangi* cult, which was dominant in Kiga society to enrol followers to help her seize her late husband's throne for her son. Having failed to do so, she attempted to seize territory in Ukinga and so clashed with British authorities there. Although she was captured in 1911, the influence of the *nyabangi* cult continued till 1919 when her successor was killed in a battle against the British.[53] Gilbert Gwassa has told the writer that women serving as *waganga* played a leading role in the Maji Maji war, in that before soldiers finally went into combat they jumped over well known women *waganga*. This act of jumping over the women *waganga* was symbolically supposed to weaken their adversaries.[54]

Me Katilili certainly played a similar but much more important role in the Giriama war, as she gave additional force to the oath in spreading the gospel of violence. Her power and influence could be linked to the Giriama past, thus giving her recognition of a special kind. Before her there had been another prophetess, Mipoho. Mipoho had foretold that white men would come to occupy their country and would bring misfortune and misery to the land. She sank into the earth at Kaloleni, but before doing so she promised to return to get rid of the white man and to restore fortune and prosperity. The Giriama people therefore saw the emergence of Me Katilili as the second coming of Mipoho. Her emergence coincided with the misery and misfortune which were brought about by the British. It is therefore easy to see why the Giriama readily accepted her message of violence.

According to the official report, the Giriama generally fulfilled the most important of the peace terms—that is, the payment of the fine, the supplying of the labourers and the evacuation of the northern bank of the Sabaki by the end of 1915. No sooner had they finished evacuating the north than a number of them began to to move back again. When he visited the area in 1917 C. W. Hobley, the Provincial Commissioner was alarmed at the large number of Giriama he found there. He proposed that the territory from which they had been required to move should be opened to private capitalists, and called on the colonial administration to ensure that the Giriama were cleared out of the area.[55] However, the governor of the time felt that the area did belong to the Giriama from earliest days and therefore ruled against his provincial commissioner's advice, allowing the Giriama to re-occupy the area. In reversing the decision of his predecessor he said:

> I cannot say that this modification of our previous decision will greatly assist the administration of the district for the moment but I feel it will at any rate make for more content amongst the members of the tribe and that in course of time the memory of the past will be distinct. I am firmly of the opinion that if injustice has been done it is our duty to repair it and in the absence of any definite evidence we should allow matters to remain as they were especially in view of the fact that the native will be enabled to grow crops and find sustenance.[56]

Certainly this is one of the most important concessions that the Giriama obtained from the colonial administration as a result of the war. Nothing like this happened with the other peoples of Kenya. The Nandi, for example, were not given back the land along the railway line which was alienated from them after the 1906 uprising. One might argue that it was easy to return the northern bank of the Sabaki river to the Giriama because, unlike the land of the Nandi, it was not coveted by settlers. Hobley, however, had insisted that it would be valuable if it were opened to private capitalists.

In addition government had as early as 1914 sanctioned the appropriation of the war fine for the development of the country; and even with regard to the deportation of some of the leaders, the District Commissioner did in 1915 recommend against their deportation, maintaining that as the rising was a concerted action of all, it would be unfair to single out a few unlucky people and leave the rest.[57]

Clearly the Giriama were able to obtain a number of concessions from the colonial administration because they had fought against them. It cannot be argued because they used violence in resisting the colonial administration, they hopelessly lost everything. As Professor Ranger writes: "Not all resistors were doomed to total failure and crushing suppression. Some of them preserved liberties, wrung concessions or preserved pride." Like the Basuto, the Shona and the Ndebele, the Giriama surprisingly wrung considerable concessions from the colonial administration. Perhaps of equal importance was the fact that by taking up arms against the British, they demonstrated how even the smallest of the peoples of East Africa valued their independence.

NOTES

1. Arthur Champion, M., *The Agiryama of Kenya* (ed. by John Middleton, 1967), VII.
2. B. G. McIntosh, "The Eastern Bantu Peoples" in B. A. Ogot and J. A. Kieran (eds.), *Zamani—A survey of East African History* (1968), 202, 268.
3. Interview with Edwin Mwinga s/o Gunga s/o Baya in G. S. Ngombo, *A Report on an Oral Research on the Giriama Rising of 1914*, 13.
   (This is a report that combines all the information and records as collected by G. S. Ngombo. It will be hereafter referred to as Ngombo, A Report on Oral Research on the Giriama War 1914.)
4. G. M. P. Hawthorn to C.S.O., Troops in British East Africa and Uganda 31 August 1914. Coast Province (C.P.), Kenya National Archives (KNA.), 5/336.
5. *Ibid.*
6. Henry Lascalles to Acting Provincial Commissioner, Mombasa. 27 August 1914. C.P. 5/336. KNA.
7. Charles Dundas, *African Crossroads* (1955), 72.
8. A. A. Hughes to O.C. Giriama Patrol 18 September 1914. C.P. 5/336. KNA.
9. P. F. Carew to O.C. Giriama Troops, 11 October 1914. C.P. 5/336. KNA.
10. Charles Dundas, "Report on the Giriama Rising" 31 October 1914.
11. Hemsted to Chief Secretary, 30 September 1914. C.P. 5/336 KNA.
12. District Commissioner Malindi to O.C. Troops, Marafa, 22 September 1914. C.P. 5/336. KNA.
13. Annual Report, Nyika District 1914/1915. C.P. 16/49. KNA.
14. *Ibid.*
15. F. Trail to P.C., 31 October 1915. C.P. 5/336.
16. *Ibid.*
17. Kilifi Political Records, Vol. 1, 1913. KNA. Rabai Sub-District C.P. 16/49. KNA.

THE GIRIAMA WAR, 1914–1915   235

18. Hardinge to Salisbury, 12 April 1896. FO. 107/51. Public Records Office, London.
19. Charles Dundas, *African Crossroads*, 73.
20. D. A. Low, "British East Africa: The Establishment of British Rule, 1894–1914" in Vincent Harlow, E. A. Chilver and Alison Smith (eds.), *History of East Africa*, 11 (1965), p. 33–4.
21. G. S. Mkangi, Interview with Kandege wa Mwachinga, 19 May 1969.
22. G. S. Mkangi, Interview with Mzee David Mwanyoya Kalipodo Hinzano, 10 May 1969.
23. For this see David Parkin's recent article in *Africa*, VI, XI, No. 3.
24. C. W. Hobley, *Kenya From Chartered Company to Crown Colony*, (1929; 2nd ed., Frank Cass, London, 1970) 164–5.
25. Charles Dundas, "Report on the Giriama Rising" C.P. 5/336. KNA.
26. Political Report, Giriama District, 1913, DC/MAL/2/1. KNA.
27. F. Bretts to P.C., 14 September 1912. 4/308. KNA. And Arthur Champion, "Memorandum on Labour Supply and the Wagiryama", 12 December 1914. C.P. 5/336. KNA.
28. W. W. A. FitzGerald, *Travels in the Coastland of British East Africa, Zanzibar and Pemba* (1898), 136.
29. Annual Report, Malindi District, 1914–15. C.P. 16/49. KNA.
30. *Ibid.*
31. Arthur Champion, "Report on Inspection of Tour of Northern Giriama", 28 October 1914. D.C. KLF/3/3. KNA.
32. *Ibid.*
33. *Ibid.*
34. *Ibid.*
35. W. McGregor Ross, *Kenya from Within* (1927; reprinted Frank Cass, London, 1968), 92, 98.
36. Annual Report, Nyika District, 1914–15. C.P. 16/49. KNA.
37. Ngombo, "Report on Oral Research on the Giriama Rising", *loc. cit.*
38. Annual Report, Rabai District, 1914–15. 16/49. KNA.
39. Interview with Edwin Mwinga in Ngombo, "Report on Oral Research on the Giriama Rising", 13.
40. Oginga Odinga, *Not Yet Uhuru* (1967), 113.
41. Charles Dundas, "Report on the Giriama Rising". C.P. 5/336, KNA.
42. G. C. Mkangi, Giriama Oral Research, Report on the 1914 Rising.
43. G. C. Mkangi, Interview with Mzee Hinzano. May 10, 1969.
44. Ngombo, "Report on the Oral Research on Giriama Rising." Mkangi, Giriama Oral Research, Report on the Giriama Rising 1914. Arthur Champion, see note 31 above.
45. Ngombo, "Report on Oral Research on the Giriama Rising," *op. cit.*
46. Arthur Champion to P.C., 18 October 1914. C.P. 5/336. KNA.
47. Ngombo, "Report on the Giriama Rising", *op. cit.*
48. D.C., South Kavirondo, to P.C., Mombasa, 18 December 1913. C.P. 9/403. KNA.
49. Arthur Champion, "Report of Inspection Tour of Northern Giriama", *op. cit.*
50. Information from Gilbert Gwassa, University of Dar es Salaam. See also John Iliffe, *The Organisation of Maji Maji.*
51. See Samuel arap Ngeny, "Nandi Resistance to the establishment of British Administration 1883–1906" in B. A. Ogot, (ed.), *Hadith 11* (1970), 104–26.

52. For a general discussion see Carl Roseberg and John Nottingham, *The Myth of Mau Mau* (1966), 243–248.

53. F. S. Brazier, "The Nyabingi Cult: Religion and Political Scale in Kigezi 1900–1930", Paper for University of East Africa Social Science Conference, January 1968.

54. Information from Gilbert Gwassa, University of Dar es Salaam.

55. C. W. Hobley to Chief Secretary, Nairobi, 26 November 1971. Malindi Political Record book. KNA.

56. C. C. Bowring to the Secretary of State for Colonies, 3 January 1918, Malindi Political Record Book, KNA.

57. Trail to P.C. 30 August 1914. C.P. 5/336. KNA.

58. T. O. Ranger, "Connections between 'Primary Resistance' Movements and Mass Nationalism in East and Central Africa, *The Journal of African History*, Vol. IX, No. 3 (1968).

10

MBIRU
POPULAR PROTEST IN COLONIAL TANZANIA
1944–1947*

Isaria N. Kimambo

INTRODUCTION

In January 1945 the Pare of north-eastern Tanzania rose in a
mass protest against a graduated local rate imposed by the colonial
government and known by the name *mbiru*. The imposition of
this tax had first been suggested by the central government, and it
had been paid by the Pare for two years before the protest began.
Then, as if something had suddenly happened, in January 1945
crowds of people began to march to Same, the district headquarters,
in protest against this tax.

In order to picture the magnitude of the whole operation, the
geography of the Pare country has to be borne in mind. The nine
chiefdoms are scattered over a range of mountains with broken
plateaux, isolated ridges and slopes which make communication
very difficult. Thus the idea of people marching all of a sudden
from all the chiefdoms and from villages far away from the
district headquarters on the plains does suggest a unique co-
ordination in this period. Within only two days thousands of demonstrators had assembled at Same. Certainly this was a dramatic
incident which forms an important chapter in the history of the
Pare people.

Traditionally, *mbiru* referred to the system of tribute used on the
Pare Mountains in the pre-colonial period. In the period preceding
the imposition of *mbiru*, there was a popular cry for the establishment of schools so that Pare children could get education. Super-
ficially, therefore, the imposition of *mbiru* seemed to be a response
to this need to raise more funds by remoulding local government
on the traditional fund-raising pattern in order to make it popular.
Yet since the inception of colonial rule on the Pare Mountains in

*First published by the East African Publishing House and reprinted
by permission.

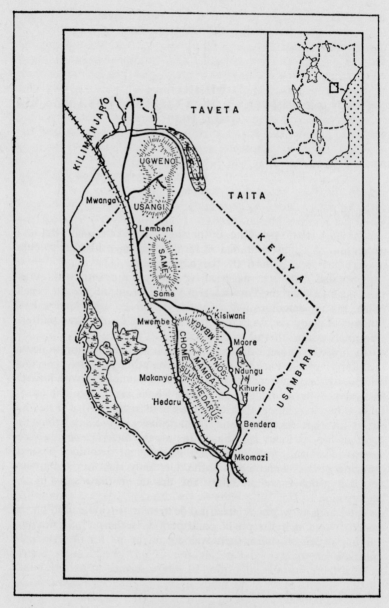

PARE DISTRICT

the 1890s, a flat rate of taxation had been imposed and people had to pay their tax whether they liked it or not. We can therefore assume that in the 1940s the Pare were not revolting against the idea of paying tax. It is true that the traditional tribute (*mbiru*) was graduated and was assessed every year just before harvest, so that every person could pay according to what his own plot was likely to produce. But in the 1940s the traditional system had been suppressed for more than forty years. As an unwillingly colonised people, the Pare naturally viewed *mbiru* as a new innovation aimed at squeezing more and more money from their meagre resources.

It has already been noted that the suggestion to impose graduated tax on the Pare Mountains came as a response to a widely felt need for an education system supported by the local government. Thus *mbiru* may appear to have been an attempt by both the central and local governments to meet a modern need (colonial education) through traditional methods. Yet the protest itself may appear to have been both "anti-modernist" as well as "anti-traditionalist". On the one hand, it tried to block the means of raising funds, the need for which had long been felt. On the other hand, it also demonstrated a revolt against an authority system fundamental for the functioning of the pre-colonial Pare society. One explanation for this contradiction can be seen in the broader issues involved in the resistance movements of this period. Clearly the Pare were protesting as much against oppressive colonial policy as against underdevelopment. But the other explanation can be obtained by studying the organisation of the movement itself. It has been assumed that the pre-mass party "tribal" revolts against colonial policies were spontaneous and unorganised. The main aim of this study is to illustrate how the *mbiru* protest reveals a clear combination of traditional methods of resistance against oppressive rulers with modern techniques learned from the colonial period to achieve specific ends. The use of petitions and literate leaders in achieving these ends makes the contradiction even more obvious. Yet it is hoped that the pattern of organisation which emerges from this study will contribute something to the understanding of the other protest movement of this period about which so little is known.

THE IMPOSITION OF *mbiru* AND ITS IMPLICATIONS

On 22 April 1941, the colonial government (through the Provincial Commissioner, Tanga) suggested to the Pare Chiefs, who constituted the Pare Native Authority, to consider instituting a graduated local rate patterned after the traditional *mbiru* in order to raise funds for the Native Treasury. On the government side, it was understood that the graduated rate would be imposed in lieu of the normal tax rebate system which had operated before, and that it was to be introduced in the Pare district only as an experimental measure. Oddly enough it is also stated that the Pare were chosen for this experiment because they had shown themselves to be progressive. It is true that North Pare at least had shown great interest in road projects on a self-help basis since the 1920s. But in general economic development, the Pare district during this period could hardly compare with either of its neighbours, Kilimanjaro or Usambara.

At any rate, the Pare chiefs, after expressing some doubt, accepted the proposal and made it their own. They petitioned the government in the following terms:

> It appears to us, the Chiefs and our advisers, that though we pay tax each year this payment is not in accordance with native custom so we thought we should bring the matter to the notice of the government in the hope that our suggestions will be considered.[1]

In short, the chiefs proposed to use the traditional *mbiru* system which divided people into fourteen different classes, each with a name and a defined amount of *mbiru*, which could then be translated into its money value. The classification, although it later proved too complicated to implement, appeared so impressive that the Provincial Commissioner, Tanga, W. O. Bonavia, praised the ability of the chiefs:

> I think it argues well for the success of the proposals that the Chiefs have been able to compile such a good memorandum embodying their views. I can see in the memorandum some of the views and suggestions of the District Commissioner and some of my own. But I am entirely satisfied that the Chiefs have given full consideration to their suggestions and thoroughly understand the implications of them.[2]

Traditionally there were office-holders whose duty it was to go through the fields and assess the amount of *mbiru* to be paid by each individual family. In their proposal, the chiefs suggested that the *mnjama* (traditionally the chief minister) in each chiefdom should, on behalf of the chief, go to each village and preside over a meeting of elders who would constitute a committee of assessment. They would assess each in the traditional grain units known as *vivale*, according to their knowledge of each individual. A person who thought the assessment was not fair would have permission to appeal to the chief, then to the Pare Tribal Council and finally to the District Commissioner whose decision would be final.

The introduction of this new rate was delayed in 1942 because of a bad harvest caused by drought. It was introduced in 1943, however, and the rate was paid for two years before the issues involved were clearly grasped. Trouble came into the open in the middle of 1944 when in every part of the country people began to question the principles on which this new tax was based. In the eyes of colonial administrators this appeared to be a sudden reaction to what seemed to have been accepted by the Pare people. An explanation was sought and found. The two years' experience had indicated that there was no fair way of assessing the rate to be paid by everybody. The government had therefore thought that the system could be improved by recording the property owned by each Pare so that assessment could be based in a more realistic value. This property recording was to have taken place in 1944 before the assessment for the 1945 rate was carried out. It was therefore assumed that the reaction in 1944 came solely from this new proposal. However, it appears that this is an oversimplified answer. Why did trouble continue even after the plan of recording property had been dropped? The fact is that in the first two assessments, the Pare people were studying the system carefully. Most of them had grown up during the colonial period and therefore knew nothing about *mbiru*. Most Wapare interviewed by this writer claim that they had never accepted the tax; they were arguing against it in village meetings as well as appealing to their chiefs. Unfortunately the chiefs were inflexible in this matter because they said it was *"amri ya Bwana D.C."* or *"amri ya serikali"*, i.e. it was the order of the government.

To make things worse, the assessment in the two years was allowed to fluctuate without proper explanation. In the first assessment, people had been assessed and their rates had been published, but they were then ordered to pay an additional fifty cents because it was discovered that the money to be raised from the new tax might be less than the previous tax rebate. In the second year the assessment was fifty cents more in each unit because the previous additional levy was to be absorbed in the assessment process. In the eyes of the Pare, the 1944 rate seemed to be fifty cents higher than that of the year before, and none of them could be convinced that he had become slightly wealthier. Various other irregularities in individual assessments were clearly pointed out and the system of appeals seldom allowed any reversal. By the time the property recording proposal was given in 1944 the Pare had come to believe that justice in this matter was unlikely to come either from their chiefs or their District Commissioner. They therefore started to send a series of petitions to the Chief Secretary to the Government in Dar es Salaam.

The District Commissioner, T. E. Pringle, and the Provincial Commissioner, W. O. Bonavia, were convinced that the heart of the trouble was a failure of authority on the part of the Pare chiefs. This is only partially true. It is true that the chiefs had authority to levy *mbiru* in the pre-colonial period. But it is also true that they had not done so since colonial rule was imposed on their country. Even the part of *mbiru* paid for rain-making had been suppressed. Therefore the authority of chiefs in levying *mbiru* had been destroyed by colonialism long before 1944. Yet all the Pare people still looked upon their chiefs as protectors of their societies and believed that even if the colonialists had bad intentions their chiefs would not let them down. Unfortunately the *mbiru* issue revealed that the chiefs were no longer playing this important function of protecting their people.

Traditionally the Pare were protected from the tyranny of their chiefs in two ways. First, if there was enough consensus about the wrong-doings of the chief the council could depose him. This kind of action happened very rarely. Secondly, if only a small group of people thought that they were oppressed, they could move away and go to a place where they were better protected. This is what happened in the nineteenth century when there was a general state of insecurity and thus people with well defined stockaded villages received refugees from the more insecure areas.

The problem for the Pare in the 1940s was that although they had seen the weakness of their own rulers, they were also convinced that there was somebody else who was corrupting them. In their meetings and petitions to Dar es Salaam, the Pare emphasised that all the bad things which were taking place in their country had been instigated by the District Commissioner. In the 1880s, just before the arrival of the colonialists, the Pare had experienced a similar kind of problem. For more than a decade before that period, Shambaa colonies had been established on the Pare plains along the caravan routes. Since these Shambaa had controlled the trade with the coast as middlemen, their success had depended on the co-operation they had been able to get from Pare rulers. Thus, as the Shambaa traders (colonists) had become more successful in their trade in slaves and ivory, the Pare people had felt that they were being oppressed by their leaders because of the evil brought by these foreigners. In one chiefdom, Mbaga, there had been a violent reaction against the Shambaa colonists who were identified with this "corrupting evil". Led by two of their men. Semboja and Mavura, the people of Mbaga had laid siege to the stockaded

village of the Shambaa traders at Kisiwani for six days until other
colonies had sent reinforcements to save it. This is one example of
a popular demonstration against oppressors, in this case the
Shambaa colonists, but resembling very much the demonstration
against the colonial district administration at Same in 1945.[3]

MOBILIZATION

The organisation against *mbiru* seems to have started in each
chiefdom. Outspoken leaders began to meet and discuss the behaviour of their rulers. In this way informal committees were founded
in many villages. Yet isolated committees of this kind could make
very little impact. Co-ordination was needed. It was achieved by
each village committee sending individuals to find out what others
were doing. As a result of these consultations a point was reached
where chiefdom meetings were openly held under such names as
"*mkutano wa raia wa Usangi*" (a meeting of the citizens of Usangi)
or "*mkutano wa raia wa Ugweno*". In these meetings they wrote
down their complaints and elected delegates to present their case
to the Pare Tribal Council in Same. At this stage mission teachers
played an important part. But it was wrong, as the government was
to discover later, to think that the mission teachers were the only
leaders. In fact, when the mission teachers saw that their activities
were endangering their own position as well as that of their
missions they retired, and leadership later lay heavily in the hands
of cultivators and traders, although many of these had obtained
education in mission schools.

The co-ordinated nature of these activities became clear when
the delegates of "chiefdom citizens" began to converge at Same
from all nine chiefdoms on 14 July 1944. They decided to meet
and put together their complaints in a petition to be put before
the Pare Tribal Council with one voice. The petition was signed
by twenty-one delegates, of whom only three were mission teachers.
The main objections raised in the petition were:

1. Assessment of *mbiru* was nothing but guesswork.
2. The tax was creating hatred simply because it was based on principles whose fairness Africans had not learned.
3. Counting property would increase the problems because there
   would be no co-operation from the people. No good Mpare would
   tell what he owned, therefore it would be a waste of time and
   hindrance to progress.
4. Graduated tax was foreign and un-African: "*Itatutoa katika haki
   za uenyeji na kututia katika haki za wageni kama Wahindi na
   Waarabu*".[4]

When no satisfactory answer was given by the Council (which mainly consisted of the chiefs), the delegates concluded that Same was the centre of the whole wickedness. They departed with a determination to appeal directly to Dar es Salaam.

The pattern of protest which seems to have emerged between July and December 1944 was that of bombarding the Chief Secretary to the Government in Dar es Salaam with letters from two groups, "Citizens of North Pare" and "Citizens of South Pare". Each letter was usually signed on behalf of these groups by three persons. Some of the letters seem to have been acknowledged by the P.C. in Tanga rather than by the Chief Secretary himself. In some instances the P.C., W. O. Bonavia, questioned the right of these people to write on behalf of the "citizens" while the chiefs were the only recognised authority in Upare. He nevertheless took the trouble to explain how useful and progressive the graduated tax was and that the Government was wholly behind it.

It is interesting to speculate what might have happened if the Chief Secretary, F. A. Montague, had responded to these appeals at this stage. To the Pare it appeared that the Provincial and District administrators were blocking their cry for justice from Dar es Salaam. Consequently, on 20 November another delegation from most Pare chiefdoms met at Same. They asked to see the District Commissioner, T. E. Pringle, who willingly gave them audience. They told him two important things. First, they said they were dissatisfied with the way the P.C. had handled their complaints. Secondly, therefore, they were handing to him their petition with a request that he forward it directly to the Chief Secretary. This petition was signed by eight persons coming from seven chiefdoms.

Meanwhile the Government was beginning to take a serious view of the petitions and the organisation behind them. On 14 November, the P.C. had visited Same and had asked all the people with complaints against *mbiru* to come and talk about them openly. Those who had signed letters to the Chief Secretary are said to have received special invitations, but none of them appeared. Instead on 20 November they went to see the D.C. Same to present the petition already mentioned. It was at this stage that the view that mission teachers were acting as ringleaders was becoming strong in the minds of the colonial administrators. Writing to the Chief Secretary, Bonavia said, "It is significant that these persons ... are Lutheran Mission teachers now paid from Government Funds".[5] At the same time, Pringle sought the help of the Government Inspector of Schools at Old Moshi to intervene. As a result quick action was taken. Seven teachers (six Lutheran and one Roman Catholic) were called to Same to meet the Inspector on 22

December 1944. They were warned that strong disciplinary action would be taken against them. In the same period the Chief Secretary, Mr. Montague, personally wrote to answer the petitioners that the Government had nothing to add to what the P.C. and D.C. had explained to them. This ended the period of written petitions. The people were completely convinced that their case had never been well explained to the "just" government in Dar es Salaam. So a new strategy was needed to make themselves heard. At the same time the colonial government was considering ways of prosecuting the so-called ringleaders. They thought they had effectively silenced the teachers and therefore could easily deal with the rest.

DEMONSTRATION AT SAME

In the eyes of colonial administrators, the most dramatic happening in this protest was the appearance of crowds of Pare demonstrators at Same on 4 January 1945. Offical reports differ greatly about the estimated size of the crowd. The highest figure given by the Director of Intelligence and Security is between 2,000 and 3,000 demonstrators. The Pare, however, estimate the crowd to have been between 10,000 and 12,000 and believe that this huge crowd had assembled by 6 January 1945. Possibly the actual number of demonstrators may lie somewhere between the official and the people's estimate

It is important to note the two main principles revealed by this demonstration. First of all the demonstration revealed to the colonial administration the popular support behind the opposition to *mbiru*. At first it was thought that the problem was caused by a few agitators (mainly mission teachers). But now even after silencing the mission teachers, the outburst could not be prevented. Other types of "ringleaders" had now to be sought. The second point, which is more important, was the realisation by the colonial administrators that they had over-rated the power of the chiefs. The D.C., Pringle, remarked:

A bad feature of the demonstration is the distrust they show to their chiefs. They regarded the local rate laws as having been introduced by their chiefs at my instigation and for some reason try to persuade themselves that it had nothing to do with the government for whom they expressed loyalty and obedience.[6]

It is possible to misunderstand this anti-chief feeling among the Pare. Pringle's remark shows clearly that he had come to realise the feelings of the people. They were against the submission of their chiefs to the "European corruption" rather than to their position as traditional leaders. This view is well supported by the loyalty displayed by the Pare to their chiefs after the *mbiru* question had been solved. It is therefore clear that this anti-chief feeling was different from the anti-chief movements which appeared in many parts of Tanzania in the 1950s with the explicit aim of replacing traditional chieftainship with different types of local government.

The demonstration had been sparked off by an incident which took place in Mamba, a chiefdom in South Pare. On 4 January 1945, the chief of the area, Daudi Sekimang'a, held a tax meeting during which his people were to turn up and pay the controversial tax. Some people attended, but did not pay. As a result he arrested 44 of them and put them on a lorry to be carried to Same for labour conscription because they had not paid their *mbiru*. About 300 other men who had attended the meeting started marching to Same to demonstrate their solidarity with the arrested men. Soon the network of informal consultations started to spread the news and two days later a huge crowd from all parts of Upare had assembled at Same. At this stage one may wonder what these people hoped to achieve. From their action in Same we can clearly see the demonstration was against the oppression of the district government. They hoped that they would obtain redress from Dar es Salaam, not from the governor, but from somebody they believed was always concerned with "Native Affairs", i.e. the Chief Secretary. We can briefly trace the drama through the following stages: (1) the organisation at Same, (2) reaction in the villages, (3) the legal fight, and (4) the last demonstration.

1. THE ORGANISATION AT SAME

The organisation at Same had two sides closely related. One side was that of the control of the huge crowd so as to produce an orderly demonstration which would make the central government more sympathetic. The second was that of opening a dialogue and negotiations directly with the Chief Secretary in Dar es Salaam. Obviously, the first one was the more difficult. Once thousands of people assembled in one spot a lot of things can happen. If violence broke out the whole plan of the Pare would have been ruined. After all, it was still during the Second World War and there would be justification to use not only the police force but also army units in order to break up the demonstration under emergency measures. Fortunately the demonstrators had superb leadership under a man called Paulo Mashambo who was able to control the crowd in such a way that colonial administrators could not but admire his talents.

A retired Seventh Day Adventist preacher, Paulo Mashambo called himself a peasant. His qualities of leadership had never been noticed until the crowd assembled at Same. His thin piercing voice, assisted by the traditional blowing of a horn, were enough to hold the whole crowd together. This was how he describes the situation:

> Actually what I was trying to do was to maintain peace. A disorder could start very easily at a place with so many people. . . . Whenever I sounded my horn . . . everybody sat down and I talked to them. I told them to pray every morning, love one another, maintain peace and return anything they find not belonging to them.[7]

What the crowd seems to have loved him for most was his spirit of defiance hidden in his demand for loyalty to the colonial government. Whenever a European came to speak to the crowd in Swahili, Paulo would translate the orders into Chasu (the Pare language), in most cases distorting the orders. Since many of the audience could speak Swahili as well, they would follow Mashambo's version with enthusiasm. For example, if the D.C. said, "You must now go home". Mashambo's translation would be, "You must now sit down". Eventually the D.C. came to realise this and in one of his reports he says:

> He persistently misrepresents what has been said by the Government Officer, and openly does not trust Government Officers. He uses his power of oratory continually to prevent the crowd from disintegrating.

Nevertheless, Mashambo was admired for his power to hold the people together for the long period of about two months during which the first demonstration lasted. Supplies of food were brought from the villages every day. Women and children, as well as the demonstrators themselves, played their part in carrying the supplies. As a rule very few women went to Same. They were supposed to remain in the villages taking care of the children and preparing food supplies for the menfolk. At Same food was shared among the group so that no demonstrator went hungry even if food from his village was late in arriving. Sanitary conditions were strictly observed as, through Mashambo's supervision, the demonstrators were willing to dig latrines without compulsion.

The second side of organisation at Same consisted of communication with Dar es Salaam. The demonstration had been necessary because petitions had achieved no results. Immediately after assembling at Same, leaders from each chiefdom met and decided to send a delegation to Dar es Salaam to talk directly to the Chief Secretary. Before the delegation left, Mashambo sent the following telegram on 20 January 1945:

> Pare citizens ask you to attend them on graduated local rate. On 4/1/45 we all arrived here but Political gave us insufficient judgement. Provincer left on 12/1/45. Till now we are here ... with twelve shillings each awaiting for justified judgement from the Government. We experience great difficulties.[9]

The message reveals two things. First, that the crowd had been addressed by both the District Commissioner, Pringle, and the Provincial Commissioner, Bonavia, and both had failed to satisfy the demands of the people. Secondly, the people were ready to pay a flat tax of twelve shillings which was two shillings higher than the flat tax they paid before the controversy. This means that the Pare had been convinced that there was a need to pay more tax in order to have more development in their area, but they were completely against the new method of raising it.

Meanwhile the deputation arrived in Dar es Salaam and met the Chief Secretary, probably on 4 or 5 February 1945. The representations of the deputation in Dar es Salaam show that the members had been well prepared. They thanked the Government for the opportunity to be heard and then they came to their arguments against *mbiru*. They insisted that they favoured a flat local rate for raising money for the local treasury but they were opposed to the *mbiru* system which was confusing the people. They enumerated the various reasons (which they had been giving since the controversy began). It seems that the Chief Secretary attempted to use this chance to break the demonstration by telling the deputation to tell the people at Same to go to their homes and then the government would consider their request. Such a message did nothing more than enrage the crowd further. But, while their leaders were still trying to keep the crowd under control, thanks to Mashambo's dynamism, a new deputation of four "cultivators", in which only one of the members of the first was included, was again sent. It arrived in Dar es Salaam on 20 February 1945 and its main strategy now was to convince the Chief Secretary that the only way of satisfying the crowd at Same and making them go home was for him to visit Same and speak to them personally. Just four days earlier, the Governor, W. E. Jackson, on his way from Arusha had stopped at Same and had addressed the demonstrators telling them to expect no change from the Government's decision and that they should obey and go home. The people wanted to see the Chief Secretary himself, for they believed he was the one who should have sympathy with "native problems". Unfortunately, while the second deputation was in Dar es Salaam, news of violence in the villages reached there; they gave up their attempt to persuade the Chief Secretary to go to Same, and rushed back to find out what had happened.

2. REACTION IN THE VILLAGES

There is no doubt that the removal of thousands of men to Same strained village life in Upare. Normal peasant activity was at a standstill. Women and children had to be mobilised in supplying the daily necessities of the demonstrators. Later, even in the legal struggle, the pleading for measures against famine in Upare was loud. But the immediate effect was a social one. Certainly the womenfolk could not feel comfortable in the village alone while their husbands were parading at Same day and night without any foreseeable results. Who was the cause of all this? The answer was clear in their minds: the chiefs and the District Commissioner. It would have been better if these "evil" people had been kept away from the enraged women. But as things went, the government had decided to collect evidence about ringleaders in order to take some legal action against them. This evidence could be obtained only if they went into the villages and planned strategy with the chiefs. Unfortunately on 20 February 1945 this exercise started in Usangi where the women were most articulate and most of their husbands had been away. This was the source of the violence which disrupted the negotiations of the second Pare deputation in Dar es Salaam.

The D.C., with Chief Kibacha and the Inspector of Police, had gone to Usangi to talk to Chief Sabuni about the ringleaders from Usangi. The Inspector of Police explained what happened:

> On leaving Usangi with Political today 20 February 1945 car was mobbed and stoned by women. We got away but Chief Kibacha and [a] Sub-Inspector of Police were cut off. Owing to lack of news from them it appears that they and Chief Sabuni are in danger and must be released. Have arranged with Moshi to send twenty men tonight with Harvey-Webb (Inspector of Police). Will proceed to Usangi to relieve the Chiefs.[10]

Actually the incident seems to have been much more harmless than that. On hearing that the D.C. was at the chiefdom head-quarters with Chief Sabuni of Usangi, the women gathered and waited—singing "traditional" Christian and Muslim songs—seeking a verbal explanation from him about what their husbands were doing in Same. It is estimated that there were about 500 women.

When the D.C. with his party left the "Baraza" they tried to leave without talking to the women. The D.C. pushed through in panic, leaving the two chiefs and the Sub-Inspector of Police behind. Chief Kibacha together wth the Sub-Inspector eventually walked through the bush and farms and got to Kisangiro safely. But for Chief Sabuni, who was in his own chiefdom, things were more worrying.

He remained in the "Baraza" until at night the police force arrived and escorted him to his house. Chief Minja of Ugweno, who was sick in the Usangi hospital, was so afraid that he too asked to be taken back home to Ugweno. Things seemed to be quiet. The women went away, but meanwhile they were planning further action. They were angry that the leaders could not spare a minute to talk to them while they were in their homes alone missing their husbands.

The following morning the women reassembled quickly. They went to Chief Sabuni's house. They surrounded the house and kept on singing. On 22 February, thirty police were sent to Usangi to free Sabuni from his own house. They dispersed the unarmed women in such a way that several complaints were to be sent to Dar es Salaam against the police action. As far as the story can be gathered from the descriptions of both sides this is what may have happened. The police used their batons in pushing the women back. As they continued to push, the crowd of women (who had to move backwards) came against all kinds of obstacles. Some fell down and others stepped over them since they were being charged by the police. It is claimed by the women that several of them were injured:

> On 22 February 1945 the D.C. came again togther with the Police Officer and two other Europeans whom we do not know. Thirty native soldiers came with them. They surrounded us on the northern side. The D.C. said to us "I give you two minutes . . . to think and if you are not prepared to go you will see something happen". A whistle was sounded and the soldiers started chasing us and beating us on our buttocks with the lower parts of their guns. Some of us had babies while we were being chased. Sixty-four women got injured; three women were admitted in hospital.[11]

Groups of Pare, even those living outside Upare, wrote to the government demanding an inquiry into the "brutal" handling of the women demonstrators in Usangi. The government, however, felt that the "people of Usangi owe a deep debt of gratitude to the police for their amazing restraint".[12]

There were two consequences of this violence in Usangi. First, it stopped the pattern of negotiation which had been started by the

leaders of the demonstration at Same. The second deputation
returned from Dar es Salaam and their leaders, including Mashambo, began to feel ashamed that their "non-violent" procedure
had been destroyed. They maintained their peaceful demonstration in Same, however, explaining away the Usangi violence
as a special provocation on the women. But since the negotiation
with Dar es Salaam had been marred by this incident, the leaders
began to think about legal representation of their case.

The second result was that the government took a more serious
view of the demonstration than it had ever done. Only 500 women
were able to shake the whole security system. What would happen
if the thousands of men at Same were to turn violent? Police
reinforcements were increased and on 24 February 1945 two companies of the King's African Rifles (K.A.R.) were moved from
Moshi to Same. The idea was to try to break the demonstration
by force under "Defence Regulations", since World War II
had not yet ended. The Attorney General in Dar es Salaam, however, advised against this and so the district administration with
the help of the police acted fast in collecting evidence against ringleaders for possible prosecution.

3. THE LEGAL FIGHT

The legal fight also had two sides. On the one hand the government tried to deal with the so-called ringleaders; on the other,
the Pare tried to get a legal representative to put their case before
the government, for they were convinced that they had a strong
case but had not been able to put it across to the authorities in a
language they could understand. On the government side, the idea
of prosecuting the ringleaders had been proposed since the beginning of the demonstration. It was argued that the leaders were
sabotaging work in rubber and sisal estates, and so they could be
prosecuted under the Defence Regulations of 1939. As we have already seen, the Attorney General advised against this. His view
was that if enough evidence could be obtained under oath, the
ringleaders could be deported by the order of the Governor
himself, using the "law and order" sections of the Penal Code.

Since the end of February the police and the district administrators had been going round the mountains taking evidence from
the chiefs, headmen and their supporters against the alleged ringleaders. The number eventually reached 24—although the D.C.
said this number was reached after a careful pruning. The names
and the evidence against them were put before the Governor, and
between April and June 1945 eight of them were deported to

various districts, far away from the Pare Mountains. The deportations were as follows:

1. Rashid Kadio to Kasulu
2. Masudi Kwandiko to Sambawanga
3. Yohana Mcharo to Njombe
4. Rafaeli Kanyapwe to Mahenge
5. Elieza Mkonda to Singida
6. Mbura Mkande to Biharamulo
7. Mbonea Singo to Mbeya
8. Mbwana Mronga to Kasulu(?)

There is uncertainty as to whether both Rashid Kadio and Mbwana Mronga went to Kasulu. What is clear is that reports from the various districts where these people went show that they were hard working and useful in various projects. Arrangements were made for those who wished, for their families to join them later. It is doubtful, however, whether these eight persons were really considered to be the master minds in the movement. Undoubtedly the action was taken to show that the government had power to do something against the demonstrators. It is particularly interesting that Paulo Mashambo, whose name had been the first among the twenty-four, was not among those deported. It is also interesting to note that the impact of these deportations was much less at the time they were carried out, since by then the Pare demonstrators had left Same, not because of these intimidations but because they had taken their own legal steps which they believed were going to secure justice for them.

The steps taken by the Pare themselves consisted of employing a lawyer to represent them before the government. Before the end of February 1945, they had sent delegates to Tanga where they sought the services of an advocate by the name of Mohamed Hussein. This lawyer visited Same on 1 March 1945. He held meetings with Pare leaders and promised to petition the government on their behalf if they would stop the demonstration and return to their homes. Thus on Saturday, 3 March 1945, the first big demonstration ended after a period of two months. Government officials have often described it in terms of fear; the Pare were scared by the arrival of the K.A.R. companies as well as by the vigorous police action in taking evidence. Most Pare informants, however, believe that they went back to their homes because they trusted that the legal action would bring quicker fruits. After all, they had been in Same for two months and nothing had happened except further disgrace (as far as they were concerned) caused by the women's violence in Usangi. Furthermore, two months of idleness in the cultivating season might re-

flect severely in terms of shortage of food in their district in the
following months. Their main task now was to raise money to
pay for the lawyer; and the main worry of the government for
several months centred on the various fund-raising meetings being
held in all chiefdoms.

At the same time the Pare sent delegations to various parts of
East Africa in order to solicit support and advice. Some went to
Moshi and Arusha. But the most important was the one sent to
Nairobi to talk to E. W. Mathu, the first African member of the
Legislative Council in Kenya. Mathu did take the trouble of
writing to the government of Tanganyika enquiring about the tax
and the Chief Secretary answered in the following terms:

> In fact the system introduced is a graduated local rate imposed
> in lieu of the normal tax rebate system, and it had been applied
> in the Pare District only, as an experimental measure, since 1943.
> All the money received from this rate accrues to the Native
> Treasury. The name "mbiru" has been applied to it in the Pare
> District and it is understood that this name was applied to a system
> of tribute paid to their chiefs and rain makers in the olden days.[13]

Possibly this reply satisfied Mathu, but meanwhile the Pare lawyer
was busy. On 13 March 1945 Mohamed Hussein wrote to the P.C.,
Tanga informing him of the action he intended to take:

> The tribe in order to show their grievance to the Government
> made a peaceful demonstration at Same and they immediately
> stopped it when I advised them that the matter has to be placed
> in a lawful manner before the authority. They have been advised
> to pay the tax pending the result of their petition to His Ex-
> cellency. They are petitioning His Excellency for this year's tax
> as well and they hope that if His Excellency be pleased to grant
> their petition for this year any tax paid by persons in excess of
> what they may be due will be refunded.
> I shall submit the petition to His Excellency in due course.[14]

Shortly the petition followed. The points presented correspond so
much with what the Pare had been arguing with the government
all along that one wonders whether this expensive business was
worth it. In fact two months later the Chief Secretary answered
the petition, saying that the lawyer had based it on wrong facts and
that the government had no intention of changing the *mbiru*
system. The Pare themselves were also becoming worried by a
number of things. The chiefs in some chiefdoms thought they had
been victorious. This kind of attitude was dangerous because almost everything done by the chief against a supporter of the
anti-*mbiru* movement was interpreted as vindictiveness. Letters

began to pour into Dar es Salaam again complaining about mis-treatment by the chiefs. This attitude tended to consolidate the anti-*mbiru* group, making the loyalists very uncomfortable. In Usangi there were complaints that traders were refusing to sell supplies to the loyalists. In several parts of South Pare physical intimidation was reported. All these were reactions showing the tension still existing in Pare society. From their point of view, the greatest disappointment was the failure of their advocate to obtain redress for them. Something had to be done about this.

By September 1945, the Pare were convinced that in order to get a reasonable hearing from the European government it was necessary to use a European who would know not only their language but also their tricks. During the time of consultations they had discovered that there was a British law firm in Moshi called Reid and Edmonds. "If the Indian has failed", said one informant, "let's get a European to fight another European". The firm was approached and an agreement reached without delay. There followed another period of raising funds. Although it is not known how much Hussein was paid, it is at least rumoured that Reid and Edmonds demanded about six to ten thousand shillings.

Reid first visited Dar es Salaam, obtained an interview with the Chief Secretary and then returned to Moshi to start his work. He held several meetings with Pare leaders in Same before and after going to Dar es Salaam. On the 27 October he sent his petition to the government. In many ways this petition was more realistic in reflecting the condition of Upare in this period than the reports of the district administrators. It revealed that there was a widespread dissatisfaction, distrust and disruption in the district as a whole, a fact which the D.C. himself had not wanted to accept. He pleaded for immediate action to restore con-ditions to their normal level. At the same time new administrators had taken over: C. Cadiz in Same and A. V. Hartnoll as P.C. Tanga instead of Bonavia. Although the new P.C. tried to refute Reid's representation, he eventually concluded:

> The desire for graduated taxation did not emanate from the people. It was first put by Government to the Chiefs who accepted it and explained it to the best of their ability to their people. It was hoped that having introduced the system it would work smoothly and would eventually be accepted as a more just imposition than the fixed rate. This anticipation had not been realized, not only because the rate was too complicated in the form originally in-troduced, but also because too much reliance was placed on the ability of the Chiefs and on their very good standing with the

people. Now that the administrative staff at Same has been increased, the District Commissioner and his assistant are able to
spare the time to give the tactful guidance and active assistance
that was previously lacking.[15]

True, the district personnel had been increased, and Cadiz
with his assistant, Chazal, was busy touring chiefdoms and super-
vising assessments for the 1946 tax. Yet rumours about "sub-
versive activities" were increasing. Meanwhile another D.C. came
in, St. G. Gray. He had hardly taken office when the tension came
out into the open and a second demonstration began at Same.

4. THE LAST DEMONSTRATION

The period betweeen November 1945 and June 1946 was full of
many attempts by the district administrators to supervise activities
in the district directly. They combined this close watch with a
severe application of the law. In some parts people were prosecuted for arson (burning houses of loyalists); in others an attempt
was made to prosecute anti-*mbiru* leaders who made speeches. On
the whole, things became worse. The distrust by the European
administrators of the chiefs were not justified for if there was a
distrust of government (in the minds of the people at least)
it was caused not by the chiefs themselves but by the European
district personnel who were the "corrupters" of the traditional
rulers.

Things came to a head on 3 July 1946. The new D.C. with his
wife had gone to Gonja (a chiefdom in South Pare) to attend a
"baraza" at Bombo. Surprisingly, the D.C. reports that he had
heard rumours that people might start a demonstration if he took
action against tax defaulters. At the "baraza" there were about
230 persons, and of these many had not paid *mbiru*. As if to
demonstrate his power, the D.C. selected, among the people, one
"ringleader". He tried him on the spot, for wilful default and sentenced him to three months' imprisonment with hard labour. The
prisoner was arrested by police accompanying the D.C., but all
the people followed and snatched him away. The D.C. could not
accept defeat, The policeman was an African. Although they
might defy an African, they certainly ought to fear "Bwana
Mkubwa". So he thrust himself into the crowd and took away the
prisoner.

The D.C., his wife and the prisoner left Bombo for Same. The
crowd followed behind them as they were walking downhill towards their lorry on the main road. When they reached the main
road, according to the D.C.'s report, the "mob" tried to obstruct

the passage so that the lorry could not move. They, however, started off slowly and managed to drive away. People followed them on foot and by 5 July 1946 a crowd had again assembled at Same. The whole provocation seemed senseless and even today, reading reports about the identification of people who had obstructed the lorry and their sentencing to imprisonment, one cannot help feeling rather itchy. At any rate, the provocation had started off a second demonstration. Although it is said that at no time did the crowd exceed 300 persons, the incident had given a chance for the tension to come out into the open. Paulo Mashambo was again in command. On 10 July 1946 the crowd under him went to see the D.C. They demanded food and wanted a latrine built for them. They also wanted to see the reply from the government to their petition sent by the lawyer, Reid. The demonstration is said to have lasted for the whole month of July.

The immediate result of this smaller demonstration was that it reminded the government of the truth contained in Reid's petition. Truly the condition of Upare was deteriorating and even the power of "Bwana Mkubwa" (as against the traditional chiefs) was not enough to restore order. The P.C., Hartnoll, started holding "baraza's" in the various chiefdoms of Upare, allowing people to address them openly. After these open "baraza" surveys it was eventually concluded after that the *mbiru* system would never work successfully in the prevailing environment:

> After having given this matter the most careful consideration and after having discussed it with the District Commissioner and the late District Commissioner, I recommend, with reluctance, that the present graduated rate rules should be repealed and not replaced, and that the previous system of rebate to the Native Treasury from flat rate Native Tax should be restored.[16]

This was the end of the whole drama. In 1947 the Pare went back to a flat rate of tax, though raised by two shillings. They felt that they had won the fight, though at a tremendous cost financially. Consequently also, by the middle of 1947 orders had been given by the Governor of Tanganyika, Sir William Battershill, to rescind the deportation orders of the eight Pare so-called ringleaders who had been in different parts of the territory.

CONCLUSION

This paper has concentrated mainly on the organisational aspect of the anti-*mbiru* movement. It has revealed that there is no justification for speaking about this movement as either "anti-modernism" or "anti-traditionalism". Although *mbiru* was initially suggested by the central government, the outcry for development (which is clearly documented by the records of the Usangi Sports ad Welfare Club),[17] antedates the suggestions and runs through the whole argument of the Pare for an increased flat rate throughout the period of the controversy. In organisation, no one can mistake such "modern" ideas as writing petitions or employing advocates. Certainly, the anti-*mbiru* movement shows how the limited tools gained from the colonial era could be employed in protesting against the colonial oppression which tended to limit the availability of such tools while at the same time corrupting the traditional channels of justice.

It is on this latter point that the irony lies. The opposition to the chiefs was certainly not intended to be in favour of the colonialists. On the contrary, the chiefs had become identified with their colonial masters, in so far as they had agreed to be corrupted. Yet pre-colonial Pare is full of examples of what can be done with an oppressive ruler. The strategy chosen, therefore, was an interesting combination of talents available in society, traditional as well as foreign. It illustrates the kind of dynamism existing in African societies which has enabled traditionalism to continue to give solutions to their problems at the time foreign ideas might cause crisis.

Moreover, the experience gained from this painful drama could not have been fruitless. Despite the divisions caused by the anti-*mbiru* movement, what was learned by the various Pare leaders about organisation and mobilisation continued to be used in the the years that followed. It is not accidental that the political organisation known as the "Wapare Union" was born before the end of 1947. This continuation of organisational skills from protest movements, however, is not a new lesson from this study. But the use of traditional patterns of organisation is likely to shed light on what have often been considered to be "spontaneous and unorganised" protest movements of the 1940s and 1950s in East African history.

ACKNOWLEDGEMENTS

The information in this publication was partly obtained through oral research among the Pare people. The author would like to thank all the informants who provided this information. He would also like to thank the keepers of the National Archives of Tanzania for permission to quote from public records.

NOTES

1. Translation of proposals by Pare Chiefs, enclosed in P.C., Tanga, to Chief Secretary, 12 July 1941, Tanzania National Archives [TNA] SMP 30030/III/407. There were nine chiefdoms on the Pare Mountains and their chiefs had met together as the Pare Native Authority since 1928.
2. *Ibid.*
3. For this incident, see Isaria N. Kimambo, *A Political History of the Pare of Tanzania* c.*1500–1900* (Nairobi, 1969), p. 175.
4. TNA SMP 16516/I/1D. There were nine delegates from North Pare, nine from South Pare, and three from Same.
5. P.C., Tanga, to Chief Secretary, 27 November 1944, TNA SMP 16516/I/5A.
6. D.C., Same, to P.C., Tanga, 6 January 1945, TNA SMP 16516/I/13.
7. Personal conversation, March 1966.
8. D.C., Same, to Chief Secretary, 24 February 1945, TNA SMP 16516/I/39.
9. Paulo Mashambo (for Wapare) to Chief Secretary, 20 January 1945, TNA SMP 16516/I/15.
10. Notes by Chief Secretary, 21 February 1945, TNA SMP 16516/I/27.
11. Women of North Pare, Usangi and Ugweno to Chief Secretary, 20 April 1945, TNA SMP 16516/I/62A.
12. D.C., Same, to P.C., Tanga, 3 March 1945, TNA SMP 16516/I/52A.
13. Chief Secretary to E. W. Mathu, 5 June 1945, TNA SMP 30030/II/273.
14. Mohamed Hussein to the P.C., Tanga, 6 March 1945, TNA SMP 16516/I/S1.
15. P.C., Tanga, to Chief Secretary, 29 November 1945, TNA SMP 16516/I/103.
16. P.C., Tanga, to Chief Secretary, 21 October 1946, TNA SMP 30030/I/366.
17. A microfilm copy of the minutes of this organisation (which began in 1935) is in the University Library, Dar es Salaam.

Notes on the Contributors

Professor Bethwell A. Ogot is Deputy Vice-Chancellor, Professor of History, Director of the Institute of African Studies, University of Nairobi. Author of *History of the Southern Luo*, Vol. I, 1967, *A Place to Feel at Home* (with F. B. Welbourn), 1966; and articles and chapters on African history in learned journals and books.

Dr. Samwiri Karugire is a Lecturer in History at Makerere University, Kampala, and has recently completed a thesis on the pre-colonial history of Nkore, which is being published by the Oxford University Press.

Dr. Donald Crummey is a lecturer in the Department of History at the Haile Sellassie I University and has contributed several articles on the history of Ethiopia to learned journals.

Dr. Robin H. Palmer is a Lecturer in the Department of History at the University of Zambia. His Ph.D. thesis on "The Making and Implementation of Land Policy in Rhodesia 1890-1936", University of London, 1968, forms the main source for this chapter.

Dr. Donald Denoon is a Lecturer in History at Makerere University, Kampala. He has recently completed a book on the history of Southern Africa since 1800.

G. C. K. Gwassa is a Lecturer in History at the University of Dar es Salaam who, for the last three years, has been engaged on a detailed study of the Maji Maji war.

Dr. William R. Ochieng' is a Lecturer in the Department of History at the University of Nairobi. He has recently completed a Ph.D. thesis on "Pre-Colonial History of the Gusii of Western Kenya".

Professor G. N. Uzoigwe formerly of Makerere University, Kampala, and now of Michigan State University, has made a substantial contribution to the history of Bunyoro-Kitara, Uganda.

Dr. A. J. Temu is an Associate Professor of History at the University of Dar es Salaam, and has contributed articles and chapters on East African history to various journals and books.

Professor Isaria N. Kimambo is Professor and Head of the Department of History, University of Dar es Salaam, as well as Chief Academic Officer of the University. He is the author of *A Political History of the Pare of Tanzania c. 1500–1900* (1967), and of numerous articles and papers on the history of East Africa.

Professor J. B. Webster was formerly a Senior Lecturer in History at the University of Ibadan. Since 1968 he has been Professor and Head of the Department of History at Makerere University. His publications include *The African Churches among the Yoruba, 1888–1922* (1964), and, with A. A. Boahen, *The Revolutionary Years: West Africa since 1800* (1967). He has now completed research on the pre-colonial history of the Iteso and Acholi of Uganda.

Index